36TH CONGRESS, 1st Session. } SENATE.

MESSAGES

OF THE

PRESIDENT OF THE UNITED STATES,

COMMUNICATING,

IN COMPLIANCE WITH RESOLUTIONS OF THE SENATE,

INFORMATION RELATIVE TO THE

COMPULSORY ENLISTMENT OF AMERICAN CITIZENS

IN THE

ARMY OF PRUSSIA, &c.

WASHINGTON:
GEORGE W. BOWMAN, PRINTER.
1860.

April 17, 1860.—*Resolved*, That the Messages of the President of the 11th and 16th of April instant, co.nmunicating, in compliance with resolutions of the Senate, information in regard to the cumpulsory enlistment of American citizens in the army of Prussia, &c., be printed together, and that five thousand extra copies thereof be printed and bound for the use of the Senate.

MESSAGE

OF THE

PRESIDENT OF THE UNITED STATES,

COMMUNICATING,

In compliance with a resolution of the Senate, information in regard to the compulsory enlistment of American citizens in the army of Prussia.

APRIL 13, 1860.—Read, ordered to lie on the table.

To the Senate of the United States:

In compliance with the resolution of the Senate of the 2d February, 1859, requesting information in regard to the compulsory enlistment of citizens of the United States in the army of Prussia, I transmit a report from the Secretary of State, and the documents by which it was accompanied.

JAMES BUCHANAN.

WASHINGTON, *April* 11, 1860.

DEPARTMENT OF STATE,
Washington, April 10, 1860.

The Secretary of State, to whom was referred the resolution of the Senate of the 2d of February, 1859, requesting the President "to communicate copies of any correspondence between the government of the United States and the government of Prussia on the subject of the compulsory enlistment of American citizens in the army of that kingdom, with such other information on the subject as the Department of State may be able to furnish," has the honor to lay before the President a copy of the papers specified in the subjoined list.

Respectfully submitted.

LEWIS CASS.

The PRESIDENT.

List of accompanying documents.

Mr. Wheaton to Mr. Forsyth, 29th July, 1840, with inclosures.

Mr. Barnard to Mr. Webster, 11th March, 1851—extract—with inclosures.

Same to same, 10th June, 1851—extract—with inclosures.

Same to same, 24th June, 1851 - extract—with inclosures.

Same to same, 28th July, 1851—extract—with inclosures.

Mr. Fay to Mr. Webster, 15th May, 1852—extract—with inclosures.

Mr. Barnard to Mr. Webster, 15th June, 1852, with inclosures.

Same to same, 13th July, 1852—extract—with inclosures.

Same to same, 20th July, 1852—extract—with inclosure.

Same to same, 3d August, 1852, with inclosures.

Same to same, 3d August, 1852—extract.

Same to same, 10th August, 1852—extract—with inclosure.

Same to same, 17th August, 1852, with inclosure.

Same to same, 12th October, 1852, with inclosures.

Mr. Fay to Mr. Webster, 26th October, 1852—extract—with inclosure.

Mr. Barnard to Mr. Everett, 7th December, 1852—extract—with inclosure.

Same to same, 14th December, 1852—extract—with inclosure.

Mr. Everett to Mr. Barnard, 14th January, 1853—extract—with inclosure.

Mr. Barnard to Mr. Everett, 8th February, 1853—extract.

Same to same, 15th February, 1853, with inclosure.

Mr. Barnard to Mr. Marcy, 22d March, 1853—extract—with inclosures.

Same to same, 5th April, 1853—extract—with inclosure.

Baron Gerolt to Mr. Marcy, 11th July, 1853, with inclosure.

Mr. Vroom to Mr. Marcy, 31st October, 1853—extract—with inclosures.

Same to same, 13th December, 1853—extract—with incloures.

Same to same, 28th February, 1854—extract—with inclosures.

Same to same, 2d May, 1854—extract—with inclosure.

Same to same, 9th May, 1854—extract—with inclosure.

Same to same, 16th May, 1854—extract—with inclosures.

Same to same, 6th February, 1855—extract—with inclosures.

Same to same, 20th March, 1855—extract—with inclosures.

Same to same, 18th September, 1855—extract—with inclosure.

Same to same, 23d October, 1855—extract—with inclosures.

Same to same, 8th January, 1856—extract—with inclosures.

Same to same, 22d January, 1856—extract—with inclosures.

Same to same, 26th February, 1856—extract—with inclosures.

Same to same, 13th May, 1856—extract—with inclosures.

Same to same, 2d December, 1856—extract—with inclosures.

Same to same, 20th January, 1857—extract—with inclosure.

Mr. Vroom to Mr. Cass, 14th July, 1857—extract—with inclosures

Mr. Wheaton to Mr. Forsyth.

No. 157.] BERLIN, *July* 29, 1840.

SIR: I have the honor herewith to inclose copies of correspondence relating to the case of Johann Philipp Knoche, a naturalized citizen of the United States, born in Prussia, and claiming to be exempt from military service on his return to his native country.

As it did not appear to me that his claim could be maintained, I had no hesitation in declining to interfere in the manner requested.

I have the honor to be, with the highest consideration, sir, your obedient servant,

HENRY WHEATON.

Hon. JOHN FORSYTH, *&c., &c.*

[Translation.]

The very humble petition of Johann Philipp Knoche, of Wunderthausen, district of Berleburg:

WUNDERTHAUSEN, *July* 19, 1840.

I emigrated to America from my birth place in my twenty-first year, in 1834, to seek my fortune in that country. I was six years in America, most of it in Baltimore, where I became an American citizen.

I did not notify my going off from here to the local authority, or the district authority, or that of the jurisdiction, nor ask their permission. It is only since about the twentieth of last month that my father wrote to me to come and fetch him, for he had also determined to emigrate to America. To my greatest astonishment, I learned that by my being here they will enrol me as a soldier, which throws me into the greatest perplexity; therefore, I make free to turn myself to your high authority, with the humble petition that you will inform me whether I must hold myself subject to the Prussian law as bound to military duty, or whether I am exempt, as an American citizen. I have an American passport and certificate of citizenship, which if it be necessary, I can send to your excellency by mail from here, where I must remain till the early part of the coming year, as my father has not yet sold his property, therefore cannot as yet emigrate.

On this subject I humbly and dutifully request as early answer as may be.

With deepest respect, I subscribe myself your excellency's most obedient servant,

JOHANN PHILIPP KNOCHE.

BERLIN, *July* 24, 1840.

SIR: I have received your application, stating that you are a native-born subject of his Majesty the King of Prussia; that you emigrated o the United States in the year 1834, being then twenty-one years old, vhere you became naturalized as a citizen; that you have since eturned to your native country, where you have been required to perorm military duty, and desiring my official interference for your relief.

In reply, I have to state that it is not in my power to interfere in he manner you desire. Had you remained in the United States, or isited any other foreign country (except Prussia) on your lawful busiess, you would have been protected by the American authorities, at ome and abroad, in the enjoyment of all your rights and privileges as naturalized citizen of the United States. But, having returned to he country of your birth, *your native domicil and national character evert*, (so long as you remain in the Prussian dominions,) and you are ound in all respects to obey the laws exactly as if you had never emirated.

I am, sir, your obedient servant,

HENRY WHEATON.

Mr. JOHANN PHILIPP KNOCHE.

Mr. Barnard to Mr. Webster.

[Extract.]

No. 14.] LEGATION OF THE UNITED STATES,
Berlin, March 11, 1851.

SIR: I have the honor to inclose a copy of a note addressed by me to Mr. Manteuffel in behalf of H. Van de Sandt, accompanied by a copy f Mr. Van de Sandt's letter to this legation.

* * * * * * * * *

With the highest respect, I have the honor to be, your obedient ervant,

D. D. BARNARD.

Hon. DANIEL WEBSTER,
Secretary of State.

Mr. Barnard to Mr. Manteuffel.

LEGATION OF THE UNITED STATES OF AMERICA,
Berlin, March 4, 1851.

MONSIEUR LE BARON: I have the honor to inclose a copy of a letter rom Mr. Sandt, who has been ordered to leave Prussia by the landath of Cleve. As he declares himself a citizen of the United States, lthough I have not yet seen his passport, I beg to present his request or a reconsideration of his case.

I avail myself of this occasion to renew to your excellency the assurance of my distinguished consideration.

D. D. BARNARD.

His Excellency BARON VON MANTEUFFEL,
Minister of Foreign Affairs, &c.

Mr. Sandt to the American Legation.

[Translation.]

BRIENENSHEN, PROVINCE OF LOWER RHINE,
Farm near Cleves, February 29, 1851.

The undersigned American citizen does himself the honor to call upon the honorable legation of the United States for the just intervention of its influence, in his most unpleasant situation.

It is only a few weeks since I came from North America amongst my kinsfolk here, on some family affairs, and now have information from the police, by order of the town councilors of Cleves, that I must at once leave the country, or otherwise, am threatened with imprisonment and compulsory banishment. Now, I have no desire to be thrust by force across the boundary like a vagabond by some uninvited attendants, my business not being, in the meantime, yet finished, so I request your honor's kind interference and counsel in this matter. The reason of this strange conduct of the police is unknown to me, as I have not been guilty of any offense, and my passport issued by Mayor Kennett, of St. Louis, was visaed at that place as correct by the Prussian consul. I cannot think what the police here can want with me.

Would your honor desire to inspect the passport referred to, I beg you will give me your kind notice of the fact.

With highest esteem,

H. VAN DE SANDT.

The LEGATION OF THE UNITED STATES OF AMERICA AT BERLIN.

Mr. Barnard to Mr. Webster.

[Extract.]

No. 24.] LEGATION OF THE UNITED STATES,
Berlin, June 10, 1851.

SIR: * * * * * *

The department has heretofore been informed that Mr. Henry Von der Sandt applied to me some time ago to interfere in his behalf with the government of Prussia. He claimed to be an American citizen in Prussia, under protection of a regular passport, and complained of harsh and unreasonable treatment, in being ordered by the authorities of Cleves to quit Prussia. In a note of the 4th of March last, I asked the government here to review the case and the decision of the local authorities.

I have received, under date of the 21st of May, a note from the department of foreign affairs, declining to reverse the decisions of the officials at Cleves, a copy of which is herewith communicated. As soon as received, a copy of this note was sent to Mr. Von der Sandt.

It would appear, from a letter received from him, dated the 25th of May, and which must have been written before the copy of the minister's note to me had reached him, that he had been promptly notified of the final decision of the government in his case, and of the necessity of his quitting Prussia. I send a copy of his letter, which is in German, remarking that it is written in a moderate tone of complaint of the legation, or the government, or somebody else, and contains an announcement of his purpose to make his grievances known both to the Prussian and American public through the newspapers.

It will be observed that Mr. Von der Sandt was not provided with a passport from the American Government, but from the mayor of St. Louis, and that he cannot be a citizen of the United States, since he emigrated from Prussia only in 1849. His motives for leaving Prussia, and the object of his return, are stated in the minister's letter to me, according to their understanding of the case; and Mr. Von der Sandt has refused to give the authorities any satisfaction in regard to the nature of the family affairs which he had said brought him back to his old home, or the length of time which he desired to occupy in his private business. The government seemed to be resolved that he should not live in Prussia as a Prussian, and yet escape all the duties of a Prussian subject, under pretense or color of being a citizen of another country.

* * * * * * *

I have the honor to be, with the highest respect, your obedient servant,

D. D. BARNARD.

Hon. DANIEL WEBSTER,
Secretary of State.

Mr. Le Coq to Mr. Barnard.

[Translation.]

BERLIN, *May* 21, 1851.

SIR: I have had the honor to receive the note you have been pleased to address to me, dated the 4th of March last, transmitting the complaint of Mr. Henry Von der Sandt, a citizen of the United States, against the order which has been given to him by the landrath of Cleves to quit the Prussian States, and I hasten to communicate to you information on this subject which I have just received from the competent authorities.

Henry Von der Sandt having, at his request, received a permit of emigration, (Entlassungs Urkunde,) left his country, in 1849, to go to America, with the sole view of screening himself by that from the performance of his military duties in the landwehr. On his return now, he wishes to avail himself of his foreign character to settle and live near his relatives, under the pretext of alleged family affairs, wishing thus to wait until the time of his military obligations shall have expired, reserving himself to get out of the way again in case circumstances should render his presence still necessary under the flag.

The passport of which he is the bearer, and which was issued to him by the mayor of the city of St. Louis, Missouri, mentions neither the object nor the duration of his journey, and being thus an insufficient means of legalization, it has been deemed necessary to come to an understanding on these two points with Mr. Von der Sandt. The latter, however, not only refuses all explanation, but will not even come forward at the summons which has been addressed to him by the landrath of Cleves.

In these circumstances, sir, the King's government could only approve and sustain the measure which Mr. Von der Sandt complains of; and I sincerely regret that I am not able to answer in a more favorable manner your intervention in his behalf.

In restoring herewith the letter inclosed in your dispatch, I have, sir, the honor to renew to you the assurance of my high consideration.

THE MINISTER OF FOREIGN AFFAIRS.

For the minister,

LE COQ.

Mr. Sandt to the legation of the United States.

[Translation.]

BREMEN, *May* 25, 1851.

To the honorable legation of the United States of North America at Berlin:

YOUR HONOR: I venture yet again, and, indeed, for the last time, to write to you, for the time for my departure is nigh at hand, and I have even until now waited in vain for a definitive answer.

It is true, I have for some time remarked a cessation on the part of the landraths in my persecution, which I attribute to your honor's interference; but nevertheless, I am assured to-day, that, according to a letter from the government, I am to be sent out of the country; but for all that, still relying on my just rights and your powerful intervention, I await your answer with good hopes.

Should, however, your honor not be in a position to protect an American citizen in this country, who, in spite of a correct passport, is persecuted without reason, then must my elevated thoughts about America vanish, and my pride in being a citizen thereof be undermined.

In that case, I may perceive it to be my special duty to become a warning to every one, and to make my condition known not only through the papers of this country, but also through publication in those of America.

I must also remark, that your honor, conformably to your last letter, is not exactly acquainted with my position; for if I had been apprized of the citation of the landraths, I should have gone blindfold into the power of the party from whom I must protect myself. Should your honor be informed of the reason of my persecution, I beg you will have the goodness to impart it to me. Under all circumstances I await your esteemed reply.

Your honor's most obedient servant,

H. VON DE SANDT.

Mr. Barnard to Mr. Webster.

[Extract.]

No. 27.] LEGATION OF THE UNITED STATES,
Berlin, June 24, 1851.

SIR:

* * * * * * * *

The decision of the government of Prussia in the case of Mr. Von de Sandt, of which the department is advised, has not satisfied that person, and he has written to me again on the subject. I send a copy of his letter, with a copy of one addressed to him in reply, by way of caution and counsel.

* * * * * * * *

I have the honor to be, with the highest respect, your obedient servant,

D. D. BARNARD.

Hon. DANIEL WEBSTER,
Secretary of State.

Mr. Sandt to Mr. Barnard.

[Translation.]

BREMEN, *June* 9, 1851.

I have received the letter of the secretary of legation, Mr. Fay, of the 26th May, and accompanying extracts from letters of the minister for foreign affairs of Prussia of the 21st May. I see, however, thereby, that you have come to an unjust conclusion, and that your decision, therefore, turns out disagreeably for me.

From the beginning: that I emigrated in 1849 is an error of fact; because, from 5th October, 1843, I threw off the bond of subjection to Prussia, and emigrated a short distance out from here. So, also, is it erroneous to say that I emigrated to get rid of the military regulations. I have fulfilled my active service period, and part of my reserve service, without fault; but if it be that I belong till my fortieth year to the first and second levy of landwehr, and could not emigrate without incurring the appearance of intention to evade my military obligations, and was the military liability the only oppression in this country, there certainly would not be here so many hundreds who, daily, secretly get across the Rhine, who are not soldiers, and who have no need to fear that; and in America, also, we are not free from the duty of service, but always bound, on any peril which may menace the land, to seize our weapons.

That my non-appearance, on the verbal request of a field-guard, to appear before the burgomasters of Kelle, half a league from here, (not before the landraths,) was given out to seem to be the principal ground of my proscription, is not justice; for, a long time after my proscription, first came this summons, and not in substitution. But the mere fear of my arrest was the reason for my non-appearance; for, had I returned the copy of my passport, which contained nothing dangerous to my personal freedom, to the burgomaster, at his request, and if my longed-for personal freedom were assured to me, I would readily enough have complied with the summons, notwithstanding the learned in the law call it indiscreet to mix up in family affairs, and occasions are not unknown here on which people have been summoned and detained by a police office.

That I desire to reside here under the name of foreigner, that I may evade the landwehr service, is also as untrue and unfounded. I wish to remain here scarcely four months longer; and thereafter, I hopefully look forward not any more to need your protection in this country. Also, yonder in America, can the time of my citizen's rights be settled and decided by competent persons, as important and not to be disturbed, so that I can, according to my oath taken, enjoy all the rights I have claim to, with that, also, of voting.

That in Prussia only one passport signed by the government in Washington is sufficient, was unknown to the person who issued my passport, as well as the Prussian consul who in good faith visaed it as the legitimate pass of an American citizen. Upon this I have made this unlucky journey, and upon this I maintain that I deserve all protection, notwithstanding all denials and intrigues.

Should your excellency, notwithstanding all this, not be in position to secure me liberty to be busy here yet a few months, this may, at least, give you a different idea of my character.

With the assurance that this letter rests on truth and justice, I remain, with the highest esteem, your excellency's most obedient servant,

H. V. DE SANDT.

The MINISTER OF THE UNITED STATES, *Berlin.*

P. S. For better faith in the foregoing language, I send, herewith, literal copies:

1. My passport, with the verification by the Prussian consul at St. Louis.
2. My oath of declaration.
3. My permit to emigrate.
4. My lately received order from the landrath of Cleves, the original whereof is with my father, H. V. de Sandt, of Bremen, where it can be seen, and to whom you may send answer.

H. V. DE SANDT.

Mr. Barnard to Mr. Sandt.

LEGATION OF THE UNITED STATES,
Berlin, June 17, 1851.

SIR: Your letter of the 9th instant has been received, and I lose no time in giving you such counsel in reply to it as your case and the positions you assume seem to demand.

Your letter and the inclosures disclose certain facts which should be noted.

In the first place, if you were a citizen of the United States already naturalized, your passport is an invalid one. A mayor of a city in the United States cannot grant a valid passport. It must come from the authority of the general government, and not from any State or city authority. With the visa of the Prussian consul, your passport proved to be sufficient to enable you to get into the country; but it was not one on which you could rely to protect you in a residence here.

But in the next place, you are not yet a citizen of the United States. Declaring your intention to become a citizen does not make you a citizen. This intention was declared so late as March, 1850, and the time required by law for your admission to citizenship after that declaration is very far short of having been accomplished.

When you ceased to be a citizen of Prussia by your permit of emigration and became a resident in the United States, the laws and government of that country became your protection so long as that residence continued. When, however, you quitted your residence there before perfecting your naturalization, and again took up your abode in Prussia, for your own purposes, your condition was a peculiar one, and required from you a peculiar and very discreet line of conduct. It was impossible for the American legation here to claim you as an American citizen; though, as a resident of the United States, who had taken the first steps in good faith to become a citizen, and whom we should hope one day to see in the full enjoyment of citizenship in that country, we might have asked, and would very gladly have been instrumental in procuring for you, the free permission of the government of Prussia to remain here for any reasonable time required by your business or your convenience.

The error in your case has been in claiming to be an Américan citizen, and in insisting on the right to remain here as such without declaring your object or business or the time of your proposed stay. I am quite persuaded, if you had presented yourself voluntarily or promptly, on being required to do so, before the proper authority or officer of the locality, and had laid frankly before him the exact truth of the case—your position as a resident of the United States, intending to become a citizen, the business or objects which had brought you back to your old home, and the probable time of your necessary stay—that on satisfying such authority or officer of the sincerity and truth of your declarations you would not have been disturbed.

Perhaps it is not too late yet. If it is still desirable to you to remain, I should advise you to try what a frank exposition of your case before the burgomaster or landrath might be able to effect for you.

But you should avoid any spirit of demand or of controversy. State exactly your position as it has now been laid down to you from this legation; state exactly wherein you have been mistaken, and ask permission, as a matter of favor and courtesy, to remain where you are till you can accomplish the business which brought you back to Prussia.

If you will put yourself on the ground here indicated, and respectfully ask to be permitted to remain in the country for the completion of the lawful objects which brought you here, I should hope that such permission might still be granted to you. I regret very much the inconvenient position in which you find yourself, and am very desirous of being of service to you by the information and advice which I give you.

Your obedient servant,

D. D. BARNARD.

Mr. VON DE SANDT.

Mr. Barnard to Mr. Webster.

[Extract.]

No. 31.]

LEGATION OF THE UNITED STATES,
Berlin, July 29, 1851.

SIR: I have the honor to inclose to you copies of correspondence, as follows:

* * * * * * * *

A letter from Mr. Bates to me, of the 19th July, with the inclosure, being a letter from a Mr. Brand, claiming to be an American citizen, and who is imprisoned at Coblentz; my letter to Mr. Bates, of the 22d July, on this subject; a letter from Mr. Bates to me, of the 25th July, referring, in the conclusion, to the case of Mr. Brand, but chiefly relating to the detention of Mr. Thomas N. Dale, an American citizen, at Aix-la-Chapelle, on the old ground of the want of a Prussian visa to his passport; my answer to Mr. Bates, of the 28th instant; and my note to the minister of foreign affairs on the question of passports, of the same date.

My letter to Mr. Bates, last referred to, together with my note to the minister, will show what action I have taken in regard to the difficulty which it seems is still sometimes made by an over-zealous police about American passports. I have the strongest assurances that steps shall be taken to correct the evil.

In regard to the case of Mr. Brand, it will be seen by Mr. Bates's letter of the 25th instant that he had, up to that day, received no further information from Mr. Brand, and that he had written to the legal officer of the king, at Coblentz, on the subject.

In a personal interview which I had yesterday with Mr. Le Coq, the under-secretary of state, (the minister being absent,) I presented the case of Mr. Brand to his notice, as far as I had information on the subject, with an earnest, though friendly, appeal in behalf of this person, if it should appear that he was an American citizen and had not been guilty of any real crime. I was met, on the part of Mr. Le Coq, with the most friendly assurances. I have handed him a copy of Mr. Brand's letter. I have great confidence that if Mr. Brand is not at once released from his confinement by the local authorities at Mr. Bates's instance, he will be released as soon as the government here can inform itself of the facts, provided the case is one which may admit of its favorable interposition. Whatever facts or information may be received from Mr. Bates will be promptly laid before the minister.

My desire being first of all to procure this man's release, if that be possible, and knowing very well how a formal correspondence (at least, it would be so here,) tends to defeat the object where one wishes to reach a particular result in the shortest time, I have purposely avoided that course in this case. In the end a correspondence may be resorted to, if the case, when all the facts shall be disclosed, seems to require it, whether the man be released or not.

* * * * * * * *

I have the honor to be, with the highest respect, your obedient servant,

D. D. BARNARD.

Hon. DANIEL WEBSTER,
Secretary of State.

Mr. Bates to Mr. Barnard.

CONSULATE OF THE UNITED STATES,
Aix-la-Chapelle, July 10, 1851.

SIR: I have just received the letter from Coblentz, a copy of which is inclosed herein. I have replied, acknowledging its receipt, and requesting the writer to send me his passport, if possible, and to state when he first went to the United States, how long he remained there, and when and where he was naturalized.

If he turns out to be an "American citizen," what shall I do in the matter?

Very respectfully, your obedient servant,

J. C. BATES,
United States Consul.

His Excellency D. D. BARNARD,
&c., &c., &c.

Mr. Brand to Mr. Bates.

[Translation.]

COBLENTZ, *July* 16, 1851.

On the 16th April, last year, I took from the authorities of New York a passport, and also an authenticated copy of my naturalization certificate. On the next day, the 17th, I sailed from New York, and in fifty-one days came by sailing vessel to London. There I stopped a while; made a visit on business to Ireland; thence back to England, where I remained some months; and then, partly on business, partly on family matters, traveled to Germany. Nearly five weeks I was in the neighborhood around Coblentz, and on the third day of my being here, at 11 o'clock at night, I was sought at my dwelling by a police sergeant, asking for my papers, which I showed him, the which he could not read, being written in English, so he took me with him to the guard-house.

Arrived here, all my effects were examined, one traveling bag, fifteen dollars, four rings, and some body linen besides, taken, whilst the rest which I had gathered in my travels I had forwarded to Liverpool. The day after the arrest I was carried before the police authorities for examination. I asked what was my offense. The official answered me I had been guilty of the offense of sending off emigrants, which is forbidden by law here.

Thereupon I denounced this as the grossest untruth, and moreover called for proof; so I was remanded to confinement, and after three days taken before the public prosecutor, when not a word was said about the beforementioned offense, but a commitment was made out for a term of eight days, with a remark that vagrancy was charged; and in this way was I robbed of my liberty, despite of my papers and passport.

In no respect have I been shown to be an offender or culprit, as has now been said.

I assert that I cannot understand the reason of this proceeding against me, and I make humble petition to your excellency as guardian and upholder of our laws, promptly to effect my liberation from this disagreeable situation, and not only help me to the recovery of my lost liberty, but to follow up all the state of facts, and especially on the foundation of the American laws, which must protect me as a citizen of the United States in a foreign country, to take all proper steps in my behalf.

In the hope of early aid, I subscribe myself, with respectful esteem,

J. W. ED. BRAND,
Doctor of Medicine.

Hon. Mr. J. C. BATES,
Consul of the United States of North America for the Rhenish Provinces.

Mr. Barnard to Mr. Bates.

[Extract.]

LEGATION OF THE UNITED STATES,
Berlin, July 22, 1851.

SIR: * * * * * * * *

I have also received your letter of July 19, with an inclosure in reference to the arrest and imprisonment at Coblentz of a person claiming to be an American citizen. If this man is really innocent of any offense, his arrest and imprisonment is a great outrage; and if he is an American citizen, as well as an innocent man, upon the facts being made known to me, I should deem it my duty to make it the subject of a grave complaint to the government.

But the first thing to be done is to get the man out of confinement, if that be possible. If you have received his passport and papers, you will know if he is a citizen of the United States. If you find he is so, I wish you would ask from the authorities at Coblentz for his immediate release from confinement, on the ground of his citizenship, and in case of refusal, that they would furnish you at once with the grounds of accusation against him, and of his imprisonment, in order that, being communicated to this legation, the matter may be laid before the government at Berlin, or such action taken upon it as the case may seem to demand.

If nothing is laid to this man's charge other than what is alleged in his letter, there is certainly very insufficient ground for his imprisonment. If he is an agent soliciting emigration, for purposes of his own, or in behalf of others in whose employ he may be, or if he be a vagabond, as he says they accuse him of being, these are hardly crimes for which he should be subjected to punishment by the Prussian authorities. They might send him out of their territories, if they think his stay here dangerous to the morals or the quiet of the country.

I ardently hope you may be able to effect Mr. Brand's release, and that without any further reference of the matter to this legation.

With great respect, your obedient servant,

D. D. BARNARD.

J. C. Bates, Esq., *Consul, &c.*

[Extract.]

Consulate of the United States,
Aix-la-Chapelle, July 25, 1851.

Sir: * * * * * * * *

Your letter of the 22d instant was received yesterday. I have heard nothing from Mr. Brand, in reply to my letter, and this morning wrote to the *procureur du roi* at Coblentz, requesting him to send, for my inspection, Mr. Brand's passport and papers, that I might determine whether he was really a citizen of the United States.

You shall be duly advised of the course of events.

I am, sir, very respectfully, &c.,

J. C. BATES.

His Excellency D. D. Barnard, *&c.*

Mr. Fay to Mr. Webster.

[Extract.]

No. 98.] LEGATION OF THE UNITED STATES,
Berlin, May 15, 1852.

SIR: * * * * * * * *

I have to inclose another case growing out of the same question: Mr. Gustavus Behne addressed a note to Mr. Barnard, under date of April 10, 1852. Not distinguishable from a private letter, it followed him to Naples, whence I have just received it.

Annexed is the copy of a note addressed by me to Baron Manteuffel, which, with its accompanying inclosure, states the case. Mr. Behne declares he was not born in Prussia at all. This may possibly procure for him a favorable reply. I have little hope of success in the application of Mr. Leopold.

I have the honor to be, with the highest consideration, your obedient servant,

THEO. S. FAY.

Hon. DANIEL WEBSTER,
Secretary of State.

Mr. Fay to Baron Manteuffel.

LEGATION UNITED STATES,
Berlin, May 13, 1852.

MONSIEUR LE BARON: Mr. Gustavus A. E. Behne had addressed to Mr. Barnard a note, extracts from which I have the honor to inclose. He declares himself an American citizen, not born in Prussia at all. About July or August, 1840, he received a summons at Dusseldorf to enter the Prussian army, with the information that the Prussian government regarded him as a Prussian subject because his father was a Prussian subject. Alarmed by an attempt to arrest him, he left for America, whence he returned last September. He is now living at Brussels, waiting the answer to his request for permission to remain some time in Prussia, without being called upon to satisfy the conscription.

I have the honor to lay this case before your excellency, with the certainty that, if no valid objections be found to exist, I shall be able to communicate a favorable reply.

I profit by the occasion to renew to your excellency the assurance of my very high consideration.

THEO. S. FAY.

His Excellency BARON VON MANTEUFFEL, *&c., &c., &c.*

Mr. Behne to Mr. Barnard.

[Extracts,]

BRUSSELS, *April* 10, 1852.

DEAR SIR: I take the liberty to address you in a matter of great importance to me, for the determination of which I ask your aid. October, 1849, I went to Germany and chose Dusseldorf for the place of my studies. At my arrival there I received what they call a "*aujenthaltskarte,*" which said that Mr. So and so, American citizen, had the permission to remain at Dusseldorf a year. At the end of July or beginning of August I received summons from the Prussian government to enter the army. I sent that invitation back, answered in the negative. * * * A few days afterwards I went to the director of the police, with whom I was very well acquainted, to learn from him the reason of this strange procedure. He told me that the Prussian government looked upon me as a Prussian subject, "because my father had been a Prussian subject, and had, when he left for America, taken only a passport, instead of a certificate of emigration." I replied, and told him to take notice of it, that my father was American citizen since six years; that, at the time of his departure, he was not any more Prussian citizen; that I was American citizen, and acknowledged as such by his own government; that I was, furthermore, not born in Prussia; and that Prussia had no claims whatever on me.

A week afterwards I left Dusseldorf to visit some friends in Province of Saxony, Prussia, and received while there a letter from a friend who lived with me, informing me that two *gen d'armes* had been at my rooms to arrest me. He gave me the advice to leave, without delay, the continent, likewise my friends and relations, and I was foolish enough to give way. Arrived at Bremen, I went to see Mr. King, American consul. * * * * *

I left the 10th of September, 1851, New York for Europe; however, without intention to remain any length of time in Prussia, or, in that case, I should have had my affairs arranged before I left. Now, however, I find it of greater advantage to me to study in Germany than in Paris. I have stayed the last six months here in Brussels, and would like to leave as *soon as possible.* Have, therefore, the kindness, sir, to give me your ideas about the subject; and, if convenient, ask the Prussian minister for an explication of the procedure against me. I hope you will succeed in arranging the matter for me, and beg your pardon for the trouble which I cause you.

I am, sir, most respectfully,

G. BEHNE.

Hon. D. D. BARNARD, *&c., &c., &c.*

Mr. Barnard to Mr. Webster.

No. 67.] LEGATION OF THE UNITED STATES,
Berlin, June 15, 1852.

SIR: I have the honor to inclose herewith a copy of a letter from the office of foreign affairs in answer to one from Mr. Fay in regard to the matter of Mr. Behne. This letter refers to another from the same office, in regard to the same matter, dated October 19, 1849, and which by mistake has not been brought to the notice of the Secretary of State at Washington at the time, for the reasons stated in a note appended to a copy thereof, which is now forwarded.

I transmit also a copy of my letter to Mr. Behne, informing him of the unsuccessful result of his application.

I have the honor to be, with the highest respect, your obedient servant,

D. D. BARNARD.

Hon. DANIEL WEBSTER,
Secretary of State.

Baron Schleinitz to Mr. Hannegan.

[Translation.]

BERLIN, *October* 19, 1849.

The predecessor of Mr. Hannegan, envoy extraordinary and minister plenipotentiary of the United States of North America, communicated, on the 23d May last, to the King's ministers a petition of Mr. Gustave Behne, citizen of the United States, residing at Dusseldorf, in which this person remonstrates against the injunction served on him to satisfy his military obligations to Prussia.

A correspondence having been opened on this subject with the ministry of the interior, and through its intermediation with the competent provincial authorities, it is only now that the undersigned finds himself in condition to apprize Mr. Hannegan of the result of the inquiries to which the remonstrance of Mr. Behne has given rise.

The father of this individual, doctor in medicine, born at Nordhausen, in Prussia, the 25th April, 1799, had resided five consecutive years at Werninghausen, in the Duchy of Saxe-Gotha. Returning to his native city in 1831, he lived there till the month of May, 1840, where, abandoning his wife and two sons, he went off to the United States of North America, without having previously obtained an emigration license. Of these two sons, one, Gustavus Edward Augustus, (who is at this moment at Dusseldorf,) was born the 1st September, 1828, at Werninghausen; the other, Oscar, the 13th of August, 1831, at Nordhausen. In the month of March, 1843, all the family emigrated, alike without the permission of the government, for North America, carrying off what little property it had in Prussia.

It follows, from this exposition, that the Behne family must be considered as belonging still to Prussia, because it has not legally broken the ties which connect it with its native land. The authority of Dusseldorf has therefore held it to be its duty to call under its flag the eldest of the two sons of Mr. Behne, who has attained the age requisite for serving in the army; and the ministry of the interior announces that it has no power to dispense with the provisions of the law.

In giving this information to Mr. Hannegan, the undersigned has the honor to offer him the assurances of his high consideration.

SCHLEINITZ.

Mr. HANNEGAN, *&c.*, *&c.*, *&c.*

N. B. This note is not recorded in the dispatch books of the legation, and does not appear to have been the subject of any correspondence. It is dated the 19th October, 1849. Mr. Hannegan had returned to his post five days previously, on the 11th, in a high state of fever. On the day of the date of the note I was myself dangerously attacked with an inflammation of the brain, which for several weeks confined me to my bed, and for several months kept me in a state of great suffering. In this way the matter was not communicated to the department.

THEO. S. FAY.

BERLIN, *June* 8, 1852.

Baron Manteuffel to Mr. Fay.

[Translation.]

BERLIN, *June* 5, 1852.

SIR: I have the honor to draw your attention, in reply to your letter of the 13th of last month, to the point that the petition of Mr. Gustavus Edward Augustus Behne, calling himself an American citizen, and who is at present at Brussels, has already been in 1849 the subject of correspondence between the legation of the United States and the king's administration. It was ascertained at that time that the Behne family must be considered as belonging to Prussia, the father, doctor in medicine, having left his native country, in 1840, without an *emigration license.*

On referring, in this matter, to the note which was addressed, 19th October, 1849, to Mr. Hannegan, I will add that, if Mr. Gustavus Behne, who in the month of May of that year resided at Dusseldorf, was not then incorporated in the army, it was because, at the moment of the summons, he undertook a little journey to foreign parts, from which he has not again returned to Prussia.

As nothing has changed since then the position of this young man, the authorization which he solicits, to be able to reënter Prussia temporarily, without being obliged to satisfy his military duties, cannot be granted to him.

In requesting you, sir, to inform the petitioner of this decision, in reply to the request he has addressed from Brussels to Mr. Barnard, I have the honor to offer you the assurance of my distinguished consideration.

For the minister of foreign affairs:

BULOW.

Mr. FAY, *&c.*, *&c.*, *&c.*

Mr. Barnard to Mr. Behne.

LEGATION OF THE UNITED STATES,
Berlin, June 11, 1852.

SIR: I regret to inform you that the government of Prussia declines positively to extend to you the right to reside in Prussia without subjecting you to the requirements of their law in regard to military services. A similar application was made to the Prussian government in your behalf in 1849, and in like manner refused.

The correspondence between this legation and the Prussian minister of foreign affairs on this subject will be forwarded, in copy, immediately to the Secretary of State at Washington.

Respectfully, your obedient servant,

D. D. BARNARD.

Mr. G. BEHNE.

Mr. Barnard to Mr. Webster.

[Extract.]

No. 71.] LEGATION OF THE UNITED STATES,
Berlin, July 13, 1852.

SIR: I have the honor to inclose to you, herewith, copies of correspondence * * * * *

Relating to Dr. Gutowsky, asking relief from an order to quit Prussia.

Relating to the case of Christian Hormann, a naturalized citizen of the United States, arrested on a demand made upon him to serve in the Prussian army.

* * * * * *

Relating to the case of B. Meyer, also a naturalized citizen of the United States, on whom a fine has been imposed, in his absence, for having left Prussia without permission, and who is threatened with being forced into the Prussian army, if he can be got hold of.

I beg leave, sir, to call your attention particularly to my letter to Baron Manteuffel in the last case here enumerated. * * I have taken occasion to submit to him some observations on the general subject of the laws of Prussia in regard to permits of emigration as attempted to be enforced against naturalized citizens of the United States, in connection with the right which she seems disposed to insist on, to compel all such citizens who have failed to obtain permission to emigrate, to enter and serve in the Prussian army, whenever she can lay her hand on them for that purpose. * * * * The object I have in view * * is to bring the Prussian government to a friendly arrangement in the matter, by which * * it will practically cease to offer * * annoyance to American citizens on this ground.

* * I had a personal and friendly interview with the minister of foreign affairs on the subject, in which I expressed to him directly and distinctly my views, * * and why I thought it important to both countries that we should come to some understanding in regard to it. He agreed with me in thinking this every way desirable, but did not for the moment see what was to be done, since so long as the Prussian laws on the subject existed, the courts must enforce them, and the government could not interfere with the courts. * *

I have the honor to be, with the highest respect, your obedient servant,

D. D. BARNARD.

Hon. DANIEL WEBSTER,
Secretary of State.

Mr. Gutowski to Mr. Barnard.

RUKOCIN, *June* 25, 1852.

SIR: The undersigned, being an American citizen, takes the liberty to ask the protection of the authorities of his country in your person; and as the police of the Prussian government in the province of Posen has, by the order of its ober-president, Mr. Putkammer, contradicted my sojourn in that country, and ordered me, without any particular reason, to quit the country in about four weeks, I thought it would be proper that I should ask you would inquire into the motives of my persecution.

I have some of my fortune here in a piece of land which I have purchased for $3,000, and upon which I am farming and cultivating. It would be impossible for me to quit it in such a short time. It is even impossible to arrange or dispose it in any convenient way.

Under such circumstances, I entreat you, sir, that you would be gracious to take it under your consideration, and obtain for me at the minister of the interior a permission to remain here for the next year, till I dispose of my property in some way; in effect of that I humbly ask your kindness that a new passport may be issued for me from your embassy visaed by the Prussian minister.

It is painful to me that during the last year I have been disturbed by the police, though I have done nothing to undergo such a treatment, and I can prove my good conduct by the testimonies of the most respectable men of this country. I came here because I am born here. I have my relations, my brother and two sisters here, still living; my parents are dead not long since. Having my own fortune, I am not at the charge of any living creature. It is true that I have lost the right of my citizenship in this country by becoming an American, but that quality makes me happy and honest wherever I am. I respect and obey the laws of the country, and I am conscious of my right conduct towards her. As to the politics, I don't take part in them, and I have not been engaged in any affairs towards any government of Europe, and consequently I am entitled to their justice and benevolence.

Your excellency will pardon me this correspondence. It was my wish to go personally to Berlin and explain the matter to you. I am designing to go there on my business, but the police refused to sign my passport, and absolutely prohibited my coming there. As the time presses, I humbly pray that your excellency would be gracious to bring my affair speedily under your consideration and result.

I remain, sir, with all due respect, your most obedient servant,

A. R. GUTOWSKI.

His Excellency Mr. BARNARD,
Minister Plenipotentiary to the Court of his Majesty the King of Prussia.

Mr. Barnard to Mr. Gutowski.

LEGATION OF THE UNITED STATES,
Berlin, June 30, 1852.

SIR: Your letter of the 25th June has been received. I will apply to the ministry of the king in your behalf.

In the meantime, I desire to learn from you more particularly than your letter discloses how long you have been in Europe, where you have resided, and how long at each place, what has been your occupation in these places, and why you reside and wish to reside in Europe instead of the United States, of which you are a citizen?

Your obedient servant,

D. D. BARNARD.

Dr. GUTOWSKI.

Mr. Barnard to Baron Manteuffel.

LEGATION OF THE UNITED STATES,
Berlin, July 1, 1852.

MONSIEUR LE BARON: I have received from Alexander R. Gutowski, doctor of medicine, at present residing at Rukocin, near Witkowo, in the Grand Duchy of Posen, a letter dated the 25th of June, asking my interposition in his behalf with the government of his Majesty the King to relieve him from the effect of an order which he has received from the local authority of the province to quit the country within about four weeks.

Dr. Gutowski informs me that no reason has been assigned to him for this order. He is an American citizen, though born in Poland, having been regularly naturalized in the United States in the year 1839. He has a regular passport at such citizen, issued at the legation in January, 1851, and visaed at the office of the ministry of foreign affairs in Berlin on the 9th February, 1851.

Born in the district of country where he now is, where his brother and two sisters now reside, and where his parents resided till their death, which happened not long since, he is the proprietor there of a farm costing three thousand thalers, which he is at present engaged in taking care of and cultivating. This is the information which he gives me. He declares that he has done nothing to deserve the order he has received; that he respects and obeys the laws of Prussia; that he has taken no part whatever in politics; and that he can prove his good conduct by the most respectable persons.

What Dr. Gutowski asks is, that he may have the permission and authority of the government of his Majesty to remain where he is for a year, or until he can dispose of his property without being obliged to sacrifice it.

I should hope that this request of a respectable and inoffensive man, as Dr. Gutowski certainly appears to be, may be considered a reasonable one, and that the permission he asks for may be granted.

I pray your excellency to receive, on this occasion, the assurance of my distinguished consideration.

D. D. BARNARD.

His Excellency Baron VON MANTEUFFEL,
Minister of Foreign Affairs, &c., &c., &c.

Mr. Barnard to Mr. Hormann.

LEGATION OF THE UNITED STATES,
Berlin, July 3, 1852.

SIR: Your letter of the 28th June, sent by mistake to the consul at Bremen, has just been received by me. I have, without a moment's delay, prepared a communication, to be sent to his Majesty's minister of foreign affairs, in regard to your case. You will be informed as soon as the result is known.

Your obedient servant,

D. D. BARNARD.

Mr. CHRISTIAN HORMANN.

Mr. Barnard to Baron Manteuffel.

LEGATION OF THE UNITED STATES,
Berlin, July 3, 1852.

MONSIEUR LE BARON: Christian Hormann, a citizen of the United States, informs me by letter, dated at Petershagen, the 28th June, that on the 26th June he was arrested at that place, taken to Minden, a distance of one German mile and a half, and placed in prison, where he was kept during the night; that the next day he was taken before the local magistrate or authority at Minden, and, on examination, discharged provisionally, and allowed to return to Petershagen, but only after his signature had been obtained to a writing which he did not comprehend, and after his passport had been taken from him and retained.

The history of Christian Hormann, as he relates it, is this: He was born in 1825, in the village of Seidfeld, belonging to the parish of Petershagen. His father emigrated to the United States in 1830, one of his sons, older than Christian, having already resided there several years. In 1838, his mother went to the United States, and he accompanied her, then being of the age of thirteen.

It had been lately resolved to dispose of the property of his father and mother in Petershagen, and he came to Prussia for this object, and with authority from them. On his arrival at Petershagen, he presented himself before the proper authorities with his passport as a citizen of the United States, and other papers, which were found in proper order.

His arrest, it appears, was upon some allegation that, as a boy of thirteen years of age, he had offended against the laws of Prussia in regard to military service, by accompanying his mother in her emigration to the United States. This seems to have been the idea of the authorities at Minden, whilst it appears that the authorities at Petershagen entertained no such opinion, but the contrary.

I beg leave to ask your excellency's attention to this case, and that I may be informed whether it is claimed that the authorities in question had any ground of justification for this harsh proceeding towards Christian Hormann. If no justifications can be alleged, I am sure his Majesty's government will not allow the case to pass without the proper rectification and redress.

I seize this occasion to offer to your excellency the assurances of my distinguished consideration.

D. D. BARNARD.

His Excellency BARON VON MANTEUFFEL.

Mr. Bates to Mr. Barnard.

UNITED STATES CONSULATE,
Aix-la-Chapelle, July 2, 1852.

SIR: Mr. B. Meyer, a native of Paderborn, in the province of Westphalia, emigrated seven years ago, at the age of eighteen, to the United States, for the purpose of becoming permanently located there; became a naturalized citizen of the same, and is furnished with a passport from the Secretary of State, dated May 6, 1852. He has returned to Germany for the benefit of his health, to see his relatives, and to attend to some private business which requires his personal presence at Paderborn.

Before emigrating, he *did not* obtain the permission of the Prussian government to do so, and since his arrival in Germany, he has been furnished with a copy of a judgment dated November 22, 1851, of the Konigliches Krieysgericht, of Paderborn, addressed to his mother, and condemning him to a fine of fifty thalers, as not having complied with the laws of Prussia with regard to military service.

This copy I inclose to you, marked A. On receipt of this document, he addressed a letter to the burgomaster of Paderborn, dated New York, 20th March, 1852, stating that he emigrated for the purpose of locating himself permanently in America, and not for the purpose of avoiding military service in Prussia, &c. * * * *

This letter was sent by him to the burgomaster, through an attorney of Paderborn, a personal friend of his. No written official answer has been received to it. The burgomaster simply stated, verbally, to the attorney by whom the letter was presented, that he could do nothing in the matter, and that Mr. Meyer would be obliged to serve in the army if found at Paderborn. Other information to the same effect has reached him through personal friends of the family, who occupy official positions at Paderborn, and he is at a loss to know what to do. Go to Paderborn *he must*, be the consequences what they may. He has a mother living there, seventy years of age, whom he has not seen for many years, and, moreover, has important business, of family affairs, to attend to. His intention is to remain in Germany about three months.

In reply to his question as to what he should do, I have given him my opinion that, as a properly naturalized citizen of the United States, he could not be liable to military service in Prussia; but that I saw no proper ground or chance for interference until some proceedings had been officially commenced against him to compel him to do so.

Not being very familiar with the Prussian military laws, I send the papers left with me to you, begging you to instruct me in the matter, both as to advising him what to do and as to the course to be pursued in case he should go to Paderborn, be arrested, and held to military service. I have informed him that I should ask your advice. It is an affair which ought to be settled amicably with the authorities, for Mr. Meyer has given me to understand that he holds some property there, which is in danger of being confiscated in the ordinary course of law.

Mr. Meyer's passport is perfectly in good order. I did not see his papers of naturalization, but he tells me that he has them here, if we wish them.

Very respectfully, your obedient servant,

JOHN C. BATES.

His Excellency D. D. BARNARD,
&c., &c., &c.

Mr. Barnard to Mr. Bates.

LEGATION OF THE UNITED STATES,
Berlin, July 5, 1852.

SIR: I have received your letter of July 2, in regard to the matter of Meyer.

My hands, just now, are full of these cases. I shall lose no time in bringing the case of Meyer to the notice of the government. I have arranged for a special interview with Baron Manteuffel to-morrow on the whole subject. The questions that arise are not without serious difficulty. I hope, however, to be able to make an amicable arrangement, which shall relieve Mr. Meyer and all other American naturalized citizens, situated as he is, from the embarrassments to which they are now subject.

I am not prepared, at this moment, to say that the counsel you have given Mr. Meyer, involving a delicate and long-mooted point of international law, is free from doubt; and I earnestly advise Mr. Meyer, at least, to wait till he hears further from this legation, and not to go to Paderborn at present, to encounter there a judgment recorded against him in a matter which the Prussian law regards as criminal, and in face, also, of the official declaration that, if he comes there, he will be put into the army.

With great respect, your obedient servant,

D. D. BARNARD.

J. C. BATES, Esq., *Consul, &c.*

Mr. Barnard to Baron Von Manteuffel.

LEGATION OF THE UNITED STATES,
Berlin, July 8, 1852.

MONSIEUR LE BARON: A person whose name is Meyer, born in Paderborn, in Prussia, in the year 1827, and now a citizen of the United States, emigrated to that country in the year 1845, when he was eighteen years of age, having been furnished with a regular Prussian passport. At the time of his emigration the subject of the military requirements of the Prussian laws, and the necessity, or propriety, of his procuring a permit of emigration was not thought of. Subsequently the subject recurred to him, and he requested his relatives and friends in Paderborn to attend to the matter, and procure for him a permit of emigration, which they promised to do.

Sometime afterwards he went from the eastern to a remote western part of the United States, where he remained for some years, and until recently, and during this period, no communication from his family in Paderborn reached him.

On his return, in the early part of the present year, to the city of New York, he learned for the first time that his friends had neglected to procure for him a permit of emigration, and that proceedings had been instituted against him for violation of the military laws of Prussia, and he had been condemned to pay a fine of fifty thalers. This judgment was rendered in the royal circle court of Paderborn on the 22d November, 1851.

On receiving this information he addressed a letter on the subject to the burgomaster of Paderborn, dated the 20th March, 1852, a copy of which I have the honor to inclose to you herewith.

He received no answer to this communication except a verbal one, through a friend, that the burgomaster could take no step in the matter, and that if he came to Paderborn he must serve in the Prussian army.

Earnestly desiring from a sense of filial duty, as well as an urgent call of business, to visit Paderborn, Mr. Meyer has arrived in Europe. He has an aged mother living at Paderborn, and there is property there in which he has an interest, which is in danger of being sacrificed without his personal presence and attention. He has no desire, I believe, to remain a moment longer than the business which calls him there may positively demand.

His request is to be permitted to visit Paderborn, and, at the same time, that such measures may be taken in his behalf that he shall be secure against arrest and all annoyance on account of the fine that has been imposed upon him, as well as on the ground of any claim upon him to enter or serve in the Prussian army. He has a regular passport as an American citizen from the proper authority at Washington.

I hope his Majesty's government may find no difficulty in acceding to this reasonable request of Mr. Meyer.

It does not admit of a doubt that this man has not been guilty of any intentional breach of the laws of Prussia. He left Prussia, as all his acts and his solemn oath demonstrate, with the *bona fide* intention of changing his residence and his country, and of becoming the subject of another State. This he has done. And it can no more be predicated of him that he left Prussia with the "intention" of avoiding his military duty, because he chanced to neglect the formality of a permit of emigration, than the same thing could be said of the thousands of others who emigrate yearly from Germany, and who may have complied with that regulation. Doubtless it is to be regretted, and Mr. Meyer himself regrets, that a permit of emigration had not been procured for him at the time of his emigration, since such is the legal regulation. But if such permit would have been granted to him without hesitation, if asked for at the time, as I presume admits of no doubt, there would seem to be no good reason, since he has been guilty of no crime, but simply of the neglect of a formal regulation, why he should not now receive such permission, or something equivalent to it, to take effect from the period of his emigration, and which shall effectually protect him from all annoyances as a citizen of the United States visiting Prussia on his lawful affairs.

I desire on this occasion, as on all occasions, to appeal to the friendly disposition of his Majesty's government towards the United States. On this ground I ask his Majesty's government to consider whether there is not something better to be done in cases of this sort which are now occurring, and likely to occur quite frequently, than to insist on the rigid application of the domestic laws of Prussia, or to insist on their applicability, under whatever notion of the abstract rights of sovereignty, even supposing them to be ever so well founded, to persons who have in the most solemn form, and in perfect good faith, following in this regard a natural and undoubting impression of their absolute right to do so, renounced their allegiance to his Majesty, and become, as they intend perpetually to remain, the subjects of a foreign and friendly State; whether there is not something to be done better than to insist on a course of proceeding from which no substantial benefit can ever be derived, but which, on the contrary, cannot fail to produce irritation and dissatisfaction, and in the end, it is to be feared, serious difficulty.

It can afford certainly no satisfaction to Prussia, if she should be able, even supposing she could have any such desire, to exact a small sum now and then by way of fine from a few American citizens who may chance to find themselves temporarily and on their proper business in this country, because from thoughtless inattention when they were mere boys they went away, or because their parents, from thoughtlessness or any other cause, led them away from Prussia to a foreign country without having first obtained a permit of emigration. Still less could Prussia derive either satisfaction or profit from the forced service, if such a thing were practicable and would be submitted to, of such American citizens in the Prussian army; though on this point I must be allowed to add, that I cannot suppose that his Majesty's government can have any design or any desire to force these citizens into its military service.

Is it necessary, then, let me ask, or can it be proper, that the local authorities in Prussia should be suffered to take advantage of the casual presence of these persons in Prussia, coming here on errands of affection or of business, to annoy and harass them by proceedings which are not at all likely to produce any beneficial result to anybody, or any practical result whatever, except such as everybody must lament; or by holding up the laws, exactions, and proceedings referred to, as a threat and a terror, to prevent or deter them from coming here, when on every consideration of justice, of humanity, and of friendly regard towards the country of their adoption, and which now owes them protection, they ought to be allowed to do so?

Mr. Meyer, as I have said, is now in Europe. He is here expressly for the purpose indicated by me, and is waiting for the proper protection to enable him to visit to Paderborn.

Accept, Monsieur le Baron, on this occasion, the asssurance of my distinguished consideration.

D. D. BARNARD.

His Excellency BARON VON MANTEUFFEL, *&c., &c., &c.*

Mr. Barnard to Mr. Webster.

[Extract.]

No. 72.]

LEGATION OF THE UNITED STATES,
Berlin, July 20, 1852.

SIR:

* * * * * * * *

I forward, also, herewith, a copy of an additional letter from me to Baron Von Manteuffel, in the case of Dr. Gutowski.

* * * * * * * *

I have the honor to be, with the highest respect, your obedient servant.

D. D. BARNARD.

Hon. DANIEL WEBSTER,
Secretary of State.

Mr. Barnard to Baron Von Manteuffel.

LEGATION OF THE UNITED STATES,
Berlin, July 14, 1852.

MONSIEUR LE BARON: Referring to my letter to your excellency of the 1st of July, 1852, in reference to Dr. Gutowski, I have the honor herewith to inclose to you, at his request, two documents, which I have just received from him, and which I doubt not will receive all due attention. These documents are:

1st. Dr. Gutowski's petition to his excellency the minister of the interior; and

2d. A certificate of guarantee for Dr. Gutowski, from the Count Skorzewski.

I renew to your excellency, on this occasion, the assurance of my distinguished consideration.

D. D. BARNARD.

His Excellency BARON VON MANTEUFFEL, *&c.*

Mr. Barnard to Mr. Webster.

No. 75.]

LEGATION OF THE UNITED STATES,
Berlin, August 3, 1852.

SIR: I have the honor to inclose to you a copy of a letter addressed by me to Baron Von Manteuffel, in the matter of Christian George Born. I do not send a copy of Mr. Born's letter to me, as he has informed me that he has already transmitted a copy to the department.

I have the honor to be, with the highest respect, your obedient servant,

D. D. BARNARD.

Hon. DANIEL WEBSTER, *&c.*

Mr. Barnard to Baron Von Manteuffel.

LEGATION OF THE UNITED STATES,
Berlin, August 3, 1852.

MONSIEUR LE BARON: I regret very much to be obliged to bring to your excellency's notice another complaint of a citizen of the United States, traveling in Prussia on his lawful business. The proceeding complained of took place at Minden, and the principal actor in the affair was an official personage whose name is Von Hassenkrug, though there were others who seem to have taken a willing part in it.

The person to whom this wrong has been done is Mr. Christian George Born, a native of Prussia, but a resident of the United States since 1837, and now a citizen of that country. He is a merchant, engaged extensively in business, and visits Germany in that capacity, though he is at the same time specially commissioned by the Department of State at Washington, as bearer of dispatches to the legation of the United States at Vienna, to which place he has now proceeded. Of his entire respectability and unexceptionable character there cannot be a doubt, nor is it easy to understand what possible excuse there could have been for making him an object of suspicion, and treating him as he was treated, like a criminal.

Mr. Born having addressed to me a full and minute statement of his grievance, and of the circumstances of his arrest, detention, and examination, I have caused a translation of the principal contents of that communication to be made into the German language, which I have the honor herewith to inclose to you, together with an appendix, containing a long list of names of respectable persons in Prussia to whom Mr. Born refers for his character and standing.

The sum of the case then, is this: Mr. Born comes to Prussia as an American merchant, visiting the merchants and manufacturers of Prussia with a view to the prosecution and extension of his lawful business, and by which the beneficial trade between the two countries would be promoted and extended. He enters Prussia with a regular passport, which is regularly visaed at Aix-la-Chapelle. Having business to transact at several different towns and places in the neighborhood of that place, three or four weeks is thus actively consumed. He then leaves Dusseldorf to go to Bremen, through Minden. At Minden he encounters Mr. Von Hassenkrug. This official from the first is imperious and rude in his behaviour. He threatens to detain him before he has seen his passport, and before he could know if there was the slightest ground for detaining him. When his passport is produced, he immediately pronounces it not in order, and yet immediately proceeds to write a visé upon it, and he renders it back to the bearer as a proper authority for his proceeding on his journey. But happening at this moment to understand that Mr. Born was on his way to Bremen, and so about to pass out of Prussia instead of remaining in it, he takes his passport from him, and angrily proclaims that he shall be detained, and his baggage minutely searched. To convince him of his error, and to show him who it was with whom he was dealing thus harshly, Mr. Born exhibits to him a document under the signature and seal of the Secretary of State of the United States, appointing him a bearer of dispatches from that government to Vienna. This document produced no change in Mr. Hassenkrug's conduct, and no effect upon him but to cause him to indulge in an expression towards the United States too vulgar and indecent to be repeated. He persists in detaining Mr. Born, and orders him and his baggage to the room of the third and fourth class passengers, where his baggage is overhauled and examined. After this he is conducted, in the custody of a police officer, an English mile and a half, to the police court of Minden, followed by a rabble, as if he had been a condemned culprit. At ten o'clock, having arrived at the station of Minden at half past four in the morning, his examination commences before an under officer of the police court. His repeated and earnest request that the land-rath, or chief of police, might be present if the papers and writings in his possession were to be examined, was not complied with. These papers and writings were opened and examined by the under officer, assisted by Mr. Hassenkrug, they possessing themselves in this way of a knowledge of all the private and business affairs and relations of Mr. Born which these papers might disclose. Finally, at near twelve o'clock, unable to find the slightest material to justify a proceeding which from the first had no foundation in reason, Mr. Born was dismissed and allowed to pursue his journey.

I am sure that this sort of unjustifiable and apparently wanton annoyance offered to citizens of the United States traveling in Prussia, or temporarily visiting this country on business, of which there have been of late too many examples, cannot meet the approval of his Majesty's government. I hardly need assure your excellency that I claim for my countrymen visiting Prussia no exemption from the just operation of the regular laws and internal regulations of Prussia which have for their object the protection of society and the government against crimes either perpetrated or devised for their overthrow or injury; but, when proceedings are instituted against them for which no justification can be alleged, or even an excuse which could stand a moment's candid examination, it becomes my imperative duty to interpose in their behalf, and in cases where some casual circumstances may have excited suspicion, enough perhaps to make it not improper that some inquiry should be instituted on the part of the local police or authorities, it is equally my duty to appeal to the government of his Majesty against proceedings which are so conducted as to confound and level all moral distinctions, all notions of right and wrong, and to place the innocent and the guilty in one common category of oppression and ignominy.

In the best and most humane systems of government or jurisprudence, legal suspicion may light on an innocent person. But if suspicion is to be made a ground of accusation and of criminal proceeding, it should at least have something better to rest upon than imagination, or a mere wild and vague conjecture; and, at any rate, when acts and circumstances affecting an individual are, to say the least of it, quite as consistent with his innocence as with any imputation of guilt, every rule of law, and every dictate of reason, justice, and humanity, require that his innocence rather than his guilt should be assumed until the contrary shall become manifest, and, if molested at all, it should only be with the most studied and delicate regard to his personal rights and his feelings as a man. This is what is due to every human being; and enlightened and humane as the government of his Majesty is well known to be, this, I assume, is what is, and always must be, accorded to his Majesty's subjects in the circumstances supposed; and this is what, in the behalf of my government, I claim shall be accorded, under the same circumstances, to the citizens of the United Stases visiting Prussia. It certainly would have been as easy and quite as efficient to have conducted the proceedings in the case of Mr. Born, in a mild, reluctant, temperate, and friendly spirit, as with the fierce zeal and vindictive temper manifested towards him. There were no appearances about him to have raised at any time even a well-grounded suspicion. He had not entered Prussia without a passport perfectly in order; and for the time that he had remained within the Prussian dominions, there was nothing which was not susceptible of the easiest explanation, and nothing which was not promptly and fully explained on the spot. There was a respectable Prussian present to answer for him, who had known him for thirty years; and if anything was still wanting to put an end to all questions about his character and pretensions, it was supplied by the commission which he bore and exhibited from the Department of State at Washington. This, however, was not only not enough to prevent his being detained and ill treated, but this very document gave occasion to Mr. Hassenkrug to vent his vulgar malignity against a government and country with which his Majesty the King, his royal master, maintains relations of peace, commerce, and amity, as they have been maintained uninterruptedly, by treaty, from the time of the Great Frederick, and from the earliest infancy of the American government.

The proceedings against Mr. Born, and his personal treatment, were altogether in a spirit of oppression and vindictiveness such as a known and undoubted criminal might perhaps have encountered without cause of complaint, and not at all in the spirit of an honest and necessary inquiry, made merely to ascertain whether there was any reason for detaining him, or regarding him as a suspected person. His examination was prosecuted in an inquisitorial manner, and as if to intimidate and entrap him. His language was misinterpreted, and his truth openly questioned and denied. He was treated throughout as a guilty person, assumed to be so, and as if nothing remained but to find in his words, or among his effects or his papers, not the proofs of his guilt, but the materials to justify the assumption of his guilt; and all this while, I feel bound to say, that Mr. Born was as innocent, whether in conduct or in thought, of any offense against his Majesty, his government, or his laws, as his accuser, or his respectable examiner, and that from the first to the last there was not the least reasonable ground for believing otherwise.

I submit this case to your excellency's consideration. It cannot fail to be regarded as one calling for the interposition of his Majesty's government, and for some suitable action on its part. The case is the more grave, because it does not stand alone. If it had been a solitary instance, it might have been looked upon in another light; but, unhappily, it is not. I cannot doubt that your excellency will agree with me that an end ought to be put to these annoyances. They produce feelings of insecurity, and of distrust and dissatisfaction. Inoffensive and respectable travelers in Prussia, from the United States, ought to be relieved from them, and from all apprehension of them; and I trust that I may have the assurance that the just influence and authority of his Majesty's government will be exerted to prevent their occurrence.

Receive, I pray you, Monsieur le Baron, on this occasion, the assurance of my very distinguished consideration.

D. D. BARNARD.

His Excellency Monsieur LE BARON VON MANTEUFFEL,
&c., &c., &c.

Mr. Born to Mr. Barnard.

BREMEN, HILLMAN'S HOTEL,
July 12, 1852.

SIR: The undersigned, Christian George Born, merchant, a naturalized citizen of the United States, carrying on business under the firm of Born, Schlieper & Haarhaus, in the city of New York, finds himself compelled to bring to your notice "the arrest and unprovoked outrages which have been practiced and perpetrated on him by Prussian officials in Minden," a frontier town and fortress of said kingdom, laying near Schaumburg-Lippe, Buckeburg, "on his arrival there by the so-called quick railroad train from Deutz, about half past four o'clock, a. m., yesterday."

Before going into a true narration of the said outrages, it seems to be proper to give you a sketch of my origin and history, and to say that I have never meddled with politics of any kind in Germany, either previous or since I am a citizen of the United States; nor have I ever been before any one of their courts of police or justice whatsoever, until yesterday.

I was born December 14, 1803, in Bergenhausen, county of Wittzenstein, Berleburg, district of Armberg, Westphalia; and when of the age of about seventeen years, I was sent into the mercantile house of John Motte & Co., in Ronsdorf, with whom I remained seven and half years; then went into the house of Gilruder Boedinghaus, manufacturer of merino, &c., in Elberfeld, with whom I stayed about four and a half years; and from them, into the business of Gilruder Colsman, large silk manufacturers in Langenberg, near Elberfeld, with whom I served five years, during which, acting for them as principal in the sale of their goods at the fairs of Leipzic and Frankfort, up to the end of August, 1837, when I left for New York, having associated myself with John H. Albers, (at present consular agent of the United States in Bremen,) who then had been carrying on business in the city of New York about fifteen years past, and which, ever since, I have continued under the firms of J. H. Albers & Born, C. G. Born & Co., Born & Schuchardt, and at present, Born, Schlieper & Haarhaus.

On my arrival in the city of New York, in October, 1837, I lawfully declared my intentions of becoming a citizen of the United States, and, after the lapse of about seven or eight years, (not leaving the Union on a visit to foreign countries until the 25th April, 1844,) the certificate of citizenship was given me, and ever since it has been my constant study and pleasure to be a true citizen of the Union in every sense in words and acts, and when abroad abstaining entirely from expressing an opinion on measures or politics of European governments.

As at the present time, I have visited Europe for business purposes in 1844, 1846, 1848, and twice in 1851, without being troubled, at any time, till yesterday, except on my arrival from New York on the 31st May, 1844, in Havre, where a custom-house officer wanted to search my pockets, which I resisted, and my conduct was approved by the collector of said port.

This time, I left New York on the 29th day of May last, in the United States steamer Atlantic, and entered Prussia, June 12th, as per visé on my passport by the police at Aix-la-Chapelle.

In Aix-la-Chapelle, Burtschied, and Duren, I remained then up to about June 18, 22, transacting business with cloth manufacturers, and then left by railroad, *via* Cologne and Dusseldorf, to Langenburg, where I stayed three days with my friends, then visiting Elberfeld, Burmen, Swheren, Ronsdorf, Lennep, and Huckeowagen on business, and returning to Langenburg, July 5. On the 6th instant proceeded to Langenburg, *via* Velbert, Werden, and Kettwig, &c., to Viersen; spent the 7th with Fred. Diergardt in Viersen, William Ditthey in Rheydt, and arrived the same evening in Crefeld.

In the morning of the 8th instant attended to business in Crefeld, and went in the afternoon *via* Dusseldorf to Deutz. Spent the morning of the 9th with Director Merrisen, at the counting-house of A. Schaaffhausen's Banking Associations, and in the afternoon went back to Dusseldorf. Spent the 10th in Dusseldorf with Feldmann Simons and lady, who are the parents-in-law of my partner Schleiper. The same day, in the evening, at 11 o'clock, left Dusseldorf in the quick railroad train taking a second-class place through to Bremen, arriving at 4½ o'clock at Minden, and there passengers were informed by the conductor that we had to change cars, and time for taking a cup of coffee. Having scarcely sat down in the first and second-class room to the coffee table, a police officer came and demanded the passport of each passenger, when it struck me that I had left mine in the trunk, and informing said officer thereof, and sitting just by the side of Mr. Frowein, a merchant from Elberfeld, who then was delivering his passport, I said, inquiringly, that this gentleman knew me well during the last thirty years, and if, in consequence, my card would suffice? To which the officer returned in rage, No; and added that he would keep me here. I then ran to the baggage-car, procured my trunk, took out in a hurry my passport, and unintentionally with it a commission which I held from the Department of State as bearer of despatches to our legation at Vienna. Coming back to the first and second-class room, I found the officer who had spoken to me, and whose name he afterwards made me understand was Commissarius Von Hassenkrug, engaged in still visaing passports, of which he had left about eight or ten laying unfinished before him, and when just done with one, I handed him mine and said, "I would be thankful for his visaing it now, and thereby enable me to finish my cup of coffee." To which he again replied, with rage, that "I had scarcely got hold of it when I wanted to be helped first," to which I remained silent, and he, meanwhile taking and looking into the same, said, "it was not in order, for having to be visaed at every place I had been staying since entering the frontier of Prussia;" to which I pleaded my ignorance in the matter, and remarking, politely, "that if such was the police regulation the hotel-keeper ought to be instructed to advise foreigners of it," to which he made no reply, but commencing to write a long line on my passport, and during which the inferior officer putting a letter-stamp on it. On his handing the same, folded, with a hard look back to me, and without my looking at what he had written, I thoughtlessly remarked that "I was going to Bremen," which word seemed to raise his suspicion, and in a furious manner he commanded the lower police officer to "retain me, with my baggage, which latter should be searched and examined very minutely," and thereupon I requested him, still politely, but earnestly, "not to give me any unnecessary delay, as everything was right with me, and that besides my passport, (which again he had taken away from me and given for safe-keeping to the lower police officer,) I was holding from my government a commission as bearer of dispatches, or courier passport, then showing it to him, in which he rejoined, "Bah, I will show you that you are in Prussia, and that we shit on your government and couriers." I then again, coolly and politely, told him that I would make the government of Prussia responsible for his violent acts and insults, to which he returned new epithets, and ordered me with my baggage to be brought to the room for the third and fourth-class passengers, apparently with the sole view of lording it over me in the presence of a more ignorant crowd of people. Here my luggage was thoroughly examined, and the delivery of my papers and scriptures to them demanded, which I resisted, saying, that "I would not separate from anything of mine." Thereupon I was informed that, after half past seven o'clock, I would be brought to the police court in the city, but twice previous to this time arriving, they wanted to take to the city my baggage without me, and and I dare say with no other view than to smuggle political papers, &c., into the same.

At last it struck 7½ o'clock, and shortly after, the lower police officer called in a porter to put in the cart my baggage, which I never left, and then I was accompanied by said officer, and was taken to the police court in the city, a distance of about one and a half English miles. In going thus through the city, the people being about, followed; and arriving at the house of police, a considerable crowd had collected, all of whom seemed to view me as a thief, a spy, or a murderer; and at this moment, sir, it would be in vain for me to attempt giving a correct description of my painful sensation of mind. On my being ushered into the police room, they again attempted, in a most ingenious manner, to separate me from my baggage, but I had made up my mind rather to die, and thanks be to a gracious God I was successful. There I was left with another inferior officer, not the same who had brought me there, until 9 o'clock, when Police Sergeant

Ruhl, as I heard him called, entered, whose business seemed to be "visaing the books of wandering professionists," of whom a number came in and left. At last, towards 10 o'clock, a young man who was called lieutenant, came in, and called me to the stand by my name; he then commenced an examination with me, and his sole aim thereby seemed to be bent on perverting and misunderstanding every word that I answered; and discovering and seeing that he was for and in coalition with my maltreator, Von Hassenkrug, I earnestly requested of him more than half a dozen times that "Herr landrath, the chief of police, would deign to be present at the examination of my papers and scriptures," to which at last he replied he would go and see about it, and actually leaving the room; but it so happening at this moment that my eyes fell on the face of the above-mentioned Mr. Ruhl, I actually thought to read in it that "Herr landrath would not be present;" and then again I repeated my request to several of the police officers going in and out, to solicit the favor for me from Herr landrath, which several promised to do, but, after half an hour's delay, the above-mentioned lieutenant came in again, accompanied by Commissarius Von Hassenkrug, and said to me the landrath was prevented by official duty to be present, and he was ordered to examine into and read my papers, unless I would deliver the same to him to be taken to the landrath, which I refused to do, saying at the same moment, it would be my duty to inform your excellency that the landrath could not, or either would not be present." I then opened my trunk, and he, in presence of Von Hassenkrug and myself, opened and read every piece of paper and writing in my possession, in all of which he could not find a single line nor word to be turned against me, except that I was carrying with me "one sealed letter" which is addressed as follows: "Herr H. Thomas, Mechaniker, Montbijin Platz, No. 10;" this letter was given to me in New York previous to my departure by Frederick Mohl, Esq., of Berlin, who spent last winter on a visit to the States, to Havana, &c., and who informed me that Mr. Thomas was furnishing machinery to cloth manufacturers, and would be the best person to tell me who of said cloth manufacturers in Silesia was turning out and finishing his goods suitable for our markets. The place of destination, for instance, "Berlin" is not written on the letter, as I am going to prove to you, sir, next week, when I hope to arrive in Berlin, from Hamburg, and have the honor of paying my respects in person to your excellency. Mr. Mohl I suppose to be also now in Berlin, in which case I will take the liberty of bringing him along with me, and introducing him to you.

The above-mentioned lieutenant and examinator told me that it was punishable carrying that sealed letter to Mr. Thomas, and I requested him to mention it in his report, as I did not wish evading to pay the fine the law imposed for carrying it.

Failing entirely to find anything else in my possession but that sealed letter without its complete address on which to hang a feather, the said lieutenant again endeavored willfully to interpret and pervert my language to Commissioner Von Hassenkrug, insinuating even that I had raised latter's suspicion by claiming to be a courier, all which is a mere contrivance of these swaggering officials, for my very first mention of holding and showing to him my commission or courier's passport was only after he had ordered me and my baggage to stay behind, and be treated as a prisoner. At last, towards 12 o'clock, I was suffered to depart free and without police accompaniment from the police court of the city back to the railroad station, where I arrived just in time for the departure of a train to this place, and though during my examination I had thought of proceeding direct to your legation at Berlin, but on consideration of the uncertainty of finding you home at once, and the pressing nature of the business I have to attend to here previous to the departure of the steamer Hermann the 16th instant, I concluded to come to this city, and inform you of my arrest and maltreatment at Minden in writing.

Sir, to the truth of every word I have written down here I am ready, at any time and place, to make oath in the presence of my God and Creator, and I now expect your excellency to act in this matter with energy and dispatch. My arrest and detention was not made in entering the territory of Prussia, but in leaving it, which is without excuse, and the more aggravating by its casting on me either the guilt of a thief or a spy, or something still worse; and as everything is likely to be resorted to by the officials of Prussia to disparage my statement and question my veracity, I herewith inclose a list of names of highly respectable persons, and subjects of Prussia, to whom I am personally known, to many of whom from childhood, and whose opinions of me can easily be ascertained. To most of the better class of inhabitants in Ronsdorf, Elberfeld, and Langenburg I am particularly long and well known.

It may perhaps be proper to mention to your excellency also, that I enjoy the honor, since the 1st day of January, 1839, of being personally and intimately known to his excellency Millard Fillmore, the faithful President of the United States.

Sir, I most earnestly deplore having been the object of such high-handed insults and outrages, the like of which amongst friendly nations I have never heard of before, and I would not dare showing my face with my fellow-citizens at home again, without having done all I can to obtain redress.

I therefore claim from the government of Prussia the payment of twenty thousand rix dollars for the arrest and insults which have been practiced on me personally in its name, and by its official servants, yesterday morning; and besides, such suitable national apology from it to our government as may be deemed sufficient and satisfactory to our President.

I have the honor to be, most respectfully, your excellency's obedient servant,

CHRISTIAN GEORGE BORN,
of New York.

His Excellency D. D. BARNARD,
Minister of the United States for Prussia.

List of names of highly respectable persons, to whom Christian George Born, now of the city of New York, is personally and well known:

<table>
<tr><td colspan="2">Prince Franz von Wittgenstein, Berleburg.</td></tr>
<tr><td>Voss. Kris Secretain,
L. H. Althaus, merchant,</td><td>In Berleburg, near Armberg.</td></tr>
<tr><td colspan="2">Charles Martin, postmaster, Erndebruck, near Armberg.</td></tr>
<tr><td>Charles Rinz, lawyer,
F. Hammer, merchant,</td><td>In Lasphe, near Armberg.</td></tr>
<tr><td>Engels Puffrath, merchant,
Julius Johanny, merchant,
Ernest Johanny, merchant,</td><td>In Hurheswagen, by Elberfeld.</td></tr>
<tr><td>J. H. Von Baur, merchant,
August Hotthausen, merchant,
William Kneip, merchant,
J. N. Siebel, merchant,
N. G. Grote, merchant,
J. E. Bleekman, merchant,
Charles Braun, merchant,
Charles Von Baur, merchant,</td><td>With many others in Ronsdorf, near Elberfeld.</td></tr>
<tr><td>William Boeddinghaus, merchant,
Henry Boeddinghaus, merchant,
William Ulinbrug, merchant,
Theodore Besenbronck, merchant,
Adrian Koehler, merchant,</td><td>With many others in Elberfeld.</td></tr>
<tr><td>Peter Schlieper, merchant,
Gustav Schlieper, merchant,
S. W. Haarhaus, merchant,
Johann Schrieck, merchant,
Edward Jung, merchant,
William Simons Koehler, merchant,
Peter Strasweg, merchant,
J. P. Ufor, merchant,
Gustav and Charles Wolff, merchants,</td><td>And many others in Elberfeld.</td></tr>
<tr><td>William Colsmann, merchant,
Edward Colsmann,
Charles Colsmann,
Aug. Feldhaff,
Gustav Hoomann,
Julius Koetgen,
Diergardt, doctor of medicine,</td><td>With many others in Langenberg, near Elberfeld.</td></tr>
<tr><td>William Weddigen, merchant,
Frederick Weddigen, merchant,
Aug. Mittelstenfcheid, merchant,
Theo. Mittelstenfcheid, merchant,
Charles Karthaus, merchant,
Gebruder Schuchard, merchant,
F. H. Wirth, merchant,</td><td>And many others in Bremen.</td></tr>
<tr><td colspan="2">Edward Busehi, merchant in Schwebun.</td></tr>
</table>

John Mohn, Vebbert.
Ernst Scheidt, merchant in Kettwig.
Frederick Diergardt, merchant, Viersen, near Crefeld.
William Ditthey, merchant, Rheydt.
G. B. Von der Herberg, merchant, Crefeld.

Feldmann Simons, rentier,
Henry Heegmann, rentier,
Conitl Leser, rentier,
Sartorius Bargmann, merchant,
} In Dusseldorf.

Edward Toenniés, merchant,
J. H. Kesselkaul, merchant,
Ernst Klinekenberg, merchant,
J. A. Bischoff, merchant,
Julius Schuremann, merchant,
} And others, in Aix-la-Chapelle.

Frederick Mohl, rentier,
B. F. Wesmer, merchant,
H. Demuth, merchant,
A. Kochne, banker,
} In Berlin.

Mr. Barnard to Mr. Webster.

[Extract.—Confidential.]

No. 76.] LEGATION OF THE UNITED STATES,
Berlin, August 3, 1852.

SIR: Mr. Born having appealed himself to the department, by sending a copy of his letter addressed to me, I proposed at first to leave his case into your hands, or at least to wait for your instructions, and I so informed him. But I have supposed on the whole that the department would prefer, in all cases of this sort, which are rather troublesome than serious, should be taken care of at the legation, at least in the first instance.

As complaints on the part of citizens of the United States, native as well as naturalized, of ill-treatment in Prussia, have multiplied of late, I have assumed a more serious tone in the case of Mr. Born, than otherwise I should have thought altogether necessary.

You will observe that the complaints which come to this legation are chiefly from the German Americans. There is no doubt that, coming back here, they are always more or less objects of suspicion. The Prussian government and its officials are always on the lookout for the German Democratic Propaganda and its agents. Slight things are enough to arouse attention; and it happens, unfortunately, that many of our naturalized German citizens visiting their native country, who are in no sense political agents, and who come here on no political errand whatever, come nevertheless with very sublimated notions of the personal liberty and independence which belong to them as Americans, and are apt to forget that Prussia is not exactly the most appropriate sphere in which to display these qualities. As a general thing, they submit with much less patience and good temper to the internal and police regulations of European counties than our native American citizens. Their high bearing and assumptions are often the commencement of the difficulties they encounter. They do not easily brook the exercise of any sort of summary authority over them. And when, having fallen into trouble, they bring their complaints to an American legation, their demands are apt to be very high and very imperious. Mr. Born, for example, one of the most respectable and well informed of the whole class of German emigrants returning to visit their native country, demands, as you will observe, twenty thousand rix thalers for his detention of six or eight hours, and very modestly informs the American minister at Berlin, that "he expects him to act in his case with energy and dispatch."

My correspondence with the department, already forwarded, will show the state of the question with Prussia and Hanover, in regard to their demand upon naturalized citizens for military services, and for fines or penalties for having avoided their military duties.

I consider the Hanoverian government as having yielded, practically, the right to exact military service of persons who have become citizens of the United States, and who may be found temporarily within the King's dominions. I hope the Prussian government will do the same thing. * * * * * * *

I have the honor, &c.,

D. D. BARNARD.

Hon. DANIEL WEBSTER,
Secretary of State.

Mr. Barnard to Mr. Webster.

[Extract.]

No. 78.] LEGATION OF THE UNITED STATES,
Berlin, August 10, 1852.

SIR: I have the honor to forward to you herewith a copy of a letter addressed by me to Dr. Gutowski, in reply to one from him urging action upon his petition to the Prussian government.

* * * * * * * *

I have the honor to be, with the highest respect, your obedient servant,

D. D. BARNARD.

Hon. DANIEL WEBSTER,
Secretary of State.

Mr. Barnard to Dr. Gutowski.

LEGATION OF THE UNITED STATES,
Berlin, August 3, 1852.

SIR: Your note of the 27th July has been received. A special application was made by me in your behalf to Baron Manteuffel on the

1st July, and on the 14th July your petition to the minister of the interior, and the certificate of guarantee which accompanied it, were sent in. No answer has yet been received. The case is in the hands of the Prussian government, which, in such matters, always moves with deliberation.

It is proper I should inform you, that having voluntarily returned to the country of your birth, where you have purchased a farm and taken up your residence, the Prussian government has a right to regard you as its subject, and so treat you in all respects. And you have now, by your petition, asked to be received again as a Prussian citizen. Under these circumstances, the government of the United States cannot claim to interpose of right in your case, as in behalf of a citizen of that country. I shall be very glad if what I have done may be of any servise to you, as I still hope it may; but the decision of your case rests with the Prussian government.

I am, sir, your obedient servant,

D. D. BARNARD.

Dr. GUTOWSKI.

Mr. Barnard to Mr. Webster.

No. 80.]

LEGATION OF THE UNITED STATES,
Berlin, August 17, 1852.

SIR: I have the honor to inclose to you herewith a copy of a note which I have received from the minister of foreign affairs in reference to my letter to him on the complaint of Mr. Born.

I have the honor to be, with the highest respect, your obedient servant,

D. D. BARNARD.

Hon. DANIEL WEBSTER,
Secretary of State.

The Minister of Foreign Affairs to Mr. Barnard.

[Translation.]

BERLIN, *April* 14, 1854.

SIR: I hastened to bring to the knowledge of the minister of the interior the facts which you indicated to me in your note of the 3d of this month, concerning the proceedure of an agent of police at Minden towards Mr. Born, merchant, citizen of the United States, and so soon as the result of the investigation I have sought on this subject shall be known to me, I shall have the honor, sir, to apprize you without delay.

I seize, meantime, this occasion, sir, to renew to you the assurance of my high consideration.

THE MINISTER OF FOREIGN AFFAIRS.
For the Minister, LE COQ.

His Excellency Mr. BARNARD, *&c., &c., &c.*

Mr. Barnard to Mr. Webster.

No. 89.]

LEGATION OF THE UNITED STATES,
Berlin, October 12, 1852.

SIR: I have the honor to inclose to you, herewith, a copy of a letter which I addressed to Baron Manteuffel on the 9th instant, in behalf of John Joseph Kracke, formerly a subject of the King of Prussia, and now claiming to be an American citizen, who has been placed in the ranks of the Prussian army, as a soldier, to serve for three years.

I send also a copy of the communication addressed to me by Mr. Kracke, and which was handed in to the legation by a Prussian military officer, who, in a private and confidential way, expressed much sympathy for this man.

I have the honor to be, with the highest respect, your obedient servant,

D. D. BARNARD.

Hon. DANIEL WEBSTER,
Secretary of State.

Mr. Barnard to Baron Manteuffel.

LEGATION OF THE UNITED STAEES,
Berlin, October 29, 1852.

M. LE BARON: I have the honor to inclose to you herewith a copy of a communication addressed to me by John Joseph Kracke.

It will be seen that Mr. Kracke, according to the simple and ingenuous account which he gives of himself, was born in Prussia in 1824; that in the fourteenth year of his age he went to reside, and to learn his trade, in Hanover; that in his seventeenth year he went to Holland, where he resided till his twentieth year; that at this time his parents emigrated to the United States; that he followed them from Holland to that country, where he has become a citizen, and the owner of lands and other property; that his health having become impaired, he has, by the advice of his physician, made a voyage to Europe; that on arriving at Recke, in the province of Westphalia, on a visit to the home of his youth, he was immediately arrested, and forced into the ranks of the Prussian army as a soldier, for a service of three years, where he now remains.

If the relation which Mr. Kracke gives of himself shall be found to be correct, I hope his Majesty's government will not hesitate to grant him a prompt discharge from the army, and liberty to return to his adopted country. I beg leave to refer your excellency to the general observations touching cases of this description, which I had the honor to submit to your consideration in my letter of the 8th of July last. I had indulged in the hope that measures might be adopted which would prevent the actual occurrence of cases like this of Mr. Kracke.

I have reliable information that Mr. Kracke is in the utmost distress at the situation in which he finds himself. He is utterly unconscious of any intentional offense against the laws or government of his native country, on account of the manner of his emigrating from it. For fourteen years, from his early boyhood, he has not resided in Prussia, and, in the meantime, he has made a home for himself in another and distant country, where he has assumed the rights and duties of citizenship, where his property is situated, and where all his interests in life are centered. Returning to visit the place of his birth, having become, as he believed, in every legal and just sense, a foreigner, he finds himself seized upon as a soldier of his Majesty the King, and he sees nothing before him but the certain sacrifice of his property, and the blasting of all his prospects in life. I am sure that no officer in his Majesty's service can exercise military authority over this unhappy man without painfully feeling the appeal which the laws of common humanity must perpetually make in his behalf.

In the application which I now present for the discharge of Mr. Kracke, I wish to avoid all reference to the abstract question of the rights of sovereignty which may be supposed to be involved in the case. I wish it to be understood, also, that I am aware of the importance, in a military point of view, which the government of his Majesty may attach to the laws of Prussia which regulate and control the emigration of his Majesty's subjects. The actual case is one of pressing and painful interest, and one in which the relief ought to come promptly. I am happy to believe it is one in which this relief may be granted without the sacrifice of any principle or any interest which Prussia may think it important to maintain, whether for her rights of sovereignty or for the efficiency of her military power.

I seize this occasion to offer to your excellency the renewed assurance of my distinguished consideration.

D. D. BARNARD.

His Excellency BARON VON MANTEUFFEL, &c.

Mr. Kracke to the American Minister.

[Translation.]

MUNSTER, *September* 29, 1852.

The humble petition of Johann Joseph Kracke, native of Recke, near Tecklenburg, some time musketeer in the second company of the musketeer battalion of the fifteenth infantry regiment at Munster, for the gracious intervention, for his discharge from the Prussian army, of the American minister.

Your excellency will graciously allow me to place the following petition before you:

I was born at Recke, near Tecklenburg; I was a royal Prussian subject according to the constitution of that time.

In my fourteenth year I left Recke, my birth place, and went to Osnabruck, in Hanover, where I learned my occupation, and labored from my seventeenth year to the twentieth in Holland. At this time my parents, at Recke, came to the determination to emigrate to the United States of North America, and I followed them from Holland.

Although I know not whether the consent of the royal Prussian government to the release from the condition of the bond of allegiance was sought by my family on my behalf, I believed, at least, that I was discharged from my condition of subject, because from my fourteenth year I had not resided within the Prussian territory, and was already naturalized and a subject of military obligations towards the United States.

Upon my arrival at New York I went on to Cincinnati, became there domiciled by a purchase of real estate, and there obtained the rights of a citizen of the United States of North America. The before-mentioned matters are established, in part, by my written depositions at the bureau of the headquarters of the regiment, partly from the official archives of the burgomaster's office at Recke, and also can be proved by searches in the municipal government of Cincinnati city. I had now lived, until this year, as a citizen of Cincinnati, and traveled by direction of my physician, on account of impaired health, back to Europe, furnished with a passport issued by that government, certified by my superior military chief.

On my arrival at Recke I was at once arrested by the police of the place, and for the fulfilling of my military obligations as a Prussian subject, which I no longer consider myself, was brought here for military service, and must moreover serve three years on military duty. My real estate in the city of Cincinnati, if I cannot go back to take care of it for three years, will be reduced to ruin, but also every probability that it will be aliened so that on return all my possessions and effects will have vanished, and I shall have become a poor man.

Under these very unfortunate circumstance I turn myself with the utmost confidence to your excellency with the humble petition that you will intercede with the Prussian royal government that I as a citizen of the United States of North America, and as such not under allegiance as subject of this country, shall be set free from military restraints.

Should, nevertheless, the impossibility of the fulfillment of this my petition be against me, then I request your excellency to give knowledge of it to the government of the United States, in order that until my return my real estate, left at the city of Cincinnati, may be taken care of.

In hopes of your highest welfare, I subscribe myself, your excellency's most obedient servant,

JOSEPH KRACKE.

Mr. Fay to Mr Webster.

[Extract.]

No. 103.] LEGATION OF THE UNITED STATES,
Berlin, October 26, 1852.

SIR: In his dispatch No. 57, [71,] under date July 13, 1852, Mr. Barnard communicated copy of a note addressed on the 8th to the Prussian government, presenting the case of Mr. B. Meyer, native of Paderborn, Prussia, who having emigrated seven years previously, without a permit of emigration, and just returned to Germany, furnished with a passport as an American citizen, dated May 6, 1852, from the Department of State, had been notified of a judgment condemning him to a fine of fifty thalers, for not having complied with the conscription law of Prussia.

His case presented circumstances of peculiar hardship, and furnished a proper opportunity for trying the question whether the government of Prussia intends to persevere in a strict application of the Prussian military law to naturalized American citizens, even having emigrated in early youth, resided long in the United States, and returned to Europe only temporarily, from the necessities of business, or the claims of private affection.

Mr. Barnard, therefore, with a strong statement of the case, addressed an application to the foreign minister, that permission should be granted Meyer to visit Paderborn upon some imperative private business, and to see his mother, aged seventy years, and requested that no measures might be taken on account of the fine, or to force him into the Prussian military service. After a lapse of three months and a half, a reply has just been received, of which a copy is subjoined.

It was not my intention to address you during the absence of Mr. Barnard, but this document is of a character to be brought to your notice without delay. The substance of it is as follows:

It flatly refuses Mr. Barnard's request that Mr. Meyer should be allowed to make a temporary sojourn at Paderborn, and declares, should he set foot on Prussian territory, he would be instantly incorporated into the army. Even upon payment of the fine, his obligation to serve in the army remains. No power can legally disengage him from the bonds attaching him to Prussia. If the government of the United States desires in future to avoid similar collisions, it should never receive as a citizen any native of Prussia, unless furnished with a permit of emigration. Finally, if the government of the King undertakes to execute the law against a Prussian subject, upon Prussian territory, that of the United States will have too high a sense of its own dignity to offer any opposition. * * *

A recent statistical publication, entitled "Hubner's Year Book for Agriculture and Statistics," estimates the German emigration of 1851 at 113,000, declaring that these are not the idle, vicious, and poor, but the industrious, the intelligent, the skillful, and the moderately thriving; and that, on an average, each individual carries from the country 200 thalers. If this be true, (and an emigrant can hardly leave this continent without some cash for his passage, &c.,) then twenty-two millions of thalers a year, and more than two hundred and twenty-six millions in ten years, are drained from Germany by the ever-increasing emigration. * * * * *

I have the honor to be, sir, with the highest consideration, your obedient servant,

THEO. S. FAY.

Hon. DANIEL WEBSTER,
Secretary of State.

Baron Manteuffel to Mr. Fay.

[Translation.]

BERLIN, *October* 22, 1852.

MONSIEUR: The letter which Mr. Barnard did me the honor to address to me, the 8th of July last, on the subject of one Meyer, a native subject of Prussia, born at Paderborn, who had emigrated to America, has given occasion for a correspondence with the minister of the interior, who has just communicated to me the report which he had called for on this matter from the proper provincial authority.

Here is the result: The person in question, born in 1827, is a son of the inn-keeper Meyer, whose widow still lives at Paderborn. In 1845, when he had scarcely attained the age of eighteen, he went to America, in the hope of finding opportunity to make a better living than in his own country, where even his mother with difficulty supported herself. Young Meyer did not at that time ask for a permit of emigration, he desired to reserve to himself the privilege of return to Prussia, in case he should not succeed in making a condition for himself in the United States. When he had attained the required age, he was summoned to return to Prussia to satisfy his military obligations, and having neglected the citation, a sentence passed 7th July last, year, condemned him to a fine of fifty crowns.

In this state of things the government cannot authorize Meyer to make a temporary sojourn at Paderborn to regulate his family affairs; it must insist, on the contrary, that this young man, if he place his foot on Prussian soil, be incorporated into the army.

I have already had the honor, sir, to cause you to observe above, that before quitting Prussia, Meyer had not asked to dissolve the ties which bound him to his native country, as he might have done, in the terms of Section 17, No. 1 of the law of December 31, 1842. On the contrary, he wished to continue to be a Prussian, to provide for the contingency of return to his country. If, notwithstanding, he has caused himself to be admitted as a citizen of the United States, he must blame himself, if by such step he has brought about collisions as to his personal relations towards two States. In his quality of Prussian subject, he is subject to military service in Prussia; not having presented himself in due time to range himself under the banners, he was duly condemned to a fine conformably with the regulations of law. Even if Meyer pay the fine which has been imposed on him, he still continues under obligation to do duty in the army, as every other subject of the King able to bear arms; and until this obligation is satisfied, he cannot lawfully be released from the bonds which bind him to Prussia. The government of the United States would be in the wrong to accuse that of the King of a want of good will, because he may make full and entire application of the law to one of his subjects who has caused himself to be received as citizen of the United States. If your government desires to avoid for the future similar collisions to that which has been brought about by the conduct of young Meyer, a simple means of attaining that end presents itself; it is only never to receive as citizen a Prussian by origin if he is not able to produce a permit of emigration. When any individual obtains naturalization in a foreign country, the government of his native country can never acknowledge that this fact, of itself, releases him from the obligations which were imposed upon him before his naturalization in his former country. I will add, that in cases like this, in which the said Meyer finds himself, it is much less a question of retaking any individual to enrol him in the army, than to maintain the respect due to the law, and to insure its execution. And if the government of his Majesty proposes to execute the law against a Prussian subject on Prussian territory, I desire to persuade myself that the government of the United States has too much respect for its own dignity to be willing to oppose itself thereto.

Accept on this occasion, sir, the assurance of my distinguished consideration,

MANTEUFFEL.

Mr. Fay,
Chargé d'Affaires of the United States.

Mr. Barnard to Mr. Everett.

[Extract.]

No. 91.] LEGATION OF THE UNITED STATES,
Berlin, December 7, 1852.

SIR: I have the honor to inclose to you herewith a copy of Baron Manteuffel's letter to me in the matter of Dr. Gutowski. My previous correspondence in this case will show the view I took of it. I allowed Dr. Gutowski to make his case and his request known to the Prussian government through me. The position in which he had placed himself did not admit of my doing more. The answer of the government shows that great pains have been taken to look into his character and pretensions, and the reasons are fully and plainly stated for the peremptory decision to which the minister of the interior has come.

* * * In my late temporary absence at Paris, Baron Manteuffel sent in his reply to my letter to him, of the 8th of July last, in the

matter of B. Meyer, a copy of which was immediately transmitted to the Department of State by Mr. Fay. In my letter to the department of 13th of July, (No. 71,) transmitting a copy of my letter of the 8th, I called the attention of the Secretary to the subject. Having received no instructions, I have supposed it was intended to leave the matter in my hands.

The case of Meyer was one where the party asked permission to visit Prussia without being subjected to a fine and to military service for having emigrated without permission. The answer refuses this permission.

With my letter of 12th October, (No. 89,) I transmitted a copy of a letter to Baron Manteuffel, in reference to the case of J. J. Kracke, claiming to be an American naturalized citizen, and then actually in forced service in the Prussian army. This case is, then, one in which the claim of the Prussian government is actually enforced and in process of execution. It remains to be seen if this case will be met in the same spirit as the other. I have a clear opinion about this doctrine of perpetual allegiance which lies at the foundation of the law and the action of Prussia in these cases, and at a proper time I may think it my duty, unless otherwise instructed, to express it in a grave and well-considered argument. * * * * * * * * *

I have the honor to be, &c.,

D. D. BARNARD.

Hon. EDWARD EVERETT,
Secretary of State.

Baron Manteuffel to Mr. Barnard.

[Translation.]

BERLIN, *November* 30, 1852.

SIR: The two letters which you have been pleased to address to me on the 1st and 14th July last, relative to Mr. Alexander Gutowski, doctor of medicine, having given rise to an exact investigation by the competent authorities, I have the honor to inform you that the minister of the interior has not found himself able to consent that the person in question may prolong his sojourn in the province of Posen, inasmuch as the information which has been gathered in regard to him is not favorable to him, and it has been proved that in his declarations Mr. Gutowski has often deviated from the truth.

It is, at the outset, uncertain that Mr. Gutowski was really born in Prussia. The only proof he has been able to produce in support of this assertion is the attestation (here annexed, in German translation,) of the curate Logowski, who is himself a Polish refugee. According to this paper, Gutowski was born the 19th January, 1816, at Malachowo, an estate in the parish of Witkowo. But this estate was never the property of the Gutowski family. It appears from the note of the death of the pretended mother of Mr. Gutowski, that such lady died the 26th May, 1822, aged fifty-seven years; she would then have been fifty-one years old at the birth of her son, which is, at least, scarcely probable. The church of Witkowo and all its records were reduced to ashes several years ago, and since then it has often happened that suspected persons have stated they were born in this parish. Gutowski will not even state the day of his birth. He says he quitted Prussia at ten or twelve years of age, to go into the kingdom of Poland; that he there frequented the college of Lublin, and from there took part in the Polish insurrection of 1830–31; that immediately afterward he emigrated to North America, and only returned to Prussia in 1851, to ask from the authorities of Bromberg letters of naturalization, which, however, were refused to him.

If Mr. Gutowski was in fact by birth a Prussian subject, which seems to be very doubtful, an absence of more than twenty years has long since caused him to lose that character; so that, by such title, he has no right he can make available in his favor.

Mr. Gutowski at first declared that he continued in the United States from 1831 to 1849. The inaccuracy of this assertion having been shown to him, he admitted that he had returned already in 1840 to France, to connect himself with the Polish emigration. In fact it is proved that Mr. Gutowski, in 1846, was at the head of the communist society known under the name of the "National Association;" that in 1848 he was leagued with the democratic Polish association. This person was also deputed in 1848 as an emissary to Cracow; sent away by order of the Austrian government, he went back there in 1849, and was again driven out. We learn also, by an avowal of Mr. Zackryewski, owner of the estate of Zabus, in the circle of Schrimm, (Grand Duchy of Posen,) that during the winter of 1847, 1848, Mr. Gutowski was secreted at his house. While this person had previously declared that, after his return to the province of Posen, in 1851, he went at once to Ruchosin, it is in proof that he first passed to Lubestrow, in the district of the regency of Bromberg. Moreover, that property is carried on by Roman Milecki, a man in ill repute for the part he took in the troubles of 1848, and who, besides, has often received in his house suspicious Polish emigrants. At Ruchocin, Mr. Gutowski has no inheritance to administer, nor any land which has descended to him to take charge of; rather he has bought a small farm for the sum of three thousand crowns, and one cannot tell what should induce him, a physician by profession, to buy such a piece of real estate.

The frequent associations Mr. Gutowski has had with Polish emigrants more or less suspected, and the ill report drawn on himself by assertions in part false, in part ill established, have induced the competent provincial authorities to send him away without delay from the province of Posen, and the minister of the interior regrets that he does not find himself in a position to revoke this order.

Receive, sir, with these explanations, the assurances of my very distinguished consideration.

MANTEUFFEL.

His Excellency Mr. Barnard,
&c., &c., &c.

Certificate of birth of Arthur Alexander Rudolph Von Gutowski.

[Translation.]

I, at the end undersigned, certify that the baptismal certificate of Arthur Alexander Rudolph Von Gutowski cannot be found here in the city of Witkowo, because on the 2d September, 1823, the church and parish records of baptism became a prey to the flames.

According to the statement of his godfather, Repemuceno Von Mozezensko, about sixty-one years old, from Przysicka, in the circle of Wongrowiecer, and of the landlord and also cook Wajeiech Zkierski, at Karscwo, over sixty years old, the said Alexander Rudolph Von Gutowski was born in the village of Malachowo, circle of Gnesener, of the lawfully married couple Katerina, born Von Koszutska and Valentin Von Gutowski, Catholics, on the 19th January, 1816, and on the 7th February of the same year, baptized in the parish church of Witkowo. His godfather and uncle, in the paternal line, Lucas Von Gutowski, died in the year 1847.

This certificate I, with my own hand, undersigned and affixed the church seal, Witkowo, the 20th November, 1851.

[L. S.]

N. LEGOWSKI,
Administrator.

Mr. Barnard to Mr. Everett.

No. 93.]

LEGATION OF THE UNITED STATES,
Berlin, December 14, 1852.

SIR: I have the honor to inclose you herewith a copy of a letter to me from Baron Manteuffel, in reply to my letter to him of the 3d of August last, in regard to the complaint of Christian George Born. It will be seen that Mr. Von Hassenkrug, the commissary of police at Minden, has on this complaint been removed from his post.

I have the honor to be, with the highest respect, your obedient servant,

D. D. BARNARD.

Hon. EDWARD EVERETT,
Secretary of State.

Baron Manteuffel to Mr. Barnard.

[Translation.]

BERLIN, *December* 12, 1852.

The reclamation of the merchant, Christian George Born, citizen of the United States, which was the subject of your note of the 3d August last, has given occasion for a correspondence with the secretary of the interior, who has made it his duty to submit it to an exact scrutiny.

It has been shown in the first instance, that if Mr. Hassenkrug, commissary of police at Minden, believed it to be his duty to search the baggage of Mr. Born, the measures was induced by the single consideration that the traveler, contrary to the existing regulations, had neglected to present his passport for visé to the competent authorities of the towns in which he had sojourned during the last four weeks of his stay in Prussia. Motives for special suspicion have not been particularized against Mr. Born. If this person pretends that Mr. Hassenkrug held in respect to him an unbecoming conduct, that is a reproach which this employé throws back upon him, it would be difficult to decide what is true in these reciprocal accusations; but as it is a fact that on former occasions Mr. de Hassenkrug has been deficient in those attentions which are due to travelers, the secretary of the interior has decided to recall him from the post he occupied at Minden.

On giving you these explanations, I have the honor to offer to you, sir, the assurance of my very distinguished consideration.

MANTEUFFEL.

His Excellency Mr. BARNARD, *&c.*, *&c.*, *&c.*

Mr. Everett to Mr. Barnard.

[Extract.]

No. 23.]

DEPARTMENT OF STATE,
Washington, January 14, 1853.

SIR: Your dispatches, with those of Mr. Fay, up to No. 95, have been duly received. The press of business upon the department since I entered it has been such as to prevent an earlier reply to any of your communications.

The question raised in the cases of Meyer and Kracke, and other similar ones, has received the particular attention of the President. They are certainly cases of suffering and hardship to those individuals, from which this government, in consideration of their quality as naturalized citizens, would gladly procure them relief. Within the jurisdiction of the United States, naturalized and native citizens possess the same rights, in the full enjoyment of which the government will protect them. It will also extend to them in foreign countries, and in the pursuit of their lawful business, the same protection which it would extend to native citizens under similar circumstances. There are, however, some points in which the positions of the naturalized and native citizens are necessarily different, and in these points the President thinks the true solution of the difficulty in such cases as those of Meyer and Kracke is to be sought.

The doctrine of inalienable allegiance is no doubt attended with great practical difficulties. It has been affirmed by the Supreme Court of the United States, and by more than one of the State courts; but the naturalization laws of the United States certainly assume that a person can, by his own acts, divest himself of the allegiance under which he was born, and contract a new allegiance to a foreign power. But, until this new allegiance is contracted, he must be considered as bound by his allegiance to the government under which he was born, and subject to its laws; and this undoubted principle seems to have its direct application in the present cases.

The Prussian government requires of all its subjects a certain amount of military service. However onerous this requirement may be, it is purely a matter of domestic policy, in which no foreign government has a right to interfere. It appears that there is no exemption from the obligation to render this service in favor of persons wishing to leave the country, unless they apply for and receive from the proper authorities what is termed "a certificate of emigration." This "emigration certificate" seems, like an ordinary passport, to be granted as a matter of course on application. When the vast extent of the Prussian military establishment is considered, and its importance in the monarchy, such a regulation, in reference to persons wishing to emigrate, who, as you are aware, now amount to many thousands annually, cannot be regarded as otherwise than liberal. But even if a different system prevailed, and if the previous rendition of a certain amount of military duty were made the condition *sine qua non* of granting the "emigration certificate," however oppressive the rule might be, a foreign government could have no right to interfere with its execution.

If, then, a Prussian subject, born and living under this state of law, chooses to emigrate to a foreign country without obtaining the "certificate" which alone can discharge him from the obligation of military service, he takes that step at his own risk. He elects to go abroad under the burden of a duty which he owes to his government. His departure is of the nature of an escape from her laws, and if at any subsequent period he is indiscreet enough to return to his native country, he cannot complain if those laws are executed to his disadvantage. His case resembles that of a soldier or sailor enlisted by conscription, or other compulsory process, in the army or navy. If he should desert the service of his country, and thereby render himself amenable to military law, no one would expect that he could return to his native land and bid defiance to its laws, because in the meantime he might have become a naturalized citizen of a foreign State.

It may be thought that this doctrine would expose our naturalized fellow-citizens to the danger of being reclaimed and given up as fugitives from justice. This, however, is by no means the case. It is unnecessary to say that there is no extradition of fugitives except for the offenses specified in the conventions under which it takes place. Escape from the obligation to render military service is not one of these offenses, and certainly never would be provided for in any extradition convention concluded by the United States. It may be added that the convention for extradition negotiated between the United States and Prussia on her own behalf and that of the other German States, which now awaits the action of the Senate, makes an exception of the case of citizens of the country on whose government the requisition is made, who are not to be delivered up even for the offenses named; and this stipulation (though the case has not arisen) would be undoubtedly held to apply to naturalized as well as native citizens. For these reasons, and without entering into any discussion of the question of perpetual allegiance, the President is of opinion, that if a subject of Prussia, lying under a legal obligation in that country to perform a certain amount of military duty, leaves his native land, and without performing that duty or obtaining the prescribed "certificate of emigration," comes to the United States and is naturalized, and afterwards for any purposes whatever goes back to Prussia, it is not competent for the United States to protect him from the operation of the Prussian law. The case may be one of great hardship, especially if the omission to procure the certificate arose from inadvertence or ignorance; but this fact, though a just ground of sympathy, does not alter the case as one of international law.

The view of the subject here presented is the same which was taken by my predecessor in reference to a subject of France, who, after having been naturalized in the United States, inquired if on his return to France he would be protected from the operation of the French law by an American passport. The answer of Mr. Webster to the inquiry is subjoined.

Although there is some diversity of circumstances in the cases which have from time to time been presented for your consideration, it is believed that the principles of the present letter will apply to them all.

* * * * * * * * *

I am, sir, respectfully, your obedient servant,

EDWARD EVERETT.

D. D. BARNARD, Esq., *&c.*, *&c.*, *Berlin.*

DEPARTMENT OF STATE,
Washington, June 1, 1852.

SIR: I have to acknowledge the receipt of your letter to Mr. Reddall of the 28th ultimo, inquiring whether Mr. Victor B. Depierre, a native of France, but a naturalized citizen of the United States, can expect the protection of this government in that country, when proceeding thither with a passport from this department. In reply, I have to inform you, that if, as is understood to be the fact, the government of France does not acknowledge the right of natives of that country to renounce their allegiance, it may lawfully claim their services when found within French jurisdiction.

I am, sir, very respectfully, your obedient servant,

DANIEL WEBSTER.

J. B. NONES, Esq., *New York.*

Mr. Barnard to Mr. Everett.

[Extract.]

No. 106.] LEGATION OF THE UNITED STATES,
Berlin, February 8, 1853.

SIR: I have the honor to acknowledge the receipt of your dispatch, No. 23, which refers to and determines the question raised in the cases of Meyer and Kracke, and some others, in regard to the competency of the United States to protect a naturalized citizen, or native subject of Prussia, who, lying under a legal obligation in that country to perform a certain amount of military duty, has emigrated to the United States without a permit of emigration, leaving that duty unperformed, and who, going back to his native land, is there subjected to the operation of the Prussian law.

The opinion and decision of the President, which is against the competency of the United States to protect a citizen thus situated, will, of course, govern my action in all cases of this description referred to. The department will not doubt that it must be a sensible relief to me to have this question definitively settled by its authority.

*   *   *   *   *   *

I have the honor to be, with the highest respect, your obedient servant,

D. D. BARNARD.

Hon. Mr. EVERETT,
Secretary of State.

Mr. Barnard to Mr. Everett.

No. 108.]

LEGATION OF THE UNITED STATES,
Berlin, February 15, 1853.

SIR: I have the honor to inclose to you herewith a copy of a letter addressed by me to the Prussian minister of foreign affairs in regard to the case of Kracke, and on the general subject of the unhappy condition of our naturalized citizens, natives of Prussia, who, with small blame, or no blame at all, have emigrated without permission, and, on their return here, are seized for Prussian soldiers.

I thought it due to the Prussian government, after the letters which I had addressed to it in several cases—those of Hormann and Meyer, and this of Kracke—that I should state to it frankly and explicitly the doctrine held by the government of the United States on the general subject, as communicated to me in your dispatch of the 14th of January, (No. 23;) and I thought it due at the same time to the United States and to the class of citizens concerned that Prussia should understand that, while her legal rights in the premises were conceded, there was a question of humanity involved, which we do not, and should not, lose sight of; that we must not be understood as wholly abandoning the sufferers, or as taking no further interest in them; and that in proper cases appealing to our just sympathies as a government and people, we must be allowed to make our voice heard in a respectful manner in their behalf. The case of Kracke being still undecided and long delayed, afforded me a proper occasion for writing this letter to the minister.

Very erroneous opinions are entertained in the United States on the general subject discussed and settled in your dispatch to me, (No. 23)—opinions which expose many of our people to involve themselves in serious difficulty, and give the government much inconvenience. Would it not be well that the government should frankly make the country acquainted with its views on the subject? The publication of your dispatch and a portion of the recent correspondence of this legation, relating to the same subject, (for example, the letter now sent you and that directed to Mr. King for the government of Bremen, in the case of Conrad Schmidt, if approved by the department,) would show what attitude had been taken by the government, and enable our people to govern themselves accordingly. I respectfully make the suggestion.

I have the honor to be, with the highest respect, your obedient servant,

D. D. BARNARD.

Hon. EDWARD EVERETT,
Secretary of State.

Mr. Barnard to Baron Manteuffel.

LEGATION OF THE UNITED STATES,
Berlin, February 15, 1853.

MONSIEUR LE BARON: In my letter to your excellency of the 9th of October, 1852, asking for the discharge of John Joseph Kracke from the Prussian army, I took occasion to remark that in making that request I I wished to avoid all reference to the abstract question of the right of sovereignty which might be supposed to be involved in the case. I said also that I wished it to be understood that I was aware of the importance, in a military point of view, which the government of his Majesty might attach to the laws of Prussia which regulate and control the emigration of his Majesty's subjects. But I abstained at that time, as I had done on previous occasions, from speaking explicitly on the question of the right of Prussia to bring under the operation of her military laws her native subjects, who, having emigrated without permits of emigration, leaving unperformed the military service to which they were legally bound, and having become naturalized in the United States as citizens of that country, afterwards return to their native land, and so fall under the jurisdiction of their original sovereign. I did not dispute the right of Prussia in these cases, though I did not in terms admit it. On a question of so much delicacy and importance I wished to speak only under the authority and advice of my government. This I am now about to do, and it is in accordance with that spirit of perfect frankness which it is the policy and practice of my government to observe in all its relations with foreign powers, that I make to your excellency the present communication.

The government of the United States considers that the laws of Prussia, which require a certain amount of military service of its subjects, and which prescribes the conditions in reference to this military service on which emigration is permitted, are a matter of domestic policy in which no foreign government has a right to interfere. It considers also that, if a Prussian subject, born and living under this state of law, emigrates to a foreign country, without a compliance with those conditions which alone can discharge him from the obligation of military service, he takes that step at his own personal risk. Going abroad under the burden of a duty still due to his native sovereign, his unauthorized emigration is in the nature of an escape from that duty, and from the laws which prescribe and enforce it, and he remains liable, in spite of any contract he may enter into in the meantime of new allegiance to a foreign power, to have these laws executed against him whenever he returns within the territorial limits and jurisdiction of his native country. In the case, therefore, of a subject of Prussia, lying under a legal obligation to perform in that country a certain amount of military service, who leaves his native land, and, without performing that service, or obtaining a permit of emigration, as the law of that country prescribes, goes to the United States, and is there naturalized, and afterwards comes back to Prussia, the government of the United States, leaving the question of perpetual or disputed allegiance wholly untouched, does not claim that it is competent for it to interpose to protect him from the operation of the Prussian law.

Having made this plain and explicit avowal and free concession, on the part of the United States, as to the legal right of Prussia in cases such as I have described, it is my duty, at the same time, to say that the United States can never fail to feel the deepest sympathy in behalf of the naturalized citizens of that country, who have, at the time of their emigration, from mere inadvertence or ignorance, or from the neglect or fault of others, failed to procure the proper permission for that purpose, and who, therefore, on returning to Prussia, wholly unconscious either of offense or of danger, are seized and placed in the ranks of the Prussian army. So much, at least, is due to them from the country of their adoption, and it can hardly be expected that the earnest expression of this sympathy in their behalf should be withheld from the Prussian government, or that the United States should abstain from urging on its attention considerations for the relief of these unhappy persons, such as one friendly power may properly address to another, in a matter of so much interest.

Your excellency is aware that a vast tide of emigration is constantly setting from the Old World to the New. This tide is as natural and irresistible as the flow of the Gulf Stream. It cannot be prevented nor diverted, and every new facility given to land and ocean travel, and to the circulation of property, information, and ideas, adds volume and vastness to this perpetual movement. This tide tends mainly to the United States, and the United States accept without hesitation their full share of whatever there may be in it of good or of evil, of present effect, or of eventual influence on the destiny of nations or of mankind.

After a fitting and sufficient probation, foreigners who desire it are admitted in the United States to the full rights of citizenship, nor does the government stop to inquire whether one or another of the hundreds of thousands who come annually to its shores may or may not have emigrated without permission of his original sovereign. If the emigration is not prevented, we conclude it is permitted. What we know is, that in a vast many cases the emigrant comes from a country where he lacked employment and bread to one where he is pretty sure of finding both; he changes a condition of want and wretchedness for one of comfort and often of prosperity. And the considerations must be obvious why no question can be made in the United States of forcing such persons back to their former country, or of not admitting them, at a proper time, to citizenship. Becoming citizens, they are incorporated with the body of our people, and thenceforward the government knows no distinction between them and native-born subjects in the duty and affection with which it cherishes and protects them. At home and abroad it throws its protection around them. The single exception, if it be an exception, to the universality of this protection is that which has been stated and admitted in this letter, arising in cases where the government considers that the parties themselves, by their own act, and by a fault or a misfortune of their own, are placed, for the time being, beyond the reach of its jurisdiction and authority as their proper sovereign. But even here the government sees among these cases at least instances in which it does not fail to follow the individuals implicated with its earnest sympathy, though it can no longer cover them with the strong arm of its power. Every one of the cases which I have had occasion to bring to the notice of the Prussian government were of this description. I refer to those of Christian Hormann, of B. Meyer, and of J. J. Kracke.

Your excellency is acquainted with these cases. The United States do not deny the legal right of Prussia to deal with them in its own way, under its laws. And considering the vast extent, and the vast importance to the monarchy of the Prussian military establishment, the United States are happy to see and recognize a very creditable degree of liberality in the legal regulations of the kingdom in reference to persons wishing to emigrate. It is undoubtedly the duty of every subject of his Majesty to comply with these regulations. But the cases to which I have adverted show that there may be failures to comply with these regulations, with scarcely a shadow of ground for an imputation of personal blame to the individual on whom the law is made to operate in the way of a most severe and terrible punishment. It is a great hardship, if failure in the observance of a legal duty, from mere want of knowledge, or want of thought, must needs be visited with such punishments. The hardship, if it must be characterized by so mild a term, is much greater if the punishment is inflicted vicariously on one person for the fault of another, as where the omission to comply with a legal regulation has been wholly the fault of a parent, and the unhappy child, grown to a man, receives the punishment.

I am aware that, in form, the condemnation in these cases follows the neglect of the party to appear at the period legally assigned for the commencement of the tour of military service, in obedience to the summons issued for that purpose. I do not suppose, however, that the authorities expect that this summons shall reach the party on the other side of the Atlantic, or, if it does, that he will voluntarily relinquish property, family, business, and the distant country, where he has been, or is about to be, adopted as a citizen, to become a soldier in the land of his birth, to which, in the meantime, he has renounced, or is about to renounce, so far at least as his will may go, all allegiance. When, therefore, on his return, for some temporary purpose, to his former home, unaware of danger, he is seized as a delinquent, his whole offense relates back to the omission to ask originally for leave to emigrate. That is the substance of the charge against him. If this permission had been obtained, which, in every one of the cases I have referred to, would have been had for the asking, the party would never have been summoned as a soldier; not having been obtained, the summons issues and the legal consequences follow.

And the whole of these consequences, the military service as well as the fine, so far at least as the individual is affected by them, are, as I have characterized them, in the nature of a punishment.

The Prussian government itself looks upon the matter in this light. In the letter which your excellency addressed to this legation in regard to the case of B. Meyer, dated the 22d of October last, it was remarked that "in such cases it was less a question of seizing a person to incorporate him in the army, than to maintain the respect due to the law and to insure its execution." It must necessarily be so. I suppose the cases are comparatively rare of emigration without permission, and it must be still more rare that persons who have thus emigrated venture back within the limits of Prussia; hardly ever, perhaps, where the legal regulations on the subject have been intentionally violated. A single soldier thus added once in a year or two, or perhaps only once in three or four years, to the large army of Prussia, could hardly be accounted as of much importance in itself, and especially when that soldier is performing a forced service, with his home and his heart in another and a distant country. When such a service is exacted, with the avowed purpose of maintaining the respect due to the law, it is plain that the service is a punishment, which is inflicted on the individual mainly with a view to its moral effect, in order that others may be deterred from the like offense of leaving the country without permission. And I am free to confess that a certain moral effect of this sort would hardly fail to follow, though unhappily, in such cases as I have named, it must necessarily be attended with another and a very different moral effect, if not in his original country, certainly in that of his adoption, among his family, and friends, and fellow-citizens, to whom the sad intelligence of his sufferings is sure to become known. There, at least, the punishment will be regarded as one of great and unmerited severity, whatever may be the political necessities to justify it in the estimation of Prussia.

His home is in another country; there he has his habitation, his family, his property, his business, and his friends; there center all his affections and all his interests; and he has no sentiment of loyalty in his heart to any sovereign or any government on earth out of his new country; nor is it possible for him to feel any sense of obligation to serve any other country or any other sovereign; and all that he possesses, and all that he holds dear, all that he has and almost all that he hopes for in life, are sacrificed, at least for the time, in the forced service to which he is subjected. It is impossible that he and those who take an interest in him should not regard his punishment as one of awful severity and terribly disproportioned—I speak of cases of involuntary omission to procure a permit of emigration—to any fault or blame which could be justly imputed to him.

Now what I have desired to say, and to show your excellency, in the observations I have made at such considerable length, is that the cases about which I have been speaking are such as call for the just and necessary sympathy of my government, and of the people of the United States, and that the expression of that sympathy on proper occasions, and in proper and courteous language, and of the sentiments and wishes to which it must give rise, is due from the United States to his Majesty's government. If the Prussian government shall still be of opinion, after all has been heard and considered, that it is a point so vital to the monarchy that the laws which regulate the emigration of the subject (which, for a military country like Prussia, are not regarded as harsh or severe in themselves) demand that their execution should be enforced by rigid and inexorable exaction in cases of alleged delinquency, such as this letter refers to, in such an alternative, I have already informed your excellency that the United States do not deny the legal rights of Prussia in the premises, and that—strong as is the interest which both government and people feel, and will always feel, in behalf of the sufferers, citizens of that country still, in spite of the remnant of authority which Prussia is entitled, and accidentally enabled, to exercise over them—my government disclaims any power or competency on its part to interfere to protect those unhappy persons from the operation of the Prussian laws. But for this very reason, the necessity is all the stronger, and the propriety the more apparent and urgent, why the government of the United States should urge on the attention of his Majesty's government such considerations in behalf of these persons as may seem to it calculated to induce some relaxation of the rigorous policy now pursued towards them. And in doing this, considering the relation in which it stands to these persons, no apprehension is entertained that any just ground can be found for imputing to it a proceeding which "the sense of its own dignity"—I quote from your excellency's letter already referred to of the 22d of October—should have hindered it from adopting.

I am not without hope, notwithstanding the ill success which has attended my previous efforts on this subject, that his Majesty's government may be led to consider whether it is not possible that the strict and rigorous enforcement of its laws in this regard may be dispensed with, or at least modified and relaxed in behalf of persons in the condition of those whose cases I have had occasion to bring to its notice, without impairing the proper and necessary authority of those laws, or the efficiency of the military system of the monarchy. If this should be so, I can only assure your excellency that the result would be received by the government and people of the United States with the highest satisfaction.

I beg leave to remind your excellency, in concluding this letter, that it is now four months since the case of Kracke was brought by me to the notice of his Majesty's government. He continues in the same lamentable state of mental distress, into which he was originally plunged by his arrest and forced service in the Prussian army, and, though he feels the silence of the government in regard to him to be ominous, he does not yield the hope that, by his Majesty's clemency, or otherwise, he may be set free, and allowed to depart to the United States. Since I have seen the Prussian law of 1842, regulating the emigration of the king's subjects, I have thought it quite probable that the investigations of the Prussian authorities into Kracke's case would relieve his Majesty's government from all embarrassment in regard to him, by showing that he had been continuously absent from Prussia for ten years, and was therefore, by the terms of the Prussian law, no longer to be regarded as in any respect a Prussian subject. But if this fact be so, certainly no time should be lost in setting this man at liberty.

I seize this occasion to assure your excellency of my very high and distinguished consideration.

D. D. BARNARD.

His Excellency BARON VON MANTEUFFEL,
Minister of Foreign Affairs.

Mr. Barnard to Mr. Marcy.

[Extract.]

No. 119.] LEGATION OF THE UNITED STATES,
Berlin, March 22, 1853.

SIR: * * * * * * * *

I inclose, also, copies of two letters from the Prussian minister of foreign affairs, in reference to the case of John Joseph Kracke, the one of later date being in reply to my letter to the minister, of the 15th of February, 1853, (vide my No. 108 to the department,) on the general subject of the forced service of German-American citizens in the Prussian army. With these, I send also a copy of anothor letter, which I have addressed to Baron Manteuffel, in regard to the case of Kracke, again urging his release from the Prussian army.

I am not without hope of eventual success in this case.

I have the honor to be, with the highest respect, your obedient servant,

D. D. BARNARD.

The Hon. SECRETARY OF STATE.

Baron Manteuffel to Mr. Barnard.

[Translation.]

BERLIN, *February* 22, 1853.

The letter which you were pleased to address to me, the 9th October, last year, on the affair of one named John Joseph Kracke, a Prussian subject, who caused himself to be naturalized in the United States before he had discharged his military obligations in his native country, has given place to a correspondence with the ministers of war and interior, as well as with the competent provincial authorities.

The circumstances under which the said Kracke left the King's territory have been maturely considered; they have, however, been found to be such, that the government does not find itself in condition to exempt him from military service, to which he was subjected after his reëntry into Prussia.

I will permit myself, sir, to present to you the facts, such as they are, stated in the report of the provincial councilor, of the circle of Tecklenburg.

The individual in question was born the 9th February, 1828, at Recke, in Westphalia. It was his duty, then, to have placed himself under the banners in 1845; but that very year he passed over secretly to the United States, after having worked during several years in Holland as a blacksmith. It was only two years afterwards, in 1847, that his parents followed him there, without having asked for either passport or permit of emigration, which, for that matter, would not have been granted, after the evasion of their son. He, not having answered the summons when, in 1845, he was cited before the proper military authority, was necessarily to be regarded as refractory. Nothing, then, more natural than that, upon his return to the province, in the autumn of 1852, he was arrested and incorporated in the army.

You will be convinced by this exposition, sir, that the said Kracke has no *right* to demand the severence of the ties which bind him to his native country, before he fulfills the obligations which are imposed upon him as a Prussian subject. Moreover, there exists no motive of *equity* or *humanity* which can be invoked in his favor. Kracke, having emigrated to America in the very year when he was about to be summoned to the standard, it is evident he only acted so in the sole intention to withdraw himself from the military service in Prussia. Without doubt, this person sets forth in the petition he has addressed to you, that he was risking the loss of his real estate in America, if he should be obliged to serve during three years in the army. But this assertion deserves no credence. It follows, from an interrogation to which the said Krache was subjected at Wesel, on the 7th December last, that his sole property in America consisted in a house, slightly mortgaged, in Cincinnati; and that, on setting out for Germany, he had directed his brother to let such house. It seems, then, the real estate of Krache could well be turned to account, until his return, by his brothers and sisters, almost all of them living in Cincinnati, who are under much obligation to him, and certainly would neglect nothing for the security of his property. In these circumstances, the royal government believes it to be a duty to hesitate the more from releasing this individual from the military service, as it behooves it to give an example to hinder (especially at a moment when emigration to America is on the increase) young people from breaking arbitrarily, and without discharging duties imposed by their condition as Prussian subjects, the ties which bind them to their country.

Accept on this occasion, sir, the assurance of my high consideration.

MANTEUFFEL.

His Excellency Mr. BARNARD, *&c.*, *&c.*, *&c.*

Baron Manteuffel to Mr. Barnard.

[Translation.]

BERLIN, *February* 28, 1853.

SIR: I have seen with lively satisfaction, by your letter of the 15th of this month, that as regards *right*, the government of the United States fully participates in the opinion announced in my note of 22d October last, in accordance with which his Majesty's government believes itself fully authorized, where a Prussian subject has caused himself to be naturalized in the United States before having satisfied his military obligations to Prussia, and without having obtained an emigration permit, to enrol him under her standard, if he returns to his former country. If then such a case should again present itself in which the Prussian government would be obliged to exercise this right, there is no longer room for apprehension that its application would foment any misunderstanding.

I understand perfectly that, when a citizen of the United States who has not dissolved the ties which bind him to Prussia, is subjected at a later day to military service in his native country, the American government will not be indifferent to the fact; that it is rather a reason for it to embrace the interests of its citizens, and to avail itself of the effect of its good officers to induce the Prussian government to be indulgent in regard to him. On my part, I can give you assurance, sir, that the King will never close his ear to such intervention; on the contrary, he will take care to submit to scrupulous examination all that can be alleged in favor of the person so commended to him. As, however, the government of the United States considers that it is not for its interest to make the admission of an emigrant as citizen dependent on the exhibition of a document proving that he had dissolved the ties by which he was attached to his old country, it is much to be feared that the government of his Majesty will still often find itself under the necessity of executing its own laws, as well as the decrees of its tribunals against Prussian subjects who have been naturalized in the United States.

Rarely will the Prussian government refuse the subsidiary issue of an emigration permit to individuals who in their infancy were taken from his Majesty's territory by their father or mother, for then the fault would be with the parents, if their children were wanting to the law. The application for such subsidiary emigration permit would only be essentially inadmissible in those cases in which Prussian tribunals had already given judgment against the emigrant; and that was the position of Christian Hormann referred to, who was the subject of my letter of the 27th of August last year.

The case is quite different as to individuals, who, when they emigrated to America, had already attained the age of seventeen, at which time their military duties commence. Generally speaking, it can never be admitted that such an one neglected to apply for an emigration permit because he was ignorant of the laws of his country.

Every Prussian subject is obliged to bear arms. This law, of forty years' standing, is known to every one; and, moreover, official notices are every year frequently published to summon the young men to their standards. Every one knows, if only through his parents or friends, that at twenty years of age it is his bounden duty to present himself to the military board called to decide whether he is fit or not to serve in the army. If, therefore, any Prussian pretends not to have known that he was held to render this service, one is clearly authorized to belive that he belies his conscience. As to those persons who wittingly attempt to evade this obligation, they certainly do not deserve that any interest should be taken in them; and it is with reason that the law decrees that such, in preference, should be enrolled in the army, because they seek to free themselves of a duty, common to all, to cast it upon their fellow-citizens. Of this number are the aforesaid B. Meyer and J. Kracke, to whom my two letters of 22d October, last year, and 22d of the present, referred.

I am pursuaded that the government of the United States, after careful examination of the conduct of these two persons, will discover that they have acted with the single purpose of evading their military duties in Prussia, and thus there is no room for complaint if the Prussian government limits itself to subjecting them to the duty which they have, of purpose, neglected. It is not a punishment inflicted upon them, it is simply the fulfillment of an obligation resting upon them in the quality of subjects of Prussia. Men like Meyer and Kracke have no right to ask that this military service should be dispensed with and they be replaced by others to keep the Prussian army full. Moreover, the service is not hard, nor of long duration. In the space of three years it is finished; and, often, even new conscripts are discharged before this term is completed.

To be willing to treat persons who have emigrated without the permission of the government with more tenderness than those who have stayed at home, would be, on one part, to encourage emigration, contrary to the public welfare, and, on the other hand, to weaken the force of laws and the respect which is due to them. Such a proceeding would be more out of place, because the law itself is so mild that it grants the right of emigration even to those subject still to service in the army, provided they are in condition to prove that, in their self-expatriation, they are not influenced by the sole intention to evade such service.

I like to believe, sir, that these explanations will give to your government the full and entire conviction that the government of his Majesty, far from having used any rigor against the said Meyer and Kracke, has only done that which it ought to do to prevent its own subjects from accusing it of treating more favorably those who violate the law than those who obey.

At the close of your note of the 15th instant, you still quote section twenty-three of the law of 21st December, 1842. I permit myself to request you will notice, sir, that the term of ten years fixed for the return to Prussia of a subject of his Majesty, only runs from the first January, 1843, and that if said paragraph authorizes the government to consider an uninterrupted absence of more than ten years as importing the loss of the quality of Prussian subject, it does not, nevertheless, dispense the absentee from duties which he ought to discharge while he was a Prussian.

Accept on this occasion, sir, the renewed assurance of my high consideration.

MANTEUFFEL.

Mr. BARNARD,
Envoy Extraordinary and Minister Plenipotentiary.

Mr. Barnard to Baron Manteuffel.

LEGATION OF THE UNITED STATES,
Berlin, March 21, 1853.

MONSIEUR LE BARON: I have received the two letters which your excellency has done me the honor to address to me—the first, dated the 22d of February, in reference to the case of John Joseph Kracke, and the other dated 28th of February, in reference to the same case, and more generally in reply to my letter of the 15th of the same month.

I had indulged the hope that his Majesty's government might have found it not incompatible with its interests, under all the circumstances of the case, and while adhering to its claim of right in the premises, to accord to my request, and to the earnest wishes of my government, the release of Kracke from the Prussian army. In this I have been disappointed; but I do not yet mean to despair of this man's release.

Kracke left Prussia when a boy of fourteen, and from that time for a period of fourteen years it appears he was never in Prussia. He learned his trade of a smith, in Hanover, and not in Prussia. He then lived and worked at his trade in Holland; and finally he passed from Holland, and not from Prussia, to the United States. There he became a naturalized citizen, acquired property, and fixed himself permanently and for life. That is his country and his home. But having ventured, after fourteen years, unconscious of offense or of danger, to set his foot as a visitor on the soil of the country where he had chanced to draw his first breath, he found himself suddenly seized and forced into the military service of that country for a term of years. This has come upon him at the age of twenty-eight, to interrupt all the plans and expectations of his life. It is at this age, just the most critical and important to him of his whole existence, that a demand is made upon him for a service of three years in the camp of a foreign country; for Prussia, in regard to such a service, is as foreign to him, to his affections, his interests, and his hopes, as Turkey would be. His labor in the United States has already had its reward. He has become the owner of a house and ground in one of the most populous and prosperous cities of that country. But this property is not wholly paid for; it is under mortgage, and he has no means of redeeming his property from that mortgage but by the earnings of his personal and continued labor. There is nobody to pay that mortgage for him, and if he is kept here, his property will almost necessarily be sacrificed.

Such is his unhappy condition. I am unable to agree with your excellency, that there is nothing in this case affording any ground either of equity or humanity on which to appeal to the Prussian government in this man's favor; and neither my government, nor the people of the United States, will be able to agree with your excellency.

On technical grounds, Kracke was still a Prussian subject when he emigrated to the United States. But he did not, in point of fact, emigrate from Prussia. He emigrated from Holland, and had then been absent from Prussia for about seven years. Intending to make the United States his permanent residence and home, and having just at his twenty-first year realized from his industry in Holland the means necessary to accomplish his voyage, it certainly can surprise nobody, whatever may have been his technical duty in the premises, that he did not first return to Prussia, either to ask for permission to emigrate, or voluntarily to undergo a military service of three years before emigrating. I think all this is matter proper for the consideration of his Majesty's government.

I have already referred, in my letter of the 15th of February, to the estimate put by the United States on the liberality of Prussia—a great military power as she is, where every citizen is a soldier—in her legal regulations in regard to persons wishing to emigrate. I hope I may now be excused for saying that there seems to me to be rather a marked contrast between that liberality and the rigor employed towards those who, as in the several instances which I have had occasion to bring to your excellency's notice, and especially in the instance of Kracke, may have failed to comply with these regulations. Although Kracke went to the United States in the "period between the end of his seventeenth and the end of his twenty-fifth year," your law only required, in order to his obtaining a free permit of emigration, that he should have obtained from the proper authority a certificate that his application did not proceed solely from a design to withdraw himself from the army. This rule is referred to and recognized in your excellency's letter of the 28th of February. I cannot doubt but that this certificate might have been readily obtained. I think his residence out of Prussia explains why he did not apply for the legal permission to emigrate, and shows, at the same time, that if he had applied, it would have been apparent to every one that his desire to dissolve his political relations with Prussia, and to find a country and home for himself elsewhere, was no new idea got up at that time merely to escape from her military service. Surely, between the liberality of the law, which would have given him, seven years ago, free permission to emigrate, and the rigorous exaction which demands from him now, at this distance of time, and under the peculiar circumstances of the case, a forced service of three years for having emigrated without that permission, there appears to be a contrast which must be acknowledged to be somewhat remarkable. At any rate, the exaction falls upon him with fearful severity.

Certainly, it is for the Prussian government to judge of the reasons of state, in reference to emigration or otherwise, which may demand such a course of action. But I trust I may be excused for suggesting that really little hope can be entertained that the constantly-swelling tide of emigration will be checked by any such measure of repression as that which is now being enforced in the person of Kracke. The only effect will be, that those who have emigrated and those who shall emigrate without leave will take warning from it to keep themselves beyond the reach of the laws and authorities of Prussia.

It seems from what is stated in your excellency's letter, that the law of the 3d December, 1843, in regard to emigration, according to the construction put upon it in Prussia, does not bear quite as liberal an interpretation as I had supposed. The law declares that "the quality of a Prussian subject is lost by a residence of ten years abroad," the rule being applied, of course, to those who absent themselves without leave.

By your excellency's construction, this term of ten years commences from the date of the law. But, at least, the equity and spirit of such a statute might be applied to a case like Kracke's without doing any violence to its letter or its intent. Certainly, it would be competent to the Prussian government, if it was so disposed, to declare that, under the peculiar circumstances of the case, and upon the equity of this law, it would consider Kracke as no longer a Prussian subject, and accordingly to discharge him from the Prussian army. I shall indulge the hope that he may yet be released, and allowed to return to the United States.

Accept, on this occasion, Monsieur le Baron, the assurance of my very distinguished consideration.

D. D. BARNARD.

His Excellency BARON VON MANTEUFFEL,
&c., &c., &c.

Mr. Barnard to Mr. Marcy.

[Extract.]

No. 121.] LEGATION OF THE UNITED STATES,
Berlin, April 5, 1853.

SIR: * * * * * * * *

I have the honor to transmit, herewith, a copy of Baron Manteuffel's reply to my letter of the 21st March, urging again on his consideration reasons for the release of J. J. Kracke from the Prussian army. The refusal to release this man seems to be final; though I think it is evident, at the same time, from the tenor of the answer, that some proper impression has been made on the minister's mind in regard to the severe operation of the Prussian law. Of course, he does not yet see * * * * its inhumanity. * * * *

I have the honor to be, with the highest respect, your obedient servant,

D. D. BARNARD.

HON. W. L. MARCY,
Secretary of State.

Baron Manteuffel to Mr Barnard.

[Translation.]

BERLIN, *March* 31, 1853.

SIR: After having already consulted with those of my colleagues who have concern in the position of the person called John Joseph Kracke, who is again the subject of your letter of the 21st of this month, I should hesitate to try new modes to obtain the exemption of this individual from military service in Prussia. Without doubt, it can be nowise convenient for Mr. Kracke to be compelled to serve in the army at the age of twenty-eight years, after having found a second country in the United States, and made the acquisition of real estate.

But this disagreeable business he should attribute only to his unreflecting and unlawful conduct from the time of his expatriation. At the age of fourteen, Kracke had obtained permission to sojourn temporarily abroad; but, in place of returning to Prussia at the age of twenty-one years completed, to enlist under the banners, as his condition of Prussian subject made it his duty to do, he chose this very time to pass secretly to the United States, and thus withdraw himself from his military obligations. After having thus openly violated the law, Kracke has no right to ask that he be released from the bonds which bind him to his native country, before he completes his service in the army. Furthermore, such request, if made in due season, would in like manner not have been acquiesced in, except in the case of his having been able to show that he was not emigrating for the purpose merely of getting rid of this service; and certainly, it would have been difficult for him to make such proof in 1845—that is to say, at the very moment when the age he had attained obliged him to serve in the army.

The harshness which is used towards refractories to incorporate them subsidiarily in the army if they return from the United States has no tendency to check emigration, it ought only to serve to convince those who desire to emigrate that the government does not mean to favor *secret and illegal* emigrations; but, on the contrary, holds out an aiding hand to those who not having satisfied the duties belonging to them as Prussian subjects before emigrating may fully comply with them on their return.

As to the bearing of the section 23 of the law of December 31, 1843, its object was to put the government in condition to withdraw the character of Prussian subjects from those who, without permission of the proper provincial authorities, have resided more than ten consecutive years abroad, but it does not authorize the admission that because a Prussian has managed to evade his duties as a subject of the King, by a sojourn of ten years abroad, the government is bound to consider him as exempt from those duties if at any time he places his foot within the territory of Prussia. There exists no motive, even in the purview of section 23 of the law before cited, to set free the said Kracke from the military service of Prussia.

Sincerely regretting not to be able on this occasion to give you a proof of my eager desire to serve you, I have the honor to offer you, sir, the assurance of my high consideration.

MANTEUFFEL.

His Excellency Mr. BARNARD, *&c., &c., &c.*

Baron Gerolt to Mr. Marcy.

PRUSSIAN LEGATION, *Washington, July* 11, 1853.

With reference to our verbal conversation, some days ago, in relation to the liabilities to which emigrants from Prussia and other German States, who have become citizens of the United States, are subjected when they voluntarily return to those States, after having left their native country without the necessary permission of emigration, and without fulfilling their military duties prescribed by law after having attained a certain age, I beg leave to inclose hereby an extract from the laws of Prussia and from the constitution of Prussia on this subject, by which you will perceive that Prussia does not pretend to enforce any allegiance upon the said emigrants, but that, if they return to Prussia, they are made responsible for having violated our laws in the cases above mentioned and are considered as criminals forfeited to the punishment of the law, from which no citizenship of any nation can liberate them.

I have the honor to be, very respectfully, your obedient servant,

FR. VON GEROLT.

Hon. W. L. MARCY,
Secretary of State of the United States, Washington.

Extract from the Laws of Prussia, of December 31, 1842, *concerning the loss of the quality of a Prussian subject.*

§ 15. The quality of a Prussian subject is lost:

1. By discharge upon the subject's request.
2. By sentence of the competent authority.
3. By living ten years in a foreign country.
4. By the marriage of a female Prussian subject with a foreigner.

§ 16. The discharge has to be asked from the police authority of the province in which the subject's domicil is situated, and is effected by a document made out by the same authority.

§ 17. The discharge cannot be granted:

1. To male subjects who are between seventeen and twenty-five years of age, until they have got a certificate of the military commission of recruitment of their district, proving that their application for discharge is not made merely to avoid the fulfilling of their military duty in the standing army.

2. To actual soldiers, belonging either to the standing army or to the reserve; to officers of the militia and to public functionaries, before their being discharged from service.

3. To subjects having formerly served as officers in the standing army or the militia, or having been appointed military employés, with the rank of officers, or civil functionaries, before they have got the consent of their former chief.

4. To the persons belonging to the militia, not being officers, after their having been convoked for actual service.

§ 18. To subjects wishing to emigrate into a State of the German Confederacy the discharge may be refused if they cannot prove that the said State is willing to receive them.—(See act of the German Confederation, Art. 18, Nro. 2, lit. A.)

§ 19. For other reasons than those specified in §§ 17 and 18, the discharge cannot be refused in time of peace. For the time of war, special regulations will be made.

§ 20. The document of discharge effects, at the moment of its delivery, the loss of the quality as Prussian subject.

§ 21. If there is no special exception, the discharge comprehends also the wife and the minor children that are still under their father's authority.

§ 22. Subjects living in a foreign country may lose their quality as Prussians by a declaration of the police authority of Prussia, if they do not obey, within the time fixed to them, the express summons for returning to their country.

§ 23. Subjects who either—

1. Leave our States without permission, and do not return within ten years, or—

2. Leave our States with permission, but not return within ten years after the expiration of the term granted by the said permission, lose their quality as Prussian subjects.

§ 24. *Entering into public service in a foreign State.*

The entering of a subject into public service in a foreign State is allowed only after his discharge (see § 20) has been granted to him. Anybody who has obtained it, is permitted to do so without restriction.

§ 25. A subject which—

1. Either takes public service in a foreign State, with our immediate permission,

2. Or is appointed in our States by a foreign power, in an office established with our permission, as, for instance, that of consul, commercial agent, &c., remaining in his quality as a Prussian.

§ 26. *General disposition.*

Subjects who emigrate without having obtained their discharge, or violate, by their entering into public service in a foreign State, the disposition of § 24, are to be punished according to the laws existing in that respect.

Given under our hand and seal, Berlin, this 31st of December, 1842.

[L. S.] FREDERICK WILLIAM.

Extract from the Constitution of Prussia, of 1850.

TIT. I. Rights of the Prussians.

Art. 1. The right to emigrate cannot be restricted by the State, except with respect to the duty of military service.

Mr. Vroom to Mr. Marcy.

[Extract.]

No. 2.] LEGATION OF THE UNITED STATES,
Berlin, October 31, 1853.

SIR: * * * * * * * *

Accompanying this is a copy of a letter from Mr. Bromberg, United States consul at Hamburg, addressed to the secretary of legation, on the subject of the holding of American citizens to military service in Germany, and some other matters, and his answer thereto.

* * * * * * * * *

I have received two letters from Mr. Bates, United States consul at Aix-la-Chapelle; one respecting the case of B. Meyer.

* * * * * * * * *

I have the honor to be, sir, very respectfully, your obedient servant,

P. D. VROOM.

Hon. WILLIAM L. MARCY,
Secretary of State, &c.

Mr. Vroom to Mr. Bates.

[Extract.]

LEGATION OF THE UNITED STATES,
Berlin, October 24, 1853.

SIR: I have received your communication of the 6th instant, in relation to the case of Mr. Meyer; and, on referring to the records of the legation, I find that my predecessor, Mr. Barnard, considered the case as settled in point of principle, and that he thereupon appealed to the government in behalf of Mr. Meyer as a matter of favor, which appeal has not been responded to. In this state of things, I do not consider it advisable to present the case anew without some change of circumstances to justify it. No new instructions have been received at this legation other than what may be considered as contained in Mr. Marcy's letter to Mr. Hulsemann, which has not yet been officially communicated; and if it had, I should deem it unwise to make that the ground for opening cases which have already been passed on and settled, unless specially instructed to do so.

* * * * * * * * *

I am, sir, very respectfully,

P. D. VROOM.

ISAAC C. BATES, Esq.,
Consul at Aix-la-Chapelle

Mr. Bates to Mr. Vroom.

[Extract.]

CONSULATE OF THE UNITED STATES,
Aix-la-Chapelle, October 6, 1853.

SIR: * * * * * * * *

I was desirous of saying a word to you more particularly on a matter which I promised to bring before you, and which is simply one of the many cases which have arisen, and one of the *more* which I think are likely to arise, regarding individuals who emigrate to America from Prussia without first receiving permission from the Prussian government to do so, and return again voluntarily to their native country after having been duly naturalized in ours.

The case is that of Mr. Meyer, which is fully stated in my communication to the legation under date of July 2, 1852, to which I respectfully beg leave to refer you.

Mr. Barnard replied to my letter on the 5th, promising to lose no time in bringing it before the government, which he did.

Not hearing from him meanwhile on the subject, I addressed him again on the 13th August, 1852, for the purpose of bringing it to mind. In reply, on the 18th August, he stated that the doctrine of the absolute and independent right of expatriation to which I had referred was not admitted by the European governments, but that this was not the only question of international law in these cases; that Mr. Wheaton, in his time, refused to interpose in behalf of a naturalized citizen, formerly a Prussian subject, who had temporarily returned to Prussia and was seized for a soldier, on the ground that his native domicil and national character reverted, and that he was bound to obey the laws in all respects, exactly as if he had never emigrated, and that the Department at Washington seems to have acquiesced in this view; but that he (Mr. Barnard) could not agree with this doctrine in the broad sense in which it was laid down; on the contrary, he thought that if an emigrant returned merely as a traveler, or temporarily on some matter of business, he should be deemed an American citizen, and treated as such, and not as a Prussian subject. He added that he had made an earnest and strong representation to induce the Prussian government to give up in Meyer's case, and altogether, their demand as well for the fine as for the military service, and hoped for a favorable result, at *least* for the military service.

Nothing more passed on the subject till October 26, when Mr. Fay advised me (Mr. Barnard being absent) that the Prussian government had just returned a negative answer to his application for Mr. Meyer to visit Paderborn temporarily without being incorporated in the Prussian army; and, in reply to my letter of 28th October, in which I asked whether the affair must be considered as definitely settled in this case and all others like it, he stated that he supposed it must, but that he could not, of course, tell what instructions would be given by the State Department in the matter, nor what would be the result of any which may be given. So the matter now stands.

Mr. Meyer was here a short time since, and desirous of going immediately to Paderborn. I read to him the correspondence which I had on the subject—the substance of all which, however, I had previously communicated him by letter—and advised him not to go. He spoke of your coming, and anticipated that you would be able to do something more effectual; and I promised to make you acquainted with his case as soon as you arrived, and to beg you to inform me if you had any instructions from Washington with regard to negotiations on this subject, and if, in your opinion, there was any hope that the result would be favorable to persons in his position. He repeated his assertion, that it was absolutely necessary for him to go to Paderborn, and that he must place himself at the mercy of the King if he could do nothing else.

It is already a question of no little importance, as recent events have shown, and is daily becoming more so, whether the government of the United States is to protect naturalized citizens who return temporarily and voluntarily to their native country, to the same extent that it would native-born citizens, and also whether any and what protection is to be afforded to individuals who have simply taken the preliminary steps and declared their intention of becoming American citizens. In my experience here, I have endeavored, in several cases, to protect *both* these classes, but have been cautious not to commit myself with regard to the latter; for I see not how they can have any *claim* whatever upon us, except a friendly one.

English legislation excludes naturalized aliens from any positive claim to the protection of their adopted country, when they are beyond its frontiers.

Our own does not; and it is highly desirable that the intention of our government in this respect be clearly made known. You will much oblige me by instructing me as to the course to be pursued in future. * * * * * *

J. C. BATES.

Mr. VROOM, *Minister at Berlin.*

[Extract.]

CONSULATE OF THE UNITED STATES,
Berlin, October 16, 1853.

SIR: * * * * * * *
I am afraid of troubling you too much, but I cannot omit to inquire if any recent instructions have been received at your legation, concerning

the right of German rulers to force their former subjects, after having become naturalized in the United States, on revisiting their native country, to bear arms. The former administration has conceded this point, and though I have been able to resist any claim of this kind, (which I believe to be wrong, and totally at variance with our naturalization laws,) yet, as the decision in favor of this claim is known, I had only last month, in a case (reported to the Hon. D. D. Barnard) of this kind, to use the utmost exertions, and to assure the syndicus that the present administration would not uphold the former decision, and I was enabled to get the person claimed unmolested to England. I have on this applied to the State Department for information, but, not having received answer, I would be obliged to you for any light on the subject.

I remain, sir, &c.,

SAMUEL BROMBERG.

O. J. Wise, Esq.,
Secretary of Legation.

[Extract.]

Legation of the United States,
Berlin, October 26, 1853.

Sir: * * * * * * * *

No instructions have yet reached this office with regard to the construction of our naturalization laws, nor with regard to the condition and rights of those unfortunate emigrants whom the Prussian government claims the right to compel to military service. As soon as such instructions are received, I will gladly communicate them to you.

Yours, truly.

O. JENNINGS WISE.

Samuel Bromberg, Esq., *Hamburg.*

Mr. Vroom to Mr. Marcy.

[Extract.]

No. 7.] Legation of the United States,
Berlin, December 13, 1853.

Sir: * * * * * * * *

On the 2d instant, I received a letter from William Parehen, a naturalized citizen of the United States, who left this country in 1848, when about eighteen years of age, and without a permit of emigration. He states that on his return a short time since to transact some family business, he was taken up, and was to be placed in the army within fourteen days, four of which had already expired. He asked the protection of the legation, and, if that could not be given, he desired to make a personal application to the King. This case appeared to be within the instructions received by the legation from the State Department in February last, and which had been communicated to the government here, and since acted on by the legation. I did not, therefore, feel at liberty to give to Mr. Parehen any positive assurance of relief. I told him that in similar cases the Prussian government had refused to listen such applications, but that I would aid him as far as was in my power; that if he desired, under the circumstances, to make an application to the King, as he had intimated, I did not wish to deprive him of the opportunity by any act of mine, without his knowledge, but that in such application he must act on his own responsibility; that if I interfered in his behalf, it would be on the ground of his rights as an American citizen, and I should expect him to await and abide the result. I have not heard from him since.—(For copies of these communications see C 1 and C 2.)

The department will perceive that complaints from our naturalized citizens of maltreatment in this kingdom continue to be frequent. I hope to be able to dispose of them satisfactorily without giving trouble. Cases of embarrassment, however, will sometimes occur, in which it will be necessary to ask for direction. The case of Parehen presents an instance. He went to the United States without a permit of emigration, and without having performed the military service required by his country. On his return a naturalized citizen, he was taken and placed in the army. The right of Prussia to do this has been formally conceded. I presume it will be proper for me to act on this principle, unless formally instructed otherwise. I did not, however, think it advisable in my letter to Parehen to commit myself by a formal abandonment of his case. It was not necessary. He emigrated with his father at the age of eighteen, when yet a minor; and an argument might have been made that in such a case a permit of emigration was not necessary. That point might have been presented without expressly admitting the principle referred to. As my interference in the case of Parehen may be requested again, I should be glad to have the views of the government on this subject at as early a day as may be convenient.

* * * * * * * * *

I have the honor to be, sir, very respectfully, your obedient servant,

P. D. VROOM.

Hon. WILLIAM L. MARCY,
Secretary of State.

[Translation.]

C. 1.] VATERODE, *November* 29, 1853.

MR. MINISTER: My father, the miller Parehen, had lived for many years at a mill convenient to the Pussian village of Vaterode, in the territory of the Prussian kingdom, in the district of the government of Erfurt, the principal city being Heiligen.

In the year 1848 he emigrated from that place to New York, North

America, taking with him myself, his eldest son, born in wedlock, then about eighteen years old.

He had obtained from the Prussian royal landrath office a permit of emigration; notice was mentioned about his release from the condition of Prussian subject; but it was resolved at the district town of Heidelberg that he only needed a passport; and on this footing he set forward with me, undisturbed, on the voyage to New York.

Afterwards, in America, I married a girl who came from Vaterode; obtained the rights of an American citizen, by the issue of letters of citizenship; was enrolled in the militia of the free States; and my wife received news in the early part of the year that an inheritance had fallen to her at Vaterode, by the will of a deceased uncle. In order to settle this inheritance, I journeyed hither with my wife about the middle of September, last year. Scarcely had I arrived at my old home, when the Hessian authorities seized me as an offender and delivered me up to the Prussians. I was taken to the royal Prussian landrath office at Heiligen, although a free American citizen, escorted by gens d'armes, and sent to the landwehr depot at Millhausen, although I had my certificate of citizenship, and my passport, verified by the American consul, Mr. Hildebrand, at Bremen. My naturalization papers were taken from me, and I was myself ordered to Erfurt; my opposition was disregarded, and under menaces of constraint and imprisonment I was put in the ranks of the thirty-first regiment of infantry. Fourteen days' leave was given me to get clothing, after I had requested it three days. It was, indeed, difficult for me competently to understand that I was subject to the requirement of the Prussian laws of December 31, 1842, and not considered as released from the obligation of subject of Prussia, in despite of the forementioned proceedings to release myself, and of my understanding that Prussia no longer had the least claim upon me since I had acquired the right of citizenship in America.

I now turn to you, Mr. Minister, in full confidence that you will give me your protection, and, as an American citizen, reclaim me from the war department of the kingdom of Prussia, and cause me to be set free from Prussian military service.

If you cannot give me the immediately-needed help, then I will be much obliged to you if you will write to me of the unlikelihood of any result from your trouble, to the care of Mr. Rechts Anwalht Schluster, at the town of Heiligen, so that I may then cause an humble petition to be addressed to his Majesty the King of Prussia.

Be assured, Mr. Minister, of my gratitude for the trouble you take in my affair, and accept the assurance of my respectful and high esteem.

WILLIAM F. PAREHEN.

Hon. P. D. Vroom,
Minister at Berlin.

Mr. Vroom to Mr. W. F. Parehen.

C 2.] LEGATION OF THE UNITED STATES,
Berlin, December 2, 1853.

SIR: I received last evening your letter of the 29th November, informing me of your unpleasant situation. It is my duty, and it will be my pleasure, to relieve you if possible. It is right I should state, however, that, in several cases very similar to yours the government has refused to interfere, and most probably it will refuse in your case; or, if relief is afforded, it may be at the end of a long correspondence.

Under these circumstances, you may think it most advisable to make a direct appeal to the favor of the King, as you suggest in your letter; and, if so, I do not wish you to be deprived of the opportunity. But in this I cannot take part. If your case is presented by me to the Prussian government, it will be on the ground of your rights as a naturalized American citizen, and you must, of course, await and abide by the result.

You will please apprize me immediately of your decision, and be assured of my best efforts to serve you.

I am, very respectfully,

P. D. VROOM.

Mr. W. F. PAREHEN.

Mr. Vroom to Mr. Marcy.

[Extract.]

No. 16.] LEGATION OF THE UNITED STATES,
Berlin, February 28, 1854.

SIR: I stated in my last dispatch, (No. 15,) that I had just received your No. 4, of the 2d instant, inclosing papers in the case of John Haben, of Syracuse, a naturalized American citizen, who was arrested and imprisoned on or about the 19th of December last, at Saarlouis, in this kingdom.

On the 22d instant, I prepared and sent to the minister of foreign affairs a communication inquiring into the facts and causes of this proceeding. No answer has yet been received. I suppose it will turn out in this case that Haben, having emigrated without permission, and being afterwards found on Prussian soil, has been condemned to punishment according to the laws of the kingdom. It will again present the question, whether persons emigrating without permission, and becoming naturalized citizens of the United States, can afterwards, if ound in Prussian territory, be compelled to serve in the army, or be rrested and imprisoned for not having performed military duty.

* * * * * * * *

I have the honor to be, very respectfully, your obedient servant,

P. D. VROOM.

Hon. WILLIAM L. MARCY,
Secretary of State.

P. S. After closing the foregoing dispatch, I received from Baron Ianteuffel a letter acknowledging the receipt of my communication especting the arrest and imprisonment of John Haben, a copy of which s herewith forwarded.

Very respectfully, &c.

P. D. VROOM.

Mr. Vroom to Baron Manteuffel.

LEGATION OF THE UNITED STATES,
Berlin, February 21, 1854.

MONSIEUR LE BARON: I have just been informed that John Haben, a itizen of the United States, was, on or about the 19th day of December ast, arrested and imprisoned by some of the public authorities of this ingdom at Saarlouis, and that he is still kept there in confinement.

It appears from the evidence furnished me, that John Haben was orn in Prussia in the year 1822; that he emigrated to the United tates from Westwellars, in the Rhine province, in 1842, and has reided for eleven years at Syracuse, in the State of New York, where he narried, and now has a wife and four children living; that he was aturalized according to law, and became a citizen of the United States n 1850; that he left Syracuse about the 1st of October, 1853, on a isit to this kingdom to recover some property inherited by him from is father, who died at Westwellars about two years since, and that oon after his arrival he was arrested and imprisoned.

At the instance of the government of the United States, I hasten to ring this matter to the notice of your excellency, and to inquire vhether it be true that such arrest has been made, and that John Iaben, the person arrested, is now confined in jail at Saarlouis or elsevhere, in the kingdom of Prussia, and, if true, upon what ground, and or what reasons such proceedings have been taken against him.

As this case involves the personal liberty of a worthy and respectale citizen, I must respectfully, but earnestly, ask for it the immediate ttention of his Majesty's government. I cannot but hope that an nquiry into the facts will show that Mr. Haben has done nothing to nerit the treatment he has received, and that he will be at once discharged.

I take this occasion to renew to your excellency the assurances of ny high consideration.

P. D. VROOM.

His Excellency BARON MANTEUFFEL.

Baron Manteuffel to Mr Vroom.

[Translation.]

BERLIN, *February* 26, 1854.

SIR: I have the honor to apprize you, in preliminary answer to your letter of the 22d of this month, that I have promptly written to the minister of the interior, inviting him to obtain information in regard to the causes of the arrest of Mr. John Haben, a citizen of the United States, detained at Saarlouis, who had come into the Rhenish province, his former country, in order to settle an affair of inheritance.

As soon as Mr. Westphalan's answer reaches me, I shall take care to inform you of its tenor.

Accept, meanwhile, sir, the assurance of my high consideration.

MANTEUFFEL.

Mr. Vroom to Mr. Marcy.

[Extract.]

No. 25.] LEGATION OF THE UNITED STATES,
Berlin, May 2, 1854.

Sir: I have at length received from the minister of foreign affairs an answer to my letter of the 22d of February last, making inquiry into the cause of the arrest and detention of John Haben, a citizen of the United States.

It appears from this communication, a copy of which is herewith sent, that John Haben, being a native of Prussia, emigrated to America in 1842, at the age of twenty years, without a permit of emigration, and without having performed the military service required of him by his country; that, in 1845, he was proceeded against for violation of law, and his property condemned; that, in 1853, he returned to the place of his birth, was arrested and imprisoned, and in January following was incorporated into the army at Saarlouis, to which town he had been transported. It further appears that he made his escape on the 26th of January, and that the government has fined him as a deserter.

Your dispatch No. 8, received this morning, informs me that Haben has returned safely to Syracuse. As he is no longer within the power of this government, no claim can be made for his release or surrender. I am, nevertheless, instructed to demand indemnification for Haben's losses and the violation of his rights, in case it shall appear that he had complied with the law of Prussia, before leaving his native country, and that he owed no military duty. As it is not alleged, or, I believe, pretended by Haben, that he emigrated with leave, or had discharged his military obligations, and as the contrary is charged by this government, there would seem to be no ground on which any claim for indemnity can be made.

* * * * * * * *

I have the honor to be, very respectfully, your obedient servant,

P. D. VROOM.

Hon. William L. Marcy,
Secretary of State.

Baron Manteuffel to Mr. Vroom.

[Translation.]

Berlin, *April* 25, 1854.

Sir: In referring to my letter of the 26th of February last, serving as a preliminary answer to that which you were pleased to address to me on the 22d of the same month, relative to the person named John Haben, a citizen of the United States, who, having returned near the end of last year into Prussia, his native land, was there arrested, I have the honor to communicate to you the reasons for this measure, as they appear from a report made by the regency of Treves.

John Haben was born on the 3d of December, 1822, at Urweiler, in the circuit of St. Wendel. He is the son of John Haben, who died on the 20th of January, 1851, and of Angela Zimmer, who is yet living. At the age of twenty, (in 1842,) this individual emigrated to America without a permit of emigration, and before he had complied with his military obligations. Prosecuted as a rebellious recruit, he was condemned on the 25th of April, 1845, by the court of Sarrebrück, to the confiscation of his present and future property in Prussia. In the course of the month of October, 1853, Haben reappeared in the place of his birth, on a visit to his relatives. He was immediately arrested, conveyed to Saarlouis, and incorporated on the 4th of January last in the fortieth regiment of infantry, in garrison at that city. In acting thus the competent authorities have strictly kept within the circle of their duties, Haben not having ceased to be a Prussian subject.

However, this individual, on the 26th of January last, succeeded in secretly leaving his garrison, to which he has not again returned. It is alleged that he has gone back to America. Consequently the government has proceeded against him as a deserter, and, on the demand of the military judge, the court of Sarrebrück, by a judgment of the 22d of February, has ordered the seizure of Haben's property in Prussia to help to satisfy the fine of 1,000 crowns which he incurred, as well as the expenses of the trial.

In giving you this information, I profit by the opportunity to offer to you, sir, the assurance of my high consideration.

MANTEUFFEL.

Mr. Vroom to Mr. Marcy.

[Extract.]

No. 26.] LEGATION OF THE UNITED STATES,
Berlin, May 9, 1854.

SIR: * * * * * * *
Inclosed is a copy of a * * * letter to the wife of William C. Parehen.

I have the honor to be, very respectfully, your obedient servant,
P. D. VROOM.

Hon. WILLIAM L. MARCY,
Secretary of State.

Mr. Vroom to Mrs. Parehen.

LEGATION OF THE UNITED STATES,
Berlin, May 4, 1854.

Your letter stating to me the unfortunate situation of your husband has been received.

I am desirous of giving you all the aid in my power, but this government has uniformly refused to grant relief in such cases.

A copy of your letter has been sent to the government of the United States.

I wish you would inform me whether your husband had his petition for release presented to the King, as he intended, and also where he now is.

Very respectfully, your obedient servant,
P. D. VROOM.

MRS. DOROTHEA PAREHEN.

Mr. Vroom to Mr. Marcy.

[Extract.]

No. 27.] LEGATION OF THE UNITED STATES,
Berlin, May 16, 1854.

SIR: I have the honor to transmit herewith the copy of a correspondence between this legation and Philip Silverstone, a naturalized citizen. It appears that Silverstone went from this country to the United States, in 1848, at about the age of eighteen years, and having resided there over five years and become naturalized according to law, he returned to his former home, and is now threatened with being placed in the army. Against this he asks to be protected.

In answer to this request, I informed him that having left his native country without leave, and without having discharged his military obligations, and having returned voluntarily and placed himself in the power of the laws he had broken, he could not be protected against the consequences of his own unlawful acts, committed before he had any claim upon the government of the United States, and whilst yet a Prussian subject. In doing this, I have conformed, I believe, to the views of the department as conveyed in your dispatch No. 7, and as further communicated in your dispatch No. 8, in relation to the case of John Haben.

The case of Parehen, who is now in the army, is entirely similar in its features, and must be governed by the same principle.

In view of these cases, it is to be regretted that the impression has so generally obtained among our naturalized citizens that they are not only absolved from all allegiance to their former country, but from all liability to answer for having broken the laws, or failed to perform the duties required of them while yet subjects, and that they may at any time and in all places call upon the agents of the United States to protect them. The same impression prevails among those who have only declared their intention to become citizens. Entertaining these opinions, they return to the land of their birth, and frequently become involved in difficulty. The number of this latter class is constantly increasing. They come, of course, without regular passports, and the peculiarity of the relation they may sustain to the United States gives rise to questions of serious embarrassment. These must be met as they occur. It seems impracticable to adopt a general rule which will apply to all cases. I shall endeavor to deal with them so as to secure protection to those which are just and right, and that will be best effected by not insisting on such as are of a doubtful character.

* * * * * * * *

I am, sir, with much respect, your obedient servant,

P. D. VROOM.

Hon. William L. Marcy,
Secretary of State.

Mr. Silverstone to Mr. Vroom.

[Literal copy.]

Santomys'l Bei Posen, *May* 7, '54.

Sir: I take the liberty to inform you in what condition I am. I am a Amerikan citizen have got my Passport and Citizen paper with me, came to this countre to visit my Realations and Friends. The Magistrate send me an order I shall go to be measure to be a *soldier*. I spoke to the Magistrat and told him I am not a Prussian only a Amerikan Citizen, he answered me that does me not any good, because I left this coutre when I was 18 *years* of age with a passport for *Hamburg* and not for Amerika, and therefore he take me for a Prussian, and does not care if I have got any Citizen paper or not, so I request your Honer to let me know if that is the law between the United States of Amerika and Prussian. I shall look for assistance to you soon, because you are our Protecter as a Amerikan Consul in this coutre I expect very respectfully a answer immediately.

Your humble servant,

PHILIP SILVERSTONE.

Mr. Vroom to Mr. Silverstone.

LEGATION OF THE UNITED STATES,
Berlin, May 8, 1854.

SIR: I have just received your letter of the 7th instant, from which I learn that you are a Prussian by birth, and emigrated to the United States at the age of eighteen years; that you are now an American citizen, and have a passport and your paper of citizenship with you; that, having come to this country to visit your relations, you are threatened with being placed in the army as a soldier.

That I may understand your situation correctly, I wish you would inform me when you left this country and went to the United States, and with whom you went; and how long you have been there; and whether you went with a permit of emigration or without leave? It would also be satisfactory to have your papers sent to me that I may see what they are; or, if you think that would be unsafe, you will send me a copy of them as soon as you can.

Respectfully yours,

P. D. VROOM.

Mr. Silverstone to Mr. Vroom.

[Literal copy.]

SANTOMYSL, *May* 10*th*, 1854.

SIR: Your worthy writing from the 8th of May I received yesterday, and can see, that you want my papers, but to take your advise I only send a Copy of them. You want to be informed of the following things: I left this country in 1848, and went directly to the United States, and staid there above 5 years. A Permitt of Emigration I hade not to leave this country for the United States, but still I have written to you in my last letter I was not but 18 Years of age, and was not at the same time old enough to be placed in the army for a soldier, bekause the do not take them here before the age of 20 years.

I would like a answer immediately of cours—the 13th May the want to put me for the Docter to be overlooked, if I am abel for the service.

Your humbly servant,

PHILIP SILVERSTONE.

Mr. Vroom to Mr. Silverstone.

LEGATION OF THE UNITED STATES,
Berlin, May 12, 1854.

SIR: I have received your letter of the 10th instant, and the papers inclosed, which appear to be regular.

It is much to be regretted that you have voluntarily come back to your native country, and put yourself in the power of her laws. These laws you violated by going away without a permit of emigration, and without having performed your military service; and being now found within the Prussian dominions, I am not authorized to protect you against the consequences of your own acts, committed whilst you were yet a Prussian subject.

Under these circumstances, it will be advisable for you to withdraw, if you can properly do it, from the Prussian territory, and return to the United States, or go to some other place where you may be protected.

So far as I can give you any aid, consistently with your rights and my own duty, it will be given with great pleasure.

Very respectfully, your obedient servant,
P. D. VROOM.

Mr. Vroom to Mr. Marcy.

[Extract.]

No. 62.] LEGATION OF THE UNITED STATES,
Berlin, February 6, 1855.

SIR: * * * * * * I transmit herewith a copy of a letter from John F. Klein, a naturalized citizen, who complains of having been arrested at Bunzlau, in this kingdom, for not having performed his military service, and also a copy of my answer. I have waited some time, in the hope of hearing further from Mr. Klein. His silence induces me to hope that he has made some arrangement with the authorities, and has been fully released.

* * * * *

I have the honor to be, very respectfully, your obedient servant,
P. D. VROOM.

Hon. W. L. MARCY,
Secretary of State.

Mr. Klein to Mr. Vroom.

[Translation.]

BUNZLAU, JURISDICTION OF LIEGNITZ,
Prussian Province of Silesia, January 15, 1855.

I beg leave to present, very respectfully, the following to the honorable minister:

Nearly six years ago I left Prussia, my fatherland, after completing my military duty to Prussia in the fifth yager battalion, at Görlitz, and was dismissed as a half-invalid of the second levy.

On my coming away, I was furnished with a foreign travel passport. Since then I have resided uninterruptedly in the United States, and am in possession of copies of the original letters of naturalization.

At present I am here, looking after the settlement of my inheritance from my father, and intending to return with my family to the United States.

Although I am a citizen of the United States, and irreproachable, I have nevertheless been three days under military arrest, because I had stayed away longer than my passport allowed. Moreover, the local magistrate here has refused to give to me the official passport issued to me at Washington, which I delivered to him, and also refuses to state the reason for such denial.

I am unwilling to expose myself to further attacks unprotected, but only to bestir myself according to the course of justice.

To your honorable legation, which I as an American citizen allow myself to recognize as my nearest lawful authority, I apply for protection to my second journey hence to America.

I moreover pray you to answer me on this matter as promptly as may be: How far the pretensions of this local authority may affect my person and other relations? Whether the local magistrate is entitled to withhold the American passport belonging to me? Whether and in what legal conditions I may reckon on the support of the honorable legation; and whether I can, before my journey to America, be furnished with a passport from the legation, when with testimonials of good conduct, I respectfully ask for it?

The honorable legation will most graciously excuse me for having prayed for the most prompt answer possible. Much depends on that, for I may fall into the embarrassment of too near approach to the Prussian authorities, or of yielding too far the rights of an American citizen.

I have the honor to be your excellency's most obedient servant,

JOHN F. KLEIN.

Mr. Vroom to Mr. Klein.

LEGATION OF THE UNITED STATES,
Berlin, January 20, 1855.

SIR: I have received your note of the 15th instant, informing me that, having been born a Prussian subject, you left your native country, about six years ago, after having performed your military duty in the fifth Prussian rifle battalion at Görlitz, and after having been declared a half invalid of the second summons; that having been provided with a passport, you went to the United States, where you were duly naturalized; that having returned to this country to attend to your paternal inheritance, with a regular passport from the government of the United

States, you have been seized and placed under military arrest, because you remained abroad longer than the period prescribed in your original passport; and that the magistrate of the place where you now are refuses to return your American passport, without assigning any reason for such refusal.

You desire to be informed—

1. How far you can be affected in person or otherwise by the just pretensions or claims of the authorities?

2. Whether the magistrates can withhold from you your American passport?

3. Whether, and in what legal mode you may look for protection from this legation?

4. Whether, before your departure for America, you can be provided with a passport from this legation, by means of a certificate of good behavior?

I have considered your case as presented, and in answer to your questions, would remark, that all persons going from this kingdom, after having performed the full military duty required of all its subjects, and complied with the municipal laws, and who shall thereafter become citizens of the United States, are entitled to, and will receive the protection of that country, wherever they may happen to be. But if they shall leave the kingdom without permission, and in violation of its laws, and afterwards return voluntarily, and place themselves within the power of the laws they have broken, they cannot be protected from the consequences of their own acts. Applying this rule, you will be able to see how far you may be legally affected, and what are the just claims that may be made against you.

As to these laws, and the due execution of them as regards your case, it will be proper for me to ask explanations of the government, unless you think that course will involve you in further difficulties; and with respect to this, you must inform me at once.

I do not understand from your letter, which is somewhat vague, that the authorities propose to enforce any other penalties against you; and I presume, therefore, the magistrates will not persist in withholding from you your American passport. If they should, after proper request made, you will inform me, and I will take such steps as may be proper to secure your safe return to the United States.

I am, respectfully, your obedient servant,

P. D. VROOM.

Mr. Vroom to Mr. Marcy.

[Extract.]

No. 68.] LEGATION OF THE UNITED STATES,
Berlin, March 20, 1855.

SIR: * * * * * * * *

I transmit a copy of a letter from Francis A. Hoffmann, a native of Prussia, now a citizen of the United States, inclosing a petition to the King for leave to visit his native country, and of my answer to it;

also a copy of a note addressed to the minister of foreign affairs inclosing the petition.

I have the honor to be, very respectfully, your obedient servant,

P. D. VROOM.

Hon. W. L. MARCY,
Secretary of State.

Mr. Hoffmann to Mr. Vroom.

CHICAGO, *February* 13, 1855.

Inclosed please find my letter to his Majesty the King of Prussia. I left Prussia some eighteen years ago, and owing at that time, as I am now informed, military service to the Prussian government, of which I was then a subject. I have acquired United States citizenship many years ago, and am desirous of visiting my native country on business.

I take the liberty of requesting you kindly to cause the delivery of my inclosed petition into the proper hands, and have the honor to subscribe myself your obedient servant,

FRANCIS A. HOFFMANN.

Mr. Vroom to Mr. Hoffmann.

LEGATION OF THE UNITED STATES,
Berlin, March 19, 1855.

SIR: I have received your favor of the 13th of February, inclosing a memorial to his Majesty the King of Prussia for leave to visit your native country. The memorial I have transmitted to the minister of foreign affairs to be laid before his Majesty. As an answer may not be returned in some time, I have deemed it proper to apprise you that the petition has been received and your request attended to. As soon as I shall be informed of the result of your application, I will give you notice.

I am, sir, very respectfully, your obedient servant,

P. D. VROOM.

Mr. Vroom to Baron Manteuffel.

LEGATION OF THE UNITED STATES,
March 19, 1855.

MONSIEUR LE BARON: The inclosed petition to his Majesty the King has been forwarded to me by the petitioner, Francis A. Hoffmann, now a citizen of the United States. Without committing myself in any way in relation to his rights as an American citizen, I have felt it my duty to transmit the memorial to your excellency, hoping that his Majesty, on viewing the same, will be pleased to grant the reasonable prayer of the petitioner.

I beg your excellency to accept the assurance of my high consideration.

P. D. VROOM.

Mr. Vroom to Mr. Marcy.

[Extract.]

No. 94.] LEGATION OF THE UNITED STATES,
Berlin, September 18, 1855.

SIR: I have the honor to transmit to you copies of the following papers:

* * * * * * * *

7. A note from the minister of foreign affairs, dated 17th instant, informing me that the petition of Francis A. Hoffmann, a citizen of the United States, for leave to visit his native country without being subjected to military requisitions or penalties has been denied.

* * * * * * * *

I have the honor to be, very respectfully, your obedient servant,

P. D. VROOM.

Hon. W. L. MARCY,
Secretary of State.

Baron Manteuffel to Mr. Vroom.

[Translation.]

BERLIN, *September* 17, 1855.

SIR: You have been so good as to cause to reach me, by your dispatch of the 19th of March last, a petition to the King, from Mr. Francis A. Hoffmann, originally a Prussian, who has settled at Chicago, in the United States, and who requests permission to return to his native country.

This request having been, by order of his Majesty, sent to the minister of the interior, information has been obtained by the president-in-chief of the province of Westphalia in regard to the antecedents of the man Hoffmann, from which it has been ascertained that that individual left Prussia in 1840, without authority of his government, and before he had complied with his military obligations. On his being prosecuted as a rebellious recruit, the court of Paderborn condemned him, on the 22d of January, 1846, to the confiscation of all his present and future property in Prussia.

Under these circumstances, the minister of the interior has deemed it his duty to hesitate in supporting Mr. Hoffman's claim before the King. The petitioner has already been directly notified of this. I have not been willing, however, to omit informing you likewise, and request you, sir, to accept, with my regrets, the assurance of my high consideration.

MANTEUFFEL.

Mr. Vroom to Mr. Marcy.

[Extract.]

No. 99.] LEGATION OF THE UNITED STATES,
Berlin, October 23, 1855.

SIR: * * * * * * *

I have the honor to transmit a copy of a letter from John Statz, a Prussian by birth, who left this country at the age of sixteen years, and returned at the age of twenty-two years, just after having been naturalized as a citizen. After being at Cologne about three months, he was taken up and placed in the army. As this case does not differ from several which have preceded it, I informed Mr. Statz, in my answer, that I would send a copy of his letter to the department, but could not hold out to him any prospect of relief. I did not think it advisable to make any application to this government, not being able to distinguish it from former cases in which interference has been refused.

* * * * * * * *

I have the honor to be, very respectfully, your obedient servant,

P. D. VROOM.

Hon. W. L. MARCY,
Secretary of State.

Mr. Statz to Mr. Vroom.

COLOGNE, *October* 12, 1855.

SIR: Forced by the arbitrary measures of the Prussian government's officers at Cologne, I, a citizen of the United States, appeal to your protection, and invoke your aid and intercession as embassador. My citizen patent and passport, here inclosed, will easily convince you of my being a citizen of the United States; nor will you, therefore, fail to give me that "lawful aid and protection" warranted to me in our Secretary of State's passport, against the *unlawful* and violent measures of subordinate Prussian officers at Cologne, whose conduct will soon, by your intercession, be disavowed and disapproved of by the Prussian government themselves. But I must first state you my case:

I was born at Cologne, Rhenish Prussia. In the year 1849, at the age of sixteen years, I left Prussia, went to the United States, and, ever afterwards, staid there until the end of April, 1855—that is, for a space of five years and a half. Having obtained, in the month of January, 1855, the quality of a citizen, I departed from my adopted country with the view of settling some pecuniary matters and family affairs at Cologne. Trusting to my quality of citizen of the United States, and sure of the aid of my adopted country's government and embassador, I arrived at Cologne, where, after an unmolested stay of about three months, I was suddenly arrested by night; my papers were strictly, but in vain, sought after; I was put into a miserable prison; and, after some days, during which I was totally cut off of all communication with any of my friends, I was forced to become, although a citizen of the United States, and now an *alien* to Prussia, a common soldier. I could not but submit to this disgraceful treatment, since all resistance, all protestations, as being no more a subject to Prussia, were in vain, and would still more deprive me of any occasion and possibility of invoking the "aid and protection" of our government's consuls and embassador. Such unworthy treatment, and the strict searches made for my papers, the superficial refusal of paying any respect to my quality of citizen of the United States, altogether inspired me with the suspicion that had those papers, by which I am enabled to prove my citizenship, been found out by the Prussian policemen, they would not have hesitated to seize them, and so to deprive me of all means of protesting and reclaiming against their arbitrary behaviour; therefore, and because I would fully be qualified in your eyes, I now intrust you with these papers that are most dear to me.

Now, as for the reasons proffered by those Prussian officers, in an at least very strange misconception of their duty and office, they are quite futile, and against all law. They say, "that when I went away I had the obligation of becoming a Prussian soldier, which duty, by going away, I had evaded, and ought now to be forced to fulfill it." But this is wholly untrue; for, *even* if I had evaded that duty or obligation, I would, by becoming a citizen of the United States, have been delivered of this as well as of any other obligation of a *Prussian* citizen. Yet my case is quite another and much more favorable for me; I never have, nor *could* have, evaded that military obligation, since when I left Prussia I was only sixteen years of age, (as I am able to prove.) Now, no Prussian *is liable* to military service before the age of nineteen, and, even *if he wished it*, can enter that service before the age of *seventeen*. Therefore, since I left Prussia, in the year 1849, and (if I had been still in Prussia) would have become liable to service in 1852, I left Prussia when I had *no such* obligation. I returned when I had broke the whole contract between Prussia and me, by becoming a citizen of the United States. So I have no Prussian citizen's obligation at all, and consequently am unlawfully retained. In the surest conscience of my being in the right, and suffering unlawful retention by a government alien to me, I now invoke and implore you, sir, in your quality of embassador of my country, to give me that "lawful aid and protection" warranted in my passport, and to do those steps which will speedily deliver me from unlawful retention; and, hoping that my case will still easier be righted than that of Koszta,

I am yours, respectfully,

JOHN STATZ,

Musketeer beim, 30th Infantry Regiment, 8th Company, Cöln.

Mr. Vroom to Mr. Statz.

LEGATION OF THE UNITED STATES,
Berlin, October 17, 1855.

SIR: I received yesterday your letter from Cologne of the 12th instant, in which you informed me that you left Prussia, your native country, in 1849, at the age of sixteen years, and went to the United States, where you have since resided; that after being naturalized, in 1855, you returned to Prussia with the view of settling up some pecuniary and family matters, when, after remaining at Cologne about three months, you were arrested and imprisoned, and then compelled to enter the Prussian army as a common soldier. I regret that, after having left this country without leave, and against the law, you should, immediately on becoming a citizen of the United States, have returned here again, and remained so long as you have done, thus exposing yourself to the danger of being apprehended and placed in the ranks. I regret still more that I cannot hold out to you any prospect of speedy relief. I am persuaded it will be useless for me to make any appeal to this government. You have returned here voluntarily, and placed yourself within the power of the Prussian laws, and these laws claim of you the performance of a military service which you owed before you became an American citizen. All I can do is to send a copy of your letter to the Secretary of State; but I have no reason to expect that, under such circumstances, the government of the United States will direct me to interfere.

Your case is entirely different from that of Koszta, to which you refer. When Koszta was seized by the Austrian authorities on the ground of his being an Austrian subject, he was not in the territory of Austria, nor within the power of her laws, but in a neutral country; and for this reason alone, independently of any other, it was proper on the part of the officers of the United States to demand and compel his delivery. If Prussia had undertaken to interfere with you in Belgium, or any other neighboring country, the cases would have been similar. You will readily see the difference between them.

I return your certificate of naturalization and passport.

Very respectfully, your obedient servant,

P. D. VROOM.

Mr. Vroom to Mr. Marcy.

[Extract.]

No. 110.] LEGATION OF THE UNITED STATES,
Berlin, January 8, 1856.

SIR: I have the honor to inclose—

* * * * * * * *

5. A copy of a letter from John Statz, and my answer to it. This unfortunate case is stated at length in dispatch No. 99. Mr. Statz seems to be of opinion, as you will perceive, that a formal demand on my part will certainly effect his release, and he will probably blame me for not making it. But I have referred him to my first views of the case, and told him they were not changed by anything contained in his letter.

* * * * * * * *

I have the honor to be, very respectfully, your obedient servant,
P. D. VROOM.

Hon. W. L. MARCY,
Secretary of State.

Mr. Statz to Mr. Vroom.

COLOGNE, *December* 19, 1855.

SIR: With much satisfaction, I received your speedy answer of Berlin, the 15th of October, to my letter of Cologne, the 12th. Although I regret very much that you cannot yourself do anything in my case without instruction from Washington, I have put my hope on the decision of our government. Awaiting this decision, I have not presumed, till now, to trouble you with any further correspondence. Now, however, I feel myself obliged to write to you again, because I now first begin to think that you possibly might have postponed that only step you could do for me, viz: to send a copy of my letter to Washington until I should directly have requested you to do so. In this case, I now request you to forward copies of both my letters to Washington. I hope, and I must hope, that our government will intercede for me; and, in order that you, sir, may become more inclined to intercede for me, I must make the following remarks on some points of your letter.

You concluded, sir, perhaps from an expression in my last letter not sufficiently clear, that I had left Prussia without leave, and against the law; yet I left Prussia with a regular "passport for one year;" therefore I can only be said to have not returned in the proper time. Even if I had not had that ardent desire and intention of becoming a citizen of the United States, I could not have returned in the term prescribed in my passport, because I had not the means; and so, you see, that, even in the eyes of a Prussian, I am not quite such a runaway as I should be if I had left Prussia without any leave and against the law.

Your letter also observes that my case is entirely different from that of Koszta. I must, however, maintain that, if there is a difference in the *right* of both cases, it is entirely to my favor. Koszta was not yet a citizen; he only had the intention. I, however, am a citizen. This, indeed, is a weighty difference.

But, that I am in Prussia, and that Koszta was on neutral ground, does not make the cases entirely different. A superficial difference it is, indeed, but it does not touch the chief question, the question of *right*. The difficulty of protecting me may perhaps seem to be greater, but then the power of the United States is such that all difficulties must vanish before their influence. A simple reclamation would deliver me directly; at least, I see no ground why the trial should not be made to deliver me. Even if the steps to be taken in my favor should seem to promise no success, yet those steps ought to be taken, for then I could confess that something had been done, or at least tried, for me.

But you remark, as a difficulty, that I owed a military service before I became a citizen of the United States. Even the case of Koszta is a splendid precedent, showing and declaring "that the United States will not only protect those that are already citizens, but also that 'citizenship' has a retrospective effect, and that even the intention of becoming a citizen has been regarded as a motive for protecting him who has that intention." Now, if this retrospective and anticipating effect of citizenship has once been acknowledged in the case of Koszta, it will also protect me and justify an intercession in my favor, for, when I first became liable to military service, I was already three years in America, with the intention, afterwards realized, of becoming a citizen. Therefore, if the government of the United States will act up to their own principles, shown in the case of Koszta, they will intercede for me also, and my intention of becoming a citizen will have protected me from becoming liable to service in Prussia.

I am sure that the slightest steps taken in my favor will deliver me directly; and the Prussian government would rather choose to dismiss a hundred persons in my situation than to give the slightest offense to the pronounced will and wish of the United States. If you, sir, would do one step in my favor, the Prussian government would probably not await the result of an official correspondence. I have strong reasons to think that they would deliver me themselves, in their own administrative way, as they do in many cases. Moreover, my being put in the ranks may easily be regarded as the act of subordinate officers, and easily be disapproved of. Awaiting, therefore, whatever will be done for me, and trusting to the protection of our government, I remain, sir, your very obedient servant,

JOHN STATZ,

Musketier beim, 30 *Inf. Reg.,* 8'*tn Compagnie, Cöln.*

Mr. P. D. Vroom,

Embassador of the United States, Berlin.

Mr. Vroom to Mr. Statz.

LEGATION OF THE UNITED STATES,
Berlin, January 5, 1856.

SIR: I have received your note of the 19th of last month, and, after carefully considering its contents, regret that I am unable to take any view of your case different from that taken in my communication of the 15th of October. Your letter to this legation and my answer to it have been transmitted without delay to the Secretary, at Washington; and whatever instructions may be given me in regard to your case will be strictly complied with. If no instructions shall be received, I shall conclude that the course I have pursued has been approved.

There is one fact stated in your last letter, and which was not mentioned in your first, that requires a single remark. It is, that you had a regular passport for a year, and therefore did not go from Prussia "without leave and against law," as I had observed in my answer. I do not perceive that this alters the case in your favor. The passport was a mere permission to be absent for a year, and it implied a promise that you would return at the end of the time. This promise you violated; and, if you took advantage of the license to become a citizen of the United States, it does not place you in a better position than if you had gone without any leave whatever. By the remark I made, I intended to be understood that you had emigrated from and abandoned your country "without leave and against law;" and this is strictly true.

I feel much concern for you in your present situation, and shall be glad, as you may well suppose, to do anything for your relief that may be consistent with my views of propriety and duty.

Very respectfully, your obedient servant,

P. D. VROOM.

Mr. JOHN STATZ, *Cologne.*

Mr. Vroom to Mr. Marcy.

[Extract.]

No. 112.] LEGATION OF THE UNITED STATES,
Berlin, January 22, 1856.

SIR:

* * * * * *

Mr. Statz, who has been placed in the army, and whose case has been before referred to on several occasions, continues to write to the legation. In his last letter he endeavors again to show that, as an American citizen, he is entitled to full protection as against the claims of this government, and wishes to know at what time he may conclude, from my not receiving any special instruction, that the course I have taken in his case has been approved by the department. I have told him, as will be perceived by a copy of the correspondence, that if any instruction was to be given, it would be done without unnecessary delay. He thinks an absolute demand should be made for his release, and that before "the pronounced will of the United States" all difficulties must vanish. My reason for not making such demand was explained to him in my first letter of the 17th of October; and in the same letter I informed him that I had no reason to suppose the government of the United States would direct me to interfere.—(See dispatch 99.)

I have the honor to be, very respectfully, your obedient servant,

P. D. VROOM.

Hon. W. L. Marcy,
Secretary of State.

Mr. Statz to Mr. Vroom.

Cologne, *January* 15, 1856.

Sir: Your note of the 5th of this month, although it did not much encourage me, yet in its conclusion confirmed me in the favorable opinion I had already conceived of your concern for me in my present situation; nothing, therefore, but the duty of utmost self-defense impels me to trouble you with another letter.

Your letter tells me that "if no instructions will be received" from Washington you will conclude that "the course you have pursued will have been approved;" but since all my other steps must be directed by the previous and certain information whether I am to expect that any instruction in my favor may possibly still arrive, I beg you will point out to me the probable term, which being elapsed, I may safely conclude that the course you pursued has been approved by the Secretary of State, and that I may give up all hope for protection by the government of the United States.

By your observation that my regular Prussian passport did not alter the case in my favor, I am indeed convinced and assent to your opinion; only this may show that I am not quite a runaway, and that if I offended the law it was only in a passive way. Yet there was another point in my last letter which you did neither refute nor mention, on which, however, I lay the greatest stress.

If I grant all other points, yet there remains the fact that the intention of becoming a citizen of the United States has a protective power, that citizenship itself therefore has a retrospective power. This has been acknowledged by our government, because they did intercede in the case of Koszta, and so I do not seem to demand unreasonably that in my own case, too, the government of the United States may act up to their own principle and protect me. This "power of the intention," or, which is the same thing, this "retrospective power of citizenship" must also have protected me against becoming liable to the military service of Prussia whilst I was staying in the United States with the intention, afterwards executed, and thus proved to be sincere, of becoming a citizen. That the difficulty of protectiug me is now greater than it was in the case of Koszta, I do not know. Besides this, all difficulties must vanish before the pronounced will of the United States. Moreover, this difficulty, that I am in the territory of Prussia, and that Koszta was in a neutral country, does not affect the chief point, the question of right in both cases; it does not make them *entirely* different. If this circumstance makes a *superficial* difference in favor of Koszta, the difference in my favor, viz: that I am a now citizen, and that Koszta only had the intention, must also be considered; and, moreover, the point in question is not whether I can be protected without difficulty, but whether I ought to be protected. If you, sir, would prove this claim of protection to be groundless, which I hope you will not, then, and only then, I shall be reduced to take the same view of my case which you took in both your communications.

Awaiting, therefore, your answer and an information about the term after which no instructions are to be expected from Washington.

I remain, sir, with thankful acknowledgment of the concern you profess to feel for me, very respectfully, your obedient servant,

JOHN STATZ,
Musketeer, 30th Infantry Regiment, 8th Company.

Mr. P. D. VROOM,
Embassador of the United States, Berlin.

Mr. Vroom to Mr. Statz.

LEGATION OF THE UNITED STATES,
Berlin, January 21, 1856.

SIR: Your letter of the 15th instant has been duly received.

I am not able to give you any satisfactory answer as to the time after which no instructions are to be expected from Washington in regard to your case. The papers have all been forwarded, and your last letter will be sent to-morrow. If, in view of the whole matter, the department shall think it advisable to give any special instruction, I am sure it will not be long delayed. Permit me to assure you again of my sympathy for you in your unfortunate situation.

Very respectfully, your obedient servant,

P. D. VROOM.

Mr. JOHN STATZ.

Mr. Vroom to Mr. Marcy.

No. 117.] LEGATION OF THE UNITED STATES,
Berlin, February 26, 1856.

SIR: * * * * * * * *

Mr. Abel French, consul at Aix-la-Chapelle, has referred to me the case of Mr. George Schlemmer, who has applied to him for protection and relief as a citizen of the United States. On examining the papers, I have informed Mr. French that an application to the government here would be entirely useless, and that I saw no mode in which Mr. Schlemmer could be relieved. The case is one of that class where persons obtaining from the government leave to go to the United States for a year, remain abroad long enough to become citizens, and on their return are compelled to perform military service. It is similar to that of John Statz, about which there has been considerable correspondence. Copies of the application of Mr. Schlemmer (through a relative) to Mr. French, of his letter to me, and my answer are forwarded with this dispatch.

I have the honor to be, very respectfully, your obedient servant,

P. D. VROOM.

Hon. W. L. MARCY,
Secretary of State.

Mr. French to Mr. Vroom.

UNITED STATES CONSULATE,
Aix-la-Chapelle, February 23, 1856.

SIR: I inclose herewith a certificate of naturalization of Mr. George Schlemmer, together with a letter which covered it, from his brother-in-law, Mr. Stahlschmidt.

I have written to Mr. Stahlschmidt that I should send his communication to you for such action as you might see fit to take, but that I feared that nothing could be done to relieve his relative from the unpleasant situation in which he has placed himself.

I have the honor to be, sir, very respectfully, your obedient servant,

A. FRENCH.

Hon. PETER D. VROOM,
United States Minister, Berlin.

Mr. Stahlschmidt to Mr. French.

The undersigned, brother-in-law of George Schlemmer, a citizen of the United States of America, naturalized on the 4th of December, 1854, wishes to claim the protection of the United States government for the said G. Schlemmer.

Said G. Schlemmer emigrated to the United States in the year 1849, with a passport of the Prussian government for one year. Pecuniary difficulty prevented his returning to Prussia, and he became in due time a citizen of the United States. Family business made his return necessary; he was provided with a United States passport, dated Washington, October, 1855. After coming home, he was taken prisoner by the Prussian government, and made a soldier against his free will, and while protesting, as a citizen of the United States, they made him swear as a soldier by force. Believing this to be against the right of nations, he claims the protection of the United States government for the said G. Schlemmer. Hoping that you, as United States consul, will do everything in your power to release him, I sign, respectfully, your servant. ——— ———

Mr. FRENCH,
United States Consul in Aachen.

Mr. Stahlschmidt to Mr. French.

[Translation.]

REUSS, *February* 22, 1856.

My brother-in-law George Schlemmer, returned some weeks ago from America, an a visit to his mother, brothers, and sisters. He is twenty-six years old, and emigrated at the age of nineteen. He tried to obtain permission to remain at Elberfeld, but it was refused to him. His American passport was taken from him, and he was sent to Dusseldorf, under the escort of gen d'armes. On his arrival there he was forthwith forced into military service. He has to undergo a great deal of drilling; is not allowed to go out without a guard, and all intercourse by letter is denied him. Those about him are strictly enjoined to watch him closely.

My brother-in-law wrote the above statement in a hurry, and requested me to copy it, and to add some explanations, and then to put it into your hands. Now, as he is in a very unfortunate position, and has, moreover, business to attend to in America, which suffers greatly on account of his absence, I solicit your kind sympathy and assistance in his behalf. I herewith inclose to you his certificate of naturalization, which I beg you will return to me, requesting that you will communicate to my address the result of your kind efforts in the matter.

Your most devoted, humble servant,

W. STAHLSCHMIDT.

A. FRENCH, Esq.,
United States Consul, Aix-la-Chapelle.

LEGATION OF THE UNITED STATES,
Berlin, February 25, 1856.

Your letter of the 23d instant, in regard to the case of George Schlemmer, has been received with the papers accompanying it. It appears that Mr. Schlemmer left Prussia for the United States in 1849, being then in his nineteenth year, with a passport from his government, giving him leave of absence for a year. Instead of returning, he remained in the United States upwards of five years, and in the meanwhile became naturalized as a citizen, in the court of common pleas for the city and county of New York, on the 4th of December, 1854, as appears by his certificate of naturalization. He has now returned voluntarily and placed himself within the power of the laws which he violated before he had any claim to protection from our government. I do not see that under such circumstances anything can be done by the legation here for his relief. I am satisfied that any application to the Prussian government for his discharge would be unavailing. The government is especially strict towards those who have taken advantage of a limited absence, granted them as a favor, to become citizens or subjects of another country.

I inclose the certificate of naturalization you sent me.

Very respectfully, your obedient servant,

P. D. VROOM.

ABEL FRENCH, Esq.,
Consul of the United States at Aix-la-Chapelle.

Mr. Vroom to Mr. Marcy.

[Extract.]

No. 127.] LEGATION OF THE UNITED STATES,
Berlin, May 13, 1856.

SIR: I have at length received from the minister of foreign affairs an answer to my note of January 4, in which was stated the case of the brothers Herzfeld, who had been ordered to leave the Prussian territory in a fortnight. This note, and the correspondence accompanying it, will be found in my dispatch No. 110. The answer of the minister is very much as I anticipated it would be. The government is induced to think, as it would seem, that these brothers obtained their permit of emigration not with a view of emigrating in good faith, but to avoid military service; and for this and other reasons which are given, it is unwilling that they shall remain longer in Prussia. The answer shows that the decree of expulsion was not executed against them, and that they were suffered to remain three months, the period requested in my note. Further time will not be granted, and I have notified them accordingly.

The minister, in his answer, states that Gustave Herzfeld, one of the brothers, was furnished with a regular passport from the government of the United States, while the other one had only a declaration of intention to become a citizen. I think the regency of Dusseldorff, who furnished information to the government here, must be under some mistake as to this, at least I hope so, because it was not represented to me that Gustave Herzfeld had such passport, and if such an one was in his possession, it must have been improperly obtained.

A copy of the note of the minister of foreign affairs, and of my letter to the Herzfelds, informing them of its purport, are sent herewith.

* * * * *

I have the honor to be, very respectfully, your obedient servant,

P. D. VROOM

Hon. W. L. MARCY,
Secretary of State.

Baron Manteuffel to Mr. Vroom.

[Translation.]

BERLIN, *May* 2, 1856.

SIR: Since the reception of your official communication of the 4th of January last, I have brought to the knowledge of the minister of the interior the reclamation of the brothers Gustavus and Maximilian Herzfeld, who form the subject of it. Mr. de Westphalen having asked the regency of Dusseldorf for a report in regard to this matter, the result is as follows:

The two individuals in question emigrated to America in 1854, with the consent of their government, so that they are no longer Prussian subjects. After an absence of from three to six months, they returned to Neuss, their place of birth. One of the brothers, Gustavus, was provided with a passport from the government of the United States in proper form; the other, Maximilian, with a certificate attesting that he had provisionally been admitted as a citizen of the United States. Having asked permission to stop at Neuss, *for the purpose of visiting their relatives there,* permits of sojourn were issued to them by the police.

The provincial councilor of the circuit, however, deemed it his duty to have investigation made into the military relations of the brothers Herzfeld; and he then learned that these two individuals had not answered the call in their native city, but that they had had themselves inscribed on the registers of the city of Cologne, from which afterwards they entirely disappeared; that Maximilian having been summoned, before his departure to America, to present himself before the commission for the recruitment of the army, he had refused to appear, claiming for himself the character of a foreigner, he having meanwhile obtained a permit of emigration; that, in order to obtain this document in the shortest possible time, the two brothers had pretended, in the course of the month of July, 1854, that the vessel in which they wished to embark for America was on the point of sailing; but that, after obtaining the permit of emigration, they had still remained in the country until the end of the year 1854.

All these maneuvers have convinced the provincial authorities that the declaration made at the time, by the two brothers Herzfeld, of wishing to emigrate to the United States, was only a trick to escape from their military obligations in Prussia.

As to the motive of his return to Neuss, Maximilian at first declared that he wished to make various purchases in the States of the Zollverein; but he afterwards'alleged that his intention was to settle his business at Neuss. Thus different motives, which have induced the regency of Dusseldorf to order Gustavus and Maximilian to be sent back. It must be stated, moreover, that, in 1848 and 1849, the house of the brothers Hersfeld at Neuss was the gathering-place of the Democratic party, so much so that Joseph Herzfeld, brother of the demandants, was prosecuted at the time for his revolutionary intrigues, and fled to America.

In this state of things, the minister of the interior thinks that the expulsion of the brothers Gustavus and Maximilian Hersfeld is fully justified, more especially as the delay of three months, which they asked for in their petition of the 18th of January last, has since expired. The regency of Dusseldorf have, therefore, just been directed to no longer extend the time which was granted to the brothers Herzfeld for their sojourn in Prussia.

In giving you these explanations, I have the honor to renew to you, sir, the assurance of my high consideration.

MANTEUFFEL.

Mr. Vroom to Messrs. Herzfeld.

LEGATION OF THE UNITED STATES,
Berlin, May 10, 1856.

I received, a few days since, from the minister of foreign affairs, a note in answer to my communication of the 4th January. The government here declines giving you permission to remain in Prussia, believing, as they say, that you have not acted in good faith, either in obtaining your permit of emigration or in returning so soon to your native place. It appears, however, that the decree of expulsion against you has been stayed for the period of three months, as was requested. Further time, the minister says, cannot be given.

Very respectfully, &c., &c.,

P. D. VROOM.

Messrs. GUSTAVE and MAX. HERZFELD.

Mr. Vroom to Mr. Marcy.

[Extract.]

No. 144.]

LEGATION OF THE UNITED STATES,
Berlin, December 2, 1856.

SIR: I have the honor to inclose to you a copy of two letters from Mr. John Statz, a naturalized citizen of the United States, who is now in the Prussian army, together with a copy of my answers. It is more than a year since Mr. Statz first made complaint that he had been apprehended at Cologne and was compelled to do military duty. Copies of the letters which have passed between him and the legation will be found accompanying my dispatches, Nos. 99, 110, 112. The case of Mr. Statz was one of those unfortunate ones, in which I felt myself precluded from demanding his release, and I deemed it impolitic and unwise to make an application which would certainly be refused. It could be of no service to Mr. Statz, and an acquiescence in the refusal of this government would only strengthen it in the maintenance of a law, the operation of which is occasionally onerous to our naturalized citizens, and which, I hope, may be at some future day repealed or modified. I supposed my answer to Mr. Statz's first letter, although not as decided as it might have been, would have satisfied him that nothing could be done for his relief, but, entertaining very decided views of his personal rights, he appears to have come to a different conclusion. He is evidently dissatisfied with my course; and, as he declares his intention to appeal to the government, and thence to the public, through the press, I have thought proper, in my answer to his last communication, to review, very briefly, the correspondence which has taken place, and present it in as simple a manner as possible. If it does not convince Mr. Statz, I hope it may assure my government and those to whom he may appeal, that I have not failed in my duty to him or to the country. I have told Mr. Statz that it is his privilege to bring his case before the government; and if he shall do so, I respectfully ask for it, in pursuance of the promise I have made him, the most favorable consideration that can be given it. If I have been in any wise mistaken in my views of what was right or expedient under the circumstances, it will be gratifying to me to conform to any directions that may be given for his benefit.

* * * * * * * *

I have the honor to be, very respectfully, your obedient servant,

P. D. VROOM.

Hon. W. L. Marcy,
Secretary of State.

Mr. Statz to Mr. Vroom.

Cologne, *July* 18, 1856.

Sir: Your letter of January 21 informed me that you then could not give me a satisfactory answer as to the time after which no special instruction was to be expected from Washington in regard to my case. I have therefore waited half a year, and now hope that you will be able to give me a *decisive* and *satisfactory* answer whether I am still to expect any such instructions or not.

Should this last and decisive answer, which I expect from you, prove to be unfavorable to my hopes, should I be cut off from your official assistance, then, relying on the sincerity of your sympathy for my unfortunate case, I presume to beg you will also inform me whether your *personal* influence with the Prussian authorities would be of service for my relief. I cannot give up my last hope, and, in every case, I shall do my utmost, and try all means, to relieve myself from involuntary retention. I hope you will regard this letter as coming from a man almost despairing, and I hope you will send me an answer, which, if not favorable, will at least be a decisive one for your obedient servant,

JOHN STATZ.

Mr. Vroom to Mr. Statz.

LEGATION OF THE UNITED STATES,
Berlin, September 10, 1856.

SIR: I have received your letter, and have delayed answering it until I could, by inquiry and other means, satisfy myself as to the best mode of rendering you assistance. I am still persuaded that it would be of no avail whatever for me officially to request your release, on the ground of your having become an American citizen. But I have come to the conclusion that the most probable way for you to obtain relief is to make an application to the King's favor, and request a remission of the residue of your term of service. This must be done by petition, in writing, to the King; and in this petition you will state your case fully, and all the hardships connected with it, and endeavor to enlist the feelings, as far as possible. If you will prepare such a document and send it to me, I will put it in the proper channel, and give to it all the assistance in my power. I cannot promise that this will be successful, for I know how strictly the military laws here are executed. But I know of no better course to advise. If application should be made to any of the military tribunals, I am sure it would be unavailing. If you should think some other mode would be better, or can suggest anything that may be of advantage, you will please write to me at once and without reserve. My object is to serve you in the best way.

Very respectfully, P. D. VROOM.

Mr. Statz to Mr. Vroom.

COLOGNE, *November* 10, 1856.

SIR: I have received your last letter, but it arrived just at time when we had set out for a field maneuver of some weeks, so I had not the time to read, less still to answer it. Now, having perused its contents, and thought about the only hope and advice you give me, viz: to petition to the King of Prussia's favor for my deliverance, which petition you promised to put into the proper channel, I feel myself very obliged to you for your well-meant intentions and advice; but I regret to say that I cannot act according to it, because I will not acknowledge the lawfulness of the treatment I have undergone, by seeking my deliverance from the favor of the King.

Declining to take the only step you advise, you ought not therefore to suppose me to have given up my hope of deliverance; for, notwithstanding your negative answers, I am not yet convinced of the impropriety of an official intercession in my favor. My opinion about the propriety of such a step has been confirmed by a precedent which has just come to my knowledge, and which I will designate to you. It is the case of Mr. Haro Haring, an adopted citizen of the United States, who, after having left his country *without leave*, and after having been sentenced "*in contumaciam*" by the governments of Prussia and Austria, *before* he became an American *citizen*, returned to Germany. He came to Hamburg in 1854, where he was arrested, upon a requisition from the aforesaid governments, but, after some days' imprisonment, he was delivered, November 27, 1854, by the intercession of Mr. Bromberg, United States consul at Hamburg, and the legation of the United States at Berlin. If I had ever entertained any doubt about the propriety of intercession in my case, it must have vanished upon the perusal of this case. I therefore again request you, most honored sir, to intercede in my behalf.

Should you, however, answer this request as you have done the others heretofore, even then I shall not be discouraged in my hope of being one day delivered. I expect assistance from my friends in America, among whom are several men of influence, to whom I have applied, after perceiving that I had no cause to expect much from your inclination to intercede in my behalf, and since you have never told me directly if the Secretary of State has sent you any instructions directly applying to my case. I have at last succeeded in finding out the means by which I can make direct application to the government of the United States, and, upon the receipt of your answer, I shall lose no time in doing so. At the same time, since I am willing to spare neither pains or money in order to be delivered, I shall interest the press of America in my behalf.

These latter details I would not have given you, had you not requested me to "write without reserve." I once more request you, sir, to intercede for me. I hope soon, sir, to have occasion to thank you for my deliverance, meanwhile, I remain your very obedient servant,

JOHN STATZ.

Mr. Vroom to Mr. Statz.

LEGATION OF THE UNITED STATES,
Berlin, November 29, 1856.

SIR: In your late letter of the 10th instant, you decline any application to the favor of the King, because, as you say, you will not acknowledge the lawfulness of the treatment you have received. I can appreciate your feelings, and am not disposed to find fault with the conclusion to which you have come. I suggested that course to you, as the only one which appeared to be open, and I did it reluctantly, and only because you seemed to think me unwilling to do anything whatever in your behalf.

I regret to find from your letter, that you still think I ought to have demanded your release of the Prussian government, on the ground that you were an American citizen. A brief review of what has taken place in reference to your complaint will show, as I hope, that you do me injustice. In October, 1855, you informed me of your situation; that you left Prussia, your native country, at the age of sixteen years, and went to the United States, where you remained five and a half years, and having been naturalized as an American citizen, you returned to your former home to arrange some family matters, and at the end of about three months, was arrested and placed in the army. I answered your letter immediately. Guided by my general instructions in similar cases, I did not feel warranted to demand your release; and I therefore informed you that, by the law of this country, you were bound to do military service here, and that this obligation rested upon you before you became a citizen of the United States; that you had returned here voluntarily and placed yourself within the power of the law, and that it would be useless for me to make any appeal in your behalf to this government. I stated to you, further, that all I could do was to send a copy of your letter to the Secretary of State, but had no reason to expect that, under such circumstances, the government of the United States would direct me to interfere. This answer was on the 17th October; on the 23d of the same month, I sent a copy of your complaint to the Secretary of State, and called his attention to it in a dispatch, and also sent a copy of my answer to you.

On the 19th December, 1855, you wrote to me a second time, and stated that you placed your hope on a decision from Washington, and feared I had delayed sending a copy of your former communication to the department. In this letter you undertook to enforce your claim to interference, by alleging that you left Prussia with a regular "passport for one year." I answered, under date of the 5th January, that I had received no instruction from Washington, and if none should be received, I should conclude my course had been approved. I also stated that your case was not strengthened by the fact of your going away with a passport for a year, as the very terms of it implied a promise that you would return at the end of that period. Both these letters were sent to the government on the 8th January.

On the 15th January, you addressed another note to the legation, in which you beg me to designate the probable time when you may safely conclude that the course pursued has been approved by the Secretary of State, and when you may give up all hope for protection from the government of the United States. On the 21st of the same month I answered that I could give no satisfactory information as to the precise time when instructions might be received, but I was sure that if the department thought it advisable to give any special instruction, it would not long be delayed. On the 22d, (the next day,) I wrote to the Secretary of State, advising him of this correspondence, and sending a copy of it, as I promised you I would do.

On the 15th of July you again wrote, wishing to know if I could give a decisive and satisfactory answer whether you were still to expect any instruction, and, if my answer should be decisive and unfavorable to your hopes, and you should be cut off from all hope of my *official* assistance, whether my *personal* influence with the Prussian authorities would not do something for your relief. In my response of the 10th September I stated why I had delayed answering your note, and suggested that an application to the King was the only probable mode of relief. I repeated my persuasion that any demand on my part for your release as an American citizen would be unavailing, as would also be any application that might be made to the military tribunals. It is true I did not in this answer say whether any instructions had been received from the Secretary of State; but, after what had already passed between us, my silence on that point could not have been misunderstood. Nor did I give a "decisive answer" to your inquiry whether any instruction was still to be expected. I could have said nothing in regard to that different from what had already been stated.

I hope this brief statement of what has passed will prove that I have not been unfaithful to your interests or to the duty I owe to the country I represent. I have acted strictly in accordance with what was believed to be the views of my government. My acts have been made known to it, and, in a case involving the personal liberty of the citizen, I am sure it would not have permitted me to remain under a mistake. Unless otherwise directed, I must continue the course I have hitherto pursued; and you must not conclude that, because I have not seen it my duty to comply with your wishes, that I have been indifferent to your situation. Such a conclusion would be both unjust and unkind. If I had known of any mode in which I could have assisted you officially or personally, consistently with my views of propriety, I would have adopted it; and I will most gladly aid you still, if an opportunity shall present.

In your last letter you refer to the case of Haro Haring, who, as you remark, was arrested at Hamburg and liberated through the interference of Mr. Bromberg, the consul at Hamburg, and of the legation of the United States at Berlin, and, upon the strength of this case, you renew your request to me to interfere. You consider yours to be similar, and calling for the same redress. I regret that in this you are mistaken. Mr. Haring's case is familiar to me. I have before me a letter from Mr. Bromberg, in which he details all the circumstances. From this it appears that Mr. Haring was arrested at Hamburg, not for the violation of the laws of that city, but for the purpose of detaining and delivering him up to some of the German powers, against whose laws it was alleged he had offended. Hamburg, through some of her authorities, claimed the right, as a member of the German Confederation, to arrest him, or at least it was alleged that the German Diet might take offense if he were released. Mr. Bromberg strenuously insisted that, unless Mr. Haring had broken the laws of Hamburg, his arrest and detention were unlawful, and demanded his immediate release. After some hesitation he was discharged. The course of Mr. Bromberg in this matter was highly commendable, and it is due to him to say that the release of Mr. Haring was effected solely by his exertions. The legation at Berlin had no other agency in the matter than to approve his conduct. Unfortunately, your case differs widely from that of Mr. Haring. If you had been arrested in Prussia for the purpose of delivering you over to Austria or Hanover, or some other German State, whose laws you were charged with having broken, your release would have been demanded instantly, and, doubtless, the government here would have yielded to the demand, as was done in Hamburg. But being a native of Prussia, and having left your country and failed to perform your duty according to her laws, you returned voluntarily within her jurisdiction and subjected yourself to the penalty which those laws prescribed. You will readily see how widely different the two cases are.

You inform me also, in your last letter, that if my answer shall be of a similar character to my former ones, that you will apply directly to the government, as you have found the way in which it may be done. This is your undoubted privilege, and I have not the smallest objection to make against it. I would rather aid you in doing it, and will solicit for your application the most favorable consideration. If I have mistaken my duty, or the views of my government, I shall be most happy to be corrected, and will carefully conform to any direction that may be given me in your behalf.

Very respectfully, your obedient servant,

P. D. VROOM.

Mr. Vroom to Mr. Marcy.

[Extract.]

No. 148.] LEGATION OF THE UNITED STATES,
Berlin, January 20, 1857.

SIR: I have had the honor to receive your dispatch No. 37, in which reference is made to the case of Mr. John Statz, now in the Prussian army. After receiving it, I prepared a note for Mr. Statz, informing him of its purport, and I now transmit a copy of the note.

* * * * * * * *

I have the honor to be, very respectfully, your obedient servant,

P. D. VROOM.

Hon. W. L. MARCY,
Secretary of State.

Mr. Vroom to Mr. Statz.

LEGATION OF THE UNITED STATES,
Berlin, January 19, 1857.

SIR: A copy of my last letter to you, of the date of the 29th November, and a copy of your note to which it was an answer, were forwarded to the Secretary of State on the 2d of December. Within a few days past, I have received a communication from the Secretary, in which he says that my proceedings in your case are approved; and that if any special instructions had been deemed necessary, they would have been given without delay. It is due to myself, as well as to you, that I should inform you of this immediately, and, in doing it, I must again express to you my regret at the situation in which you are unfortunately placed, and at my inability to relieve you.

Very respectfully, your obedient servant,

P. D. VROOM.

Mr. STATZ.

Mr. Vroom to Mr. Cass.

[Extract.]

No. 163.] LEGATION OF THE UNITED STATES,
Berlin, July 14, 1857.

SIR: * * * * * * *

Bonifaz Glahn, alleging himself to be a naturalized citizen of the United States, has recently been apprehended at Weisenfels, in the province of Saxony, and subjected to military service as a Prussian subject. In a letter addressed to the legation, dated the 3d instant, but which was not received until the 9th, he complains of this treatment, and asks for relief and protection. He states that he left Prussia in 1849, at the age of fifteen and a half years, and went to the State of Illinois, where he learned a trade, and was about to commence business for himself, but desired first to visit his parents in Germany. Having become naturalized in the United States, and bearing a passport and certificate of citizenship, he returned to his birth-place after an absence of eight years, and was there immediately apprehended and placed in the ranks.

As this case, however unfortunate it may be for Mr. Glahn, differs in no respect from others that have occurred, and in which the government has declined to interfere, I have advised him that I am not authorized to demand his discharge, for reasons which are fully set forth in my answer to his letter, and that he must not therefore expect any relief from the legation.

I stated, however, that I would send a copy of his complaint to the Department of State, but without any expectation that I would be instructed to take any measures in his behalf.

This being the first case of the kind that I have had occasion to present to your notice, I have thought it advisable to refer to it somewhat in detail, in order that the principle adopted and hitherto acted on might be more distinctly brought to the view of the department.

If I had the least hope that any application for a remission of even part of Mr. Glahn's term of service would meet with favor, I should feel encouraged to make one. But knowing, as I well do, the views and feelings of the Prussian government on this whole subject, I am persuaded that an application, made now, would not only be unavailing, but injuriously affect any effort that may be made for his release at a future time.

A copy of the correspondence with Mr. Glahn, and also of my letter first referred to, are herewith transmitted.

* * * * * * * *

I have the honor to be, most respectfully, your obedient servant,

P. D. VROOM.

Hon. LEWIS CASS,
Secretary of State.

Mr. Glahn to Mr. Vroom.

[Translation.]

WEISENFELS, *July* 3, 1857.

The humble petition of Bonifaz Glahn for his gracious relief from Prussian military service:

HONORABLE MINISTER: In the year 1849, I emigrated, when not more than fifteen and a half years old, and long before, according to the Prussian laws, I was subject to military duty, to America, where I settled in the State of Illinois and learned a trade, and was on the eve of setting up in business. Before, however, I entered upon this, the desire to see my old father and beloved sister induced me to travel to Germany. On the 26th of May, I arrived, as a foreigner, at my old father's and sister's, at my birthplace. Two hours after my arrival at the paternal home, I went to the local authorities to verify before them my passport and certificate of citizenship, but was, on the instant, despite my verifications, despite my citizenship, which my father and a relation offered to prove to the authorities, I was by them arrested like a robber or murderer, and sent to the royal depot at Korbis, from which I was transferred to the major of the Muhlhauser landwehr battalion, who sent me to the military authority at Erfurt, by which last authority, notwithstanding my American citizenship, I was placed in the ranks of the sixth company of the second musketeer battalion of the thirty-first regiment of infantry stationed here at Weisenfels. I must also further humbly remark, that the local authorities of Kolungen, my birthplace, took from me not only my passport, but also my certificate of citizenship, and as yet it is not returned to me. It was my purpose to have passed a few weeks with my relations, and then again to have returned to America and set up business for myself. Now, I see at once the whole scheme of my future happiness destroyed by enlistment in the Prussian military service, which separates me for many years from my most important interests in America, where I acquired property by the sweat of my brow, and was betrothed to an acquaintance whom I may easily lose through many years of absence. As I am already an American citizen, I hold it, therefore, against justice to place me here in military service, and therefore humbly pray your excellency that you will earnestly labor at the royal department of war at Berlin to have me let go. In full confidence that your excellency will take up my case favorably and earnestly, and help me to recover my just rights, I subscribe myself,

Your excellency's most obedient, humble servant,

BONIFAZ GLAHN.

To the Hon. AMERICAN MINISTER AT BERLIN.

Mr. Vroom to Mr. Glahn.

LEGATION OF THE UNITED STATES,
Berlin, July 11, 1857.

SIR: I have received your letter of the 3d from Weisenfels, informing me that you went to America in 1849, when fifteen and a half years old, and have lived in the State of Illinois, where you were about to settle yourself in business; that before doing so, you concluded to make a visit to Germany, and arrived at your native place on the 26th May last, having a passport and certificate of citizenship; that, notwithstanding these, you have been arrested and sent to the military authority at Erfurt, and subsequently placed in the thirty-first infantry regiment at Weisenfels. You apply to me for relief on the ground that you are an American citizen, and as such cannot be subjected to military service in Prussia.

It was very proper for you to give me notice of your situation, and I sincerely regret that it is not in my power to afford you the relief you ask. Being a Prussian by birth, the obligation to perform the military service required by her laws rested upon you as it does upon all Prussian subjects. You left your country without discharging that obligation, and you left it, as I conclude from your statement, without having first obtained leave to emigrate. In so doing, and in being absent at the time military service was required of you, you violated the laws of the country, and made yourself liable to the penalty of such violation. Had you remained in the United States, you would have been safe. The Prussian government could not have interfered with you when visiting any other German kingdom or State except Prussia. The authorities of Prussia could have had no legal claim upon you, and you would have been entitled to the protection of your adopted country. But you have thought proper to return voluntarily to your native land, and place yourself within her jurisdiction and the power of her laws. These laws claim of you the performance of an obligation which rested upon you before you became a citizen, and from this your naturalization does not release you. Under such circumstances, I am not authorized to demand your discharge as a matter of right, and it will be entirely unavailing to ask it as a favor. I would most gladly do anything that I could with propriety to assist you in your unfortunate difficulty. At present there appears to be no way open. I will immediately send a copy of your letter to the Secretary of State, at Washington, but without any expectation that he will direct me to interfere in your behalf.

Very respectfully, your obedient servant,

P. D. VROOM.

Mr. BONIFAZ GLAHN.

Mr. Wright to Mr. Cass.

[Extract.]

No. 2.] LEGATION OF THE UNITED STATES,
Berlin, September 19, 1857.

SIR: * * * * * * *

In consequence of similar cases being presented to this legation, your attention is respectfully called to the case of Bonifaz Glahn, stated in the dispatch of my predecessor No. 163, of the date of July 14, 1857. I shall be pleased to hear from the department in reference to said case.

I have the honor to be, very respectfully, your obedient servant,

JOSEPH A. WRIGHT.

Hon. LEWIS CASS,
Secretary of State.

Mr. Wright to Mr. Cass.

[Extract.]

No. 39.] UNITED STATES LEGATION,
Berlin, September 21, 1858.

SIR: Having received no response to the cases of Eugene Dullyé and John Henne, the presumption is that the State Department acquiesces in the views taken of these cases by the Prussian authorities. I cannot, therefore, but suggest to our government the propriety of making some radical change in relation to the claims of the Prussian government upon citizens of the United States for military services, as well as providing some remedy for the protection of our citizens who are ordered away from Prussia without notice, trial, &c. It is well known at this very hour, there are United States citizens serving in the Prussian army against their will; others desire to return to the land of their birth, which they left in infancy; some to settle up their estates; some to see their aged parents; others, in the language of John Henne, "to weep over the grave of his father." Yet all this is refused under the present ministry. Had this occurred with our Irish emigrants under the English government, it may be well said that we would have found a remedy. Why not find one with Prussia? The cases presented are numerous, and must, in the nature of things, increase. Cannot an appeal be presented from our government, asking at least for some exceptions to this rule? May not the infant from Prussia, raised under our flag from childhood to three score and ten, return to his native land, see his relatives, settle up his business; and may not the American citizen, settled in business in Prussia under existing treaties, claim the right to be tried by the Prussian courts before he is ordered out of the country? In short, may not our government at once recognize the importance of vindicating the inviolability of the United States citizen in Germany, and take some prompt and decisive steps to bring this subject before the Prince of Prussia?

Believing that something may be accomplished, and that the auspicious moment will be at the time of the ushering in of the Prince of Prussia, as he has shown already some clear indications favorably recognizing the rights of the citizen, I await the views of the government, with the firm belief that some protection and aid may be attained at this time for this large class of our adopted and worthy citizens.

* * * * *

I have the honor to be, most respectfully, your obedient servant,

JOSEPH A. WRIGHT.

Hon. LEWIS CASS,
Secretary of State, Washington City.

Mr. Wright to Mr. Cass.

[Extract.]

No. 40.] LEGATION OF THE UNITED STATES,
Berlin, September 28, 1858.

SIR: * * * * May we not ask successfully, under the new order of things, for some change in the treatment of our adopted citizens who return to Prussia, particularly those who left in infancy? Is there not reason to hope that we may at least expect some exceptions to the present rigorous rule?

The department has before it the cases of John Henne and Eugene Dullyé.

Among the numerous cases presented to the undersigned is the one of Captain Paul Borner, who was shipwrecked on the coast of Africa and returned to New York, his adopted home, enfeebled and sick. He was advised by his physicians to return to the land of his birth, Breslau, in Prussia, where his parents reside. After three months rest and kind treatment there, his health was restored. When he sought to leave for his adopted home, however, the authorities there gave him to understand that his military duty in Prussia must be discharged.

It is said that, at this time, there is a person serving in the Prussian army against his will who was one of our soldiers in the war with Mexico, and who is a citizen of the United States.

No American consul or minister can shield from impressment a United States citizen who has the misfortune to be born in Prussia. Is it possible that there is no remedy for this state of things? My opinion is, that if a decided and firm stand be taken by our government, during the present peculiar position of affairs in Prussia, it will lead to good results. It is certainly worthy of a trial, and my energies and time shall be devoted to furthering the work.

I have the honor to be, very respectfully, your obedient servant,

JOSEPH A. WRIGHT.

Hon. LEWIS CASS,
Secretary of State.

Mr. Wright to Mr. Cass.

[Extract.]

No. 45.] LEGATION OF THE UNITED STATES,
Berlin, November 2, 1858.

SIR: * * * * * * * *

Almost every week, to my knowledge, citizens of the United States who return to Prussia are either placed in the army or are compelled to avoid the same by leaving the country. This morning, two young men, Marcus Collman and Otto Rhein, who went to the United States when fifteen and seventeen years of age, called upon me with American passports—one of them being the only son of a widow. I said to these young men that I could not encourage them to remain in Prussia one hour, with any assurance that I could afford them aid if they were once within the power of the police of this country. The parents of Collman are aged and infirm, and he has been absent for some years past from Prussia; but, like a true son, he is determined to see his father and mother, and if he is arrested by the police, I will afford him all the aid and protection within my power.

May I not hope that these cases will urge the department to find some relief under the administration of the Prince of Prussia?

* * * * * * * *

I have the honor to be, very respectfully, your obedient servant,

JOSEPH A. WRIGHT.

Hon. LEWIS CASS, *Secretary of State.*

Mr. Wright to Mr. Cass.

[Extract.]

No. 50.] LEGATION OF THE UNITED STATES,
Berlin, December 4, 1858.

SIR: * * * * * * * *

Herewith is a copy of a report by the "royal public attorney," at Stralsund, Prussia, in reference to those who neglect their military duty before leaving Prussia, &c. By reference to my dispatch No. 32, dated August 27, 1858, the department will see the full object of these proceedings, and the manner by which the Prussian authorities punish the estates of the heirs who are out of the country.

You will learn, by reference to the case of John Henne, that, notwithstanding the payment of the fine by his mother, he was refused admittance into Prussia by the late minister of foreign affairs. Though such proceedings are reprehensible, they are not so severe as the present avowed rule, which is, to require from a father, with sons under age, on his way to the United States, a declaration, placed in his Prussian passport, that the sons, when of age, are to fulfill their military duty.

We cannot countenance this doctrine of the right of a parent to make prospective obligations for his minor children. No parent has the right to bind his son to perform such duties. The obligation is of no force, and should be treated as such. I await the views of the department upon these questions.

I have the honor to be, very respectfully, your obedient servant,

JOSEPH A. WRIGHT.

Hon. LEWIS CASS, *Secretary of State.*

[Translation.]

Inquiry by the "Royal Public Attorney," at Stralsund, Prussia, October 14, 1858.

1. The tanner, Henry Robert Plettner, of Stralsund.
2. The seaman, John C. H. Schiffman, of Stralsund.
3. The seaman, John Joach Fred. Witt, of Damgarten.
4. The seaman, Anton Hans Fred. Dübb, of Damgarten.
5. The weaver, John Chris. Theodore Galitz, of Papenhagen.
6. The seaman, Charles Peter Ebert, of Zingst.

Note.—Nos. 1 to 6 were born in the year 1828, in Prussia.

7. The seaman, Ernst Brassen, of Bisdorf.
8. The shoemaker, John Lewis Ulrich Lustig, of Stralsund.
9. The seaman, Rudolph William Adolf Borman, of Stralsund.
11. The seaman, John Henry Kraefft, of Prerow.

Note.—Nos. 7 to 11 were born in the year 1829, in Prussia.

12. The seaman, Charles Ernst Wilde, of Cummerow.
13. The goldsmith, John Burmeister, of Stralsund.
14. The seaman, Charles Chr. Bründler, of Stralsund.
15. The shoemaker, Henry G. Groth, of Stralsund.
16. The seaman, John Charles Grey, of Stralsund.
17. The seaman, John Fred. Schutt, of Bartelshagen.
18. The seaman, Charles Hermann Schutt, of Born.
19. The seaman, Hans Nich. Vierow, of Damgarten.
20. The seaman, Gus. Henry Gottschalk, of Fuhlendorf.
21. The seaman, Joachim Peter Utech, of Prerow.
22. The seaman, John Henry Mierke, of Zingst.
23. The sailor, John Daniel Schutt, of Zingst.

Note.—Nos. 12 to 23 were born in Prussia, A. D. 1830.

These have left the kingdom without permission, in order to avoid the performance of their military duty.

The late quartermaster, William Haase, of the second class of landwehr, of Stralsund.

The sub-officer of the second class of landwehr, of Stralsund, John Ehrbecker.

The soldier of the second class of landwehr, Gundlach, of Starkow.

These landwehrmen had leave of absence temporarily, but they emigrated in 1857 without permission.

All those persons herein named are summoned to appear at midday on the 21st of February, 1859, before this court, (royal,) first section, and to bring with them all evidence which can serve for their defense.

Against those who do not appear the sentence of disobedience will be passed.

ROYAL DISTRICT COURT, FIRST SECTION,
Stralsund, October 14, 1858.

Mr. Cass to Mr. Wright.

No. 14.]

DEPARTMENT OF STATE,
Washington, December 10, 1858.

SIR: Your several dispatches concerning the cases of Eugene Dullyé and of John Henne, and also conveying your views respecting the condition of American citizens, natives of Prussia, returning to that country, have been under consideration of the department.

Cases have heretofore occurred, and have been brought before this government for its action, which involved the question of the power of European governments over their returned subjects, who had acquired the character of American citizens, and the views of the United States upon some of the points were made known in dispatches from Mr. Webster and Mr. Everett. A copy of the communication of Mr. Everett will be found in the archives of your legation; and they must also contain the views of Mr. Wheaton, arising out of a case, in which application was made for his official aid, while he was minister at Berlin. In these several communications it is admitted, indeed, it cannot well be contested, that obligations may be imposed by the law, and actually existing at the time of expatriation, which are not canceled by naturalization, but which may be enforced against the party in the event of his return.

There are serious practical difficulties connected with this whole subject, which the government is very desirous entirely to remove, and if that cannot be effected, to render less annoying and unacceptable. Some of these are indicated in your correspondence, and they exhibit pretensions on the part of Prussia so contrary to our notions of political rights, that they are calculated to excite strong feelings of disapprobation in this country, as well as much sympathy for those who have suffered by their enforcement. If it depended upon this government alone, adequate protection would soon be provided against these acts of hardship. But in dealing with foreign governments, our first duty is to ascertain our rights, and after being satisfied upon that subject, then it becomes us to maintain and enforce them, and especially when they concern the personal security of our citizens, whether native-born or naturalized. And even where we are not entitled to make a peremptory demand, we may be justified in appealing to the sense of justice and the friendly feelings of another power for a change of measures which press with undue severity upon our citizens.

It was the case of Eugene Dullyé—who was charged with having disturbed the proceedings at a public banquet, by hissing when a toast was given to the King's health—which first occasioned your interposition with the Prussian government; and you appear surprised that you did not receive the views of this government concerning the position taken by you immediately after you had reported the circumstances. Upon this subject, it is proper to inform you that your report of this case, and copies of your correspondence with the Prussian minister of foreign affairs, were received at this department on the 16th of February last. The note of Baron Manteuffel evinced no disposition on the part of the Prussian government to make any change in the decision of Mr. Dullyé's case, nor to recognize the principles you contended for; and the spirit manifested did not indicate that the time was favorable for urging those modifications in the Prussian system which circumstances called for. Repeated conversations with the Prussian minister here confirmed this impression. The last note of Baron Manteuffel, dated January 12, 1858, was a positive denial of the existence of any just claim in this case upon the Prussian government, and a distinct avowal that no action in favor of Mr. Dullyé would take place. This position was so decided, that you considered any further efforts on your part useless, and therefore you referred the matter to your government and awaited its instructions.

The first consideration which presented itself was, whether the application to the Prussian government was an appeal to its justice, in which the treaty rights of the United States were involved, or an appeal to its comity, conveying the views of a friendly power in a matter in which it felt an interest. On a careful consideration of the case, I felt myself compelled to differ from you in opinion, and became satisfied that, as a matter of right, Prussia could not be required to reverse the proceedings against Mr. Dullyé. Had the conclusion been otherwise, you would have been instructed to present the firmest representations to the Prussian government against its action, and to make a peremptory demand for redress. Not being entitled, therefore, to urge this case as a violation of a treaty stipulation, the government felt unwilling to invoke the favorable action of the Prussian government at that time, in the face of the manifestation of its indisposition to make any such change as we desire in its established policy. The subject had been presented by you with much force, and little could be added to the considerations you had urged showing the hardship of such cases.

With respect to the question of right involved in the proceedings against Mr. Dullyé I have to observe, that it is connected with certain general principles of administration which require a brief notice. Every independent state has the right to regulate its internal concerns in its own way, taking care to avoid giving just cause of offense to other nations. In almost all the European states there are police and administrative powers exercised by the governments, which enable them to exert a very arbitrary authority over residents, whether natives or foreigners. When our citizens enter those countries, they enter them subject to the operation of the laws, however arbitrary these may be, and responsible for any violation of them. Our treaty with Prussia recognizes this obligation, and provides that the inhabitants of each of the said countries shall be at liberty to reside in the territories of the other party, and shall enjoy the same security and protection as natives, "on condition of their submitting to the laws and ordinances there prevailing."

The Prussian secretary of foreign affairs, in answer to your representations, informed you that Mr. Dullyé committed an act which, by the laws of Prussia, subjects him to the jurisdiction of the administrative authority, with power to order him out of the country. Baron Manteuffel, as you remark, stated that Mr. Dullyé had not been accused of an act which the law makes a crime or offense. I do not understand with you, however, that this admission concedes that Mr. Dullyé had [not] offended against the laws of Prussia, but that the act with which he was charged does not constitute a crime or offense cognizable by the judicial tribunals, whose proceedings are public, but that it was a violation of public order, for which he was responsible to the administrative tribunals to whose proceedings publicity is not given. I do not perceive that you call in question these principles of Prussian law, either with regard to their prohibitions or administration. The Prussian law being thus laid down authoritatively, this government has no right, especially in the absence of all other information, to doubt the accuracy of the statement. It must consider that point established.

With respect to the application of the law to the facts, in the exercise of the power of the administrative tribunal, I have no hesitation in saying that the considerations you present strongly incline me to believe that Mr. Dullyé was an injured man, and was not guilty of the conduct which was so severely visited. But his guilt or innocence was a subject for the determination of the Prussian authorities, necessarily resulting from the jurisdiction conferred upon them. It appears by the statement of Baron Manteuffel, that the Prussian government investigated this subject with a good deal of care, and became convinced that Mr. Dullyé had rendered himself obnoxious to the administration of the law.

In your dispatch of August 7, which was received here on the 28th, you present the case of John Henne, and again call the attention of the department to that of Dullyé, and it appears by your dispatch of September 21 following, which reached here October 11, that you had then expected the reception of the views formed here respecting those cases. Such an expectation was hardly compatible with these dates, even had there been no obstacle to prevent an immediate reply from the department sustaining you in your views, as you desired. Such an obstacle however, did exist. You had asked of the ministers of foreign affairs that Mr. Henne, born a Prussian subject, but become an American citizen, should be permitted to return to Prussia to revisit his friends and relatives. To this the Prussian minister answered that he had consulted two of his colleagues of the cabinet, whose administrative duties embraced this application, and they reported that Mr. Henne was a "*refractaire*," a person owing military service, and not having performed it, and that it was an established principle that no person in that situation should be permitted to return to Prussia without being compelled to fulfill his military obligation. You correctly remark that this decision is in accordance with the views previously held by the Prussian government, and which have not been contested by the United States. If Mr. Henne actually owed an existing service at the time he left Prussia, from which duty he had not been absolved, it was hardly to be expected that the government would adopt a principle of action which would free him from the consequences of an obligation already commenced.

You informed me a short time since that the expected inauguration of a regency in Prussia would probably afford a favorable opportunity to bring this subject of the condition of our citizens in that country to the attention of the government, with the hope that modifications in the present police and administrative systems might be assented to, which would remove some of the inconveniences now complained of. That event, which has already taken place, may render it expedient to submit to the consideration of the present government the desire of the United States that some changes may be introduced into the Prussian administration which will meliorate the condition of our citizens. Upon this subject, I shall communicate further with you after the receipt of your answer to this dispatch. In one of your communications you state, that some of our citizens are serving against their will in the Prussian army, but you omit to mention the circumstances of this compulsory service. I am not, therefore, able to form a judgment whether the course of the Prussian government in this respect gives just cause of offense to the United States. Cases may occur in which such service may be claimed and enforced without any violation of our rights, as when it is the consequence of obligations, legally imposed and existing at the time of emigration. Under such circumstances, an emigrant by becoming an American citizen does not free himself from preëxisting liabilities in the event of his return. I have the same difficulty in forming a judgment upon the case of Captain Paul Bonner, reported in your letter of September 25, 1858, because the facts are not stated, and I have no means of ascertaining what were the reasons which induced the Prussian authorities to give him notice not to leave the country until his military duties were discharged. I should feel obliged by your transmitting me a statement of the facts in all these cases, that we may be able to judge whether the interposition of the government is called for by the violation of obligations which Prussia has contracted with the United States. I desire, also, to know whether the notice to Captain Bonner has been followed by any coercive act compelling his service.

The Constitution of the United States, with one exception, makes no difference between a native-born and a naturalized citizen, nor does the government recognize any difference between them in the treaties into which it enters. Obligations of the nature adverted to may create liabilities on the return of Prussian-born subjects, but we have a right to expect that these will be enforced with as little individual injury as may be consistent with a just system of administration, and especially as the doctrine of inalienable allegiance has been abandoned by Prussia, and therefore this general subject cannot be embarrassed by any question arising out of that pretension.

I regret to see in Baron Manteuffel's note to you of November 9, 1857, a disposition unfavorable to the return, under any circumstances, of Prussian emigrants, who have been naturalized in the United

States. Though no intention is avowed to exclude them, such a feeling on the part of the Prussian authorities may render their residence in Prussia very unpleasant, as well as useless for purposes of business, if not, indeed, liable to still graver objections. Even where a government is not restricted by treaty engagements, it is still a harsh measure to exclude the naturalized emigrant from his native country, or to subject him to penalties in the event of his return, even for a brief period, or when yielding to imperative circumstances. Business, anxiety to see near and valued relatives, a natural desire to visit the land of their birth—these and other motives, laudable in themselves, may well induce this class of our citizens to return to their native countries. It is difficult to perceive what national objection can exist to the gratification of such feelings. Surely no danger can be apprehended to the public peace, for the governments possess ample power for its preservation, even if there were a disposition, a very improbable supposition, on the part of these few individuals to disturb the tranquillity of the country. These remarks are not made in defense of the right of naturalized citizens of the United States, natives of Prussia, to revisit and reside there—that right is secured by treaty—but this government relies upon the justice and friendship of that of Prussia not to permit any unfavorable impression respecting these returned naturalized citizens to work them injury. Your views upon the general subject are accompanied by the remark, that if our naturalized citizens of Irish birth had causes of complaint against the British government similar to those which the same class of Prussian emigrants have against theirs, a remedy would be found; and you ask, significantly, why not find a remedy in the latter case? I am constrained to believe that this remark, which has been read by the President with regret, was made without due consideration. To find a remedy for cases of hardship is precisely what you have been striving to do, and what the government is anxious to accomplish. Where there are violations of our rights, either international or conventional, the United States will not hesitate to use all proper means to secure a remedy. But there are many cases of hardship in which no such rights are violated, and here our appeal must be made to the justice and good feeling of the proper government; and when they occur in Prussia, of course, to the Prussian government.

The government of the United States is not influenced in the treatment of our naturalized citizens, or in the protection it affords them, by any considerations growing out of their respective places of birth, and I am at a loss to understand why you should have thought it necessary to intimate a different opinion.

In looking into this subject, I feel the want of an accurate knowledge of the Prussian law respecting service in the army. Almost all the complaints which have reached the government from naturalized citizens in Prussia have originated in demands arising out of the system of compulsory service. The process by which the necessary supply of men is provided for the military establishments of continental Europe is contrary to our ideas of personal right, but we have no right to ask that it be changed, and made to accommodate itself to our standard. If it affect our citizens injuriously, it may fairly be made the subject of friendly representation. According to the Prussian system, which has some peculiar features, the whole population is compelled to serve in succession in the army. You will oblige me by communicating to me all the details connected with this branch of the Prussian administration, which may be useful in forming a judgment of its operation upon our returned citizens; and especially at what time the military service actually commences, and at what age persons are considered liable to be enrolled, or so connected with the service that the obligation cannot be dissolved, without the action of the government.

In addition, I shall be pleased to learn any other features of this scheme of policy which may exhibit its bearing upon our citizens.

It is understood that a document is issued by the authority of the Prussian government to all its subjects desirous of leaving the country, with a view to establish themselves elsewhere, called a certificate of emigration, which exonerates such persons from the penalties arising out of their liability to serve in the army, should they return to Prussia. If such a certificate is fairly issued, as a matter of course upon application, and with reasonable fees only to the proper officers making out the papers, and if its legal effect be to remove the obligation which would otherwise exist, I can conceive no just reason why any person not ignorant of his ability to obtain such a protection should leave Prussia without providing himself with it. I am desirous of learning the provisions of the Prussian law in this respect. How are these certificates granted, and how far do they remove existing or contingent liabilities? Are they granted to persons of tender age upon application made for them, or how are such persons considered by the law? It may happen, that by some accident or misconception, a person may leave Prussia without this muniment of safety; but unless so prevented such emigrant is inconsiderate in his departure, and still more inconsiderate in his return.

Information upon the above points is indispensable to the formation of a correct judgment upon the true condition of our returned citizens in Prussia, and of the proceedings and views of that country. As soon as it is received the whole subject will be fully considered. We shall then be better enabled to judge what causes of complaint fairly exist, and what modifications we ought to ask of the Prussian government. There is one position you have taken which I entirely approve, and that is that the evidence upon which a decision is given against an American naturalized citizen should be communicated to the minister of the United States upon his application. Involving as it must the treaty stipulations between the two countries, it is a demand which ought not to be contested. I shall, however, again advert to this topic when your report reaches here, and furnish you with the views of the government respecting it, as well as those it may be enabled to form from the information received concerning the measures it may be proper to adopt.

I am, sir, your obedient servant,

LEWIS CASS.

JOSEPH A. WRIGHT, Esq.,
&c., &c., &c., Berlin.

Mr. Wright to Mr. Cass.

No. 56.] LEGATION OF THE UNITED STATES,
Berlin, January 18, 1859.

SIR: I have the honor to forward herewith copies of a correspondence with the minister of foreign affairs on the subject of the military service in Prussia, as suggested in your dispatch No. 14, dated December 10, 1858.

I endeavored, in my communication to the minister, to embrace the points alluded to in your dispatch No. 14, and, though his answer does not embody them all as satisfactorily as might be desired, I hasten to forward it to the department.

In presenting, heretofore, the case of Eugene Dullyé, in addition to the desire to seek relief in his case, I hoped to induce some change in the police regulations of Prussia, in their operation upon our naturalized citizens. Hence my language: "I beg leave to submit whether some action should not be taken by our government which may result in a change in this respect." The charge against Mr. Dullyé may be in itself "no crime or offense," to employ the language of the late minister of foreign affairs; but the removal, in this summary manner, without notice or trial, of an American citizen engaged in active business, under our present treaty stipulations with Prussia, surely involves in its operation and effect a charge which is most serious in its consequences. In the case of Eugene Dullyé, it was quite impossible to present the department with all the details of the charge and prosecution; yet the facts communicated showed, in the language of your last dispatch, "that Mr. Dullyé is an injured man, and not guilty of the conduct which was so severely visited."

The department will readily perceive, from the language of the former minister of foreign affairs relative to citizens of the United States returned to Prussia, so forcibly answered in your last dispatch, what will be the practical working of such views upon our citizens who are returned to Prussia.

I beg leave to submit to the department whether an arrangement by treaty stipulations, that American citizens residing in Prussia shall not be ordered out of the country without notice or trial, is asking too much of a government like this, united so closely by intercourse and increasing commerce to our own.

My object in communicating the case of John Henne was to present to the department the two questions which had arisen. I used the following language in my dispatch dated August 7, 1858: "Mr. Henne states that when seventeen years of age he left Prussia, the land of his birth, in company with his uncle, for the United States." Thus Mr. Henne left before he was subject to military duty.

It is very seldom that a citizen of the United States, who has received a permit of emigration from Prussia, desires to return. Those receiving permits of emigration, who are of age, take with them their families and relatives. Those under age embraced in these permits of emigration, when they reach adult age in our country, find their kindred and friends around them. Hence, the great majority of those returning to Prussia belong to a different class from either of these.

The department will observe the requirements of the Prussian law, "who leaves Prussia without permission and avoids thereby the service in the active army or the landwehr, incurs a fine of fifty to one thousand thalers, and the payment of the fine, or the imprisonment, does not dispense with the obligation to discharge the military duty."

I have endeavored, after the fullest consultation with the consuls at Bremen, Hamburg, and Stettin, to arrive at some satisfactory data as to the number of Germans annually returning to this country from the United States. I have embraced in my inquiries all who were born in the Zollverein States, their age when they left, &c. I have ascertained from these investigations that not less than ten thousand Germans return annually, more than one third of whom left before incurring any liability for military duty, and not one in ten of these minors have taken with them a permit of emigration. Another class must not be omitted, viz: those who left the country ignorant of their duty, and who believe that an American passport will protect them from their neglect of duty in not obtaining a permit of emigration, and against all the demands of any foreign government. It will be observed that the mere fact of not obtaining a permit of emigration is, of itself, such a violation of the Prussian code as to bring the offender under the penalty of the law. Prussia keeps a register of the birth of every child born within its limits; and no government takes more pains, and is more accurate with all its statistical tables. Hence, were forwarded with my dispatch, No. 50, a list and a memorandum concerning those against whom sentence will be pronounced for neglect of duty, "because they did not appear at a certain time before the recruiting committee in order to be examined as to their fitness to do duty." The proper officer has only to examine the register of births, and from this he makes out his report of the list of delinquents. Although an individual may have been for ten years previous to his twentieth year residing in the United States, yet, if not protected by a permit of emigration, on his return to Prussia, he is liable to the sentence of the law; and if he can be found at any time, imprisonment is his doom, and service in the army, against his will, his certain reward. I do not believe that Prussia succeeds in one case in twenty in placing in its army our returned citizens. It is a pretension of but little value to them, while to us it is most unacceptable and annoying.

The department had, doubtless, my dispatch, No. 45, upon the 10th of December. The young men therein named, Marcus Collman, residing in Detroit, and Otto S. Rhein, residing in New York, the latter the son of a widow of this city, left Prussia without permits, neither of them being liable to military duty at the time of their emigration. Rhein remained six weeks in Berlin, in seclusion, with his mother; but Collman did not venture to tarry but one night with his aged parents. Both of them succeeded in returning to their adopted homes in America.

In communicating to me the correspondence in reference to the young man who desired to return to Oldenburg, a copy of which is herewith attached, the consul at Bremen uses the following forcible language: "I could present you with numerous instances in which the hardships of the existing laws in relation to military duty, as applied to those who left this country under age, have come under my own observation. Indeed, it is the rule, and not the exception, that when the poor wanderer, covered by the broad ægis of our country's nationality, arrives within the limits of my consulate, I am forced to tell him thus far you can go, but no further. He may be almost within sight of the house of his father, or the white tomb of his mother's grave; yet all around my consular district, he is hemmed in by the bayonets and police of foreign powers, who jealously exclude him from the blessed privilege of meeting with his long absent friends, around the hearthstone of his boyhood's home." Again: "In at least three out of five cases, persons residing in other States are obliged to come within the limits of my consulate to see their children or brothers."

In answer to the inquiry about those serving in the army against their will, I would refer the department to the case of John Statzer or Statz, mentioned in detail by my predecessor in his dispatch, No. 144, dated December 2, 1856. It seems that Statz left Prussia, the land of his birth, when sixteen years of age, was placed in its army on his return, against his will, and as far as I am advised, is still discharging military duty.

I am not advised as to the result of the case of Captain Paul Bonner.

The department will perceive that the reply of the minister of foreign affairs does not meet the question as to the course of proceedings taken against those who leave Prussia under age, without having performed their military duty. In a conversation with said minister, on the 3d day of December last, I understood him to say that obligations were taken from the parent leaving the country for the performance of this duty. It seems, however, that I misunderstood him. I have since had an interview with him, expressly upon this subject, and he informs me that "the government seldom gives permits of emigration, where the sons are nearly of age at the time of the application, and never when they believe the object in view is to avoid this duty; but that it may in some cases make such a stipulation." This report will account for what I stated in my dispatch, No. 50, dated December 4, 1858.

The Prussian army consists of three divisions:

1. The standing army, numbering about one hundred and twenty-five thousand.

2. The landwehr. This consists of two parts: the first levy includes all the serviceable men from twenty-five to thirty-two, and the second levy is composed of all the fighting men between thirty-two and forty.

3. The landsturm. This is composed of all men capable of bearing arms who are from seventeen to fifty, and who are neither in the standing army nor in the landwehr.

The government of Prussia is peculiarly a military one, and while we have no right to ask for a change in this respect, or seek to have her accommodate herself to our standard, still, with all due respect, I would submit the question, whether we have not the right to deny at least all retrospective obligations, and to demand the suspension of judicial proceedings against those who left this country during minority?

I not only witness cases of great hardship, but hear of others well calculated to excite any citizen of our country. In my communication upon this subject, I have been surprised, not at the action of the department, but at the fact that so little has been done by our representatives abroad to bring this subject properly before the department.

The number of Germans returning to their fatherland is constantly increasing; therefore, whatever course is finally settled upon in this matter for the future by Prussia, will be adopted by all the States of the Zollverein.

I suggest to the department the propriety of presenting the following points for the consideration of the Prussian government:

1. The abandonment of the claim of military duty upon all American citizens returning to Prussia, who left this country before the liability accrued.

2. No proceedings to be taken against absent Prussians, residing in the United States, who left before they were of a certain age, say twenty.

3. Some additional restrictions giving American citizens, residing in Prussia, the right of trial in a Prussian court, before enforcing their expulsion.

4. The right to copies of all papers in either of the departments of Prussia, in any way affecting an American citizen.

Prussia is surrounded by free cities and small governments, and her railroad facilities are great; therefore, the young and adventurous Prussians who leave for our happy country have but little trouble in making their way thither. These are the most numerous class who, in riper years, return to the land of their birth. One says, "to weep over the grave of his father," another "to see an aged mother," and another "on business connected with his father's estate."

The United States is not a party to the arrangements by which the sovereigns of Europe claim to hold these subjects in perpetual bondage, and by which they deny to them the right to choose and select for themselves a new home and free institutions. If these subjects, in pursuit of their undoubted rights, choose our free country as their home, conform to its laws, are nurtured and raised under our institutions, perfect their citizenship, and are admitted to a perfect equality with the native citizen, it would seem to be our part of the contract to defend them while abroad; at least those against whom no liability had accrued when they left the land of their birth.

I have great confidence that our government will be able to devise means of a pacific but firm character, which will remove these unjust and inhuman restrictions.

If I have been mistaken in my views of what is right or what is expedient, it will be my pleasure to conform to those of the department, and to coöperate with it in doing all I can to relieve this numerous class of our adopted citizens.

* * * * * * * * *

I have the honor to be, very respectfully, your obedient servant,

JOSEPH A. WRIGHT.

Hon. Lewis Cass,
Secretary of State.

Mr. Wright to Baron Schleinitz.

LEGATION OF THE UNITED STATES,
Berlin, December 31, 1858.

The undersigned would be pleased to receive from your excellency some accurate information respecting the military service in the Prussian army, embracing all the details which may be useful in forming a correct opinion of its operation upon citizens of the United States who were born in Prussia; and especially upon the following points: At what time does the military service actually commence, and at what age are persons liable to be enrolled, or so connected with the service, that the obligation cannot be dissolved without the action of the government? I should be pleased to receive any other information which shall disclose the principal features of the Prussian military system which affect citizens of the United States.

Your excellency will please furnish me, also, with a copy of the document issued to subjects leaving Prussia called a "certificate of emigration." I allude to those certificates which exonerate persons from the penalties arising out of their liability to serve in the army, should they return to Prussia. I hope to learn from your excellency, also, how these certificates are granted, and how far they remove existing or contingent liabilities; and whether they are granted to persons of tender age upon application being made for them; or how are such persons considered by the law. I inclose your excellency a list of the persons against whom notice has been issued for neglect of military duty.

I beg to be informed if such proceedings are taken against all persons who have left Prussia without performing their military duty, without regard being had to their age at the time of removal.

The undersigned would be pleased to receive from your excellency, at as early a day as may be found convenient, information upon these subjects.

I pray your excellency to receive herewith the assurance of my highest consideration.

J. A. WRIGHT.

His Excellency BARON DE SCHLEINITZ,
Minister of Foreign Affairs, &c., &c., &c.

[Translation.]

BERLIN, *January* 6, 1859.

SIR: In your letter of 31st of last month you expressed a desire to obtain some information about the military service of Prussia.

After causing such information to be collected, I have had it condensed in the memorandum which I have the honor, sir, to transmit to you herewith.

In returning to you, at the same time, the citation which was annexed to your letter, I seize the occasion to offer to you, sir, the assurance of my high consideration.

SCHLEINITZ.

Mr. WRIGHT,
Envoy Extraordinary and Minister Plenipotentiary, &c., &c.

Memorandum.

[Translation.]

By the terms of section 1 of the law of 3d September, 1814, (collection of laws for the year 1814, p. 79,) every Prussian subject who has attained the age of twenty full years is obliged to serve in the army.

In consequence, in each year all the young men of that age must present themselves at a certain time before the military commission of the circle in which they are domiciled, to be examined as to their fitness to render service, and designated, the case happening, to the detachment in which they are to be incorporated.

This obligation to present themselves for service is not extinguished by time. Whoever does not appear at the point indicated, is held to serve at a more advanced age; and if he can be got hold of, is enrolled under the flag before any other.

Service in the army, in active employ, lasts three years.—(Section 6 of the law above-mentioned.)

During the two years following, the soldier is dismissed on leave, and belongs to the reserve; thenceforward he is not called into service until a war, or an increase of the active force requires it.

After the expiration of these two years, the soldier passes for seven years into the first levy of landwehr, (land-guard,) which, in time of peace, musters only annually for some weeks of drill.

These seven years completed, the soldier becomes a member for seven years longer of the second levy of the landwehr, which is only called out in time of war.

Whoever evades the duties of the landwehr is obliged to take part therein at a later time, and his more advanced age does not exempt him from such call.

Emigration is not permitted, except with express leave from the government. This permission cannot be granted to males between seventeen and twenty-five years of age, unless they produce a certificate from the commission for recruiting the army, testifying that they do not propose to expatriate themselves for the sole purpose of evading their military obligations.—(Section 17 of the law of 31st of December, 1842, on the mode in which the quality of subject of Prussia is acquired and lost. Bulletin of the laws of the year 1843, p. 15, *et seq.*)

This certificate serves also as a guide when it is required to determine if there is reason to grant to minors authority to emigrate with their parents.

Soldiers belonging to the army in active service, or to the reserve, do not obtain leave to expatriate themselves until they have been dismissed.

On the other hand, the service in the first or second levy of the landwehr does not prevent the person who may still be subject to such service from disengaging himself from the ties which bind him to his native land; one exception alone is made to this regulation, which is when the landwehr is called into active service.

Whoever leaves Prussia without permission, and thereby evades service either in the army, in active service, or the landwehr, incurs a penalty of 50 to 1,000 crowns, or incurs an imprisonment of one month to one year.—(§ 110 of the penal code of April 14, 1851.)

But the payment of the penalty or the infliction of the punishment of imprisonment does not dispense with the obligation to render the military service. This obligation continues the rather until he who may have neglected his duty discharges it completely.

Proceedings are taken against such persons the moment it is perceived that they are unlawfully absent, and without regard to the age they may meantime have attained.

The permission to emigrate, of which a formula is annexed to this memorandum, puts an end to the quality of Prussian subject, (§ 20 of the law of December 31, 1842,) and whoever has obtained it is no longer under any obligation to serve in the army. Unless there be a formal exception, this permission embraces also the wife of the individual to whom it has been granted, as well as the minor children who are still subject to the paternal authority.

BERLIN, *January* 6, 1859.

Form.

[Translation.]

The undersigned royal government certifies hereby that a permit of emigration has been granted to, [name, profession, residence,] at his request, and for his emigration to ——— with his wife, formerly Miss ———, and the following minor children, still being under the authority of the father:

[Name and time of their birth.]

This permit of emigration causes the loss of the quality of Prussian subject from the date of its delivery, only, however, for those persons expressly named therein.

The day of —— ——.

ROYAL PRUSSIAN GOVERNMENT.

[SEAL.]

(No. —.)

Mr. Diller to Mr. Thyen.

CONSULATE OF THE UNITED STATES,
Bremen, May 7, 1858.

DEAR SIR: Can a person who left Oldenburg before he was fifteen years of age, and before 1849, return on a visit of one month to said dukedom, if he is a citizen of the United States? Is there a law of Oldenburg that the only son of a widow is exempt from military service? If such is the law, or if it is not, can such a son get permission from the Grand Duke to visit his mother for a month or six weeks?

Excuse me for troubling you, and accept assurances of esteem from yours, very truly,

ISAAC B. DILLER,
United States Consul at Bremen.

O. THYEN, Esq., *Consul for Oldenburg.*

Mr. Thyen to Mr. Diller.

BREMEN, *June* 15, 1858.

SIR: You are aware that, on the 7th ultimo, in consequence of your note of the same date, I immediately requested the Oldenburg ministry to give me information on the subject of your inquiry; to which I have at last, to-day, received an answer, of which the inclosed is a copy. I am sorry not to have been able to give it sooner.

Begging you to accept the assurances of my regard, I am, sir, your most obedient servant,

O. THYEN,
Consul for Oldenburg.

ISAAC B. DILLER, Esq.,
United States Consul.

[Translation.]

MINISTRY OF STATE OF THE GRAND DUKE OF OLDENBURG,
Oldenburg, June 11, 1858.

In answer to the inquiry of the United States consul, dated the 7th of May, as well as to his other interrogatories in respect to the laws of this country upon "military duty" and "emigration," the ministry, observing at the same time that, in the absence of official relations between the said consul and the government of the Grand Dukedom, and between Consul Thyen, respectively, the communication can only be regarded as a private one, reply as follows:

1. That an Oldenburg subject, even if he have left his native country before his fifteenth year, not only does not, by that circumstance, lose

his quality of subject, but remains bound to perform his military duty as such subject, and cannot, of himself, escape this obligation by becoming a citizen of the United States. For such an abandonment of duty, he is liable to be visited by the penalties of the law; and if he, or a part of his property, can be laid hold of, legal proceedings must be instituted against him. There is, however, nothing to prevent his return to this country; and a summary arrest will be dispensed with, in case he receive "free escort" from his Royal Highness the Grand Duke, or give satisfactory security that he will hold himself ready, at all times, to meet the requirements of the law.

2. According to existing laws, the only son of a widow is not exempt from performing military duty; and this rule was, under the former laws, only otherwise when the son supported his mother in such a manner that she, in the event of his entering the service, must have fallen a burden upon the "general poor box;" but even this ground of exemption is wanting to those who have not properly announced themselves, or have been condemned for avoiding duty.

3. Permission from the Grand Duke to return to their native land, without the infliction of legal punishment, cannot be granted to those subjects who have violated the laws for the military service. A remission or mitigation of the legal punishment, by sovereign grace, can only be taken into consideration after the party in question has submitted to legal proceedings, followed by judgment.

Department of foreign affairs, represented by

VON BERG.

Mr. O. Thyen,
Consul of the Grand Duke of Oldenburg at Bremen.

Mr. Wright to Mr. Cass.

[Extract.]

No. 57.] Legation of the United States,
Berlin, January 26, 1859.

Sir: * * * * * * * *

I omitted to inform the department, in my last dispatch, that, among others who have lately been placed in the Prussian army, with American passports, are Joseph Orthaus and Raphael Fisher. The latter has been relieved by the clemency of the Prince Regent. The application of Mr. Orthaus for relief has not yet been decided. They both left the country, I am advised, after their liability for military service had accrued.

I have the honor to be, &c., &c., &c.,

JOSEPH A. WRIGHT.

Hon. Lewis Cass, *Secretary of State.*

Mr. Wright to Mr. Cass.

[Extract.]

No. 62.] LEGATION OF THE UNITED STATES,
Berlin, March 12, 1859.

SIR: * * * * * * * *

Since my dispatch of the 18th of January, (No. 56,) several cases have come before me in relation to "military service." I have presented two of these, by petition to the Prince Regent, for relief, but have received no definite answer yet.

* * * * * * * *

I have the honor to be, &c., &c., &c.,

JOSEPH A. WRIGHT.

Hon. LEWIS CASS, *Secretary of State.*

Mr. Wright to Mr. Cass.

[Extract.]

No. 66.] LEGATION OF THE UNITED STATES,
Berlin, April 9, 1859.

SIR: * * * * * * * *

Numerous cases have been presented, since my dispatch of January 18, 1859, No. 56, on the subject of military service claimed from our citizens. I have presented petititions, in some of them, to the Prince Regent. In reply to one of them, he reduced a sentence of nine months' imprisonment to three, for a case of desertion.

At this time, the application of Francis A. Hoffmann, a distinguished citizen of Chicago, Illinois, is before the Prince Regent, and I have strong hopes of his receiving a full pardon. Mr. Hoffmann has not been arrested.

I have not, thus far, presented any case for clemency where the party left this country before any liability accrued.

I have the honor to be, &c., &c., &c.,

JOSEPH A. WRIGHT.

Hon. LEWIS CASS, *Secretary of State.*

Mr. Wright to Mr. Cass.

[Extract.]

No. 76.] UNITED STATES LEGATION,
Berlin, June 4, 1859.

SIR: * * * * * * * *

I am just in receipt of your dispatch No. 18, dated May 12. It shall receive my most earnest and constant attention.

During the present crisis, it will be impossible to turn the attention of the government to these interesting and, to us, deeply important questions. As an evidence of the disposition of the Prince Regent to avoid this class of subjects at present, I cite the case of Francis A. Hoffmann, mentioned in my dispatch No. 66. In this case, the ministers of war, justice, interior, and foreign affairs, have all united in favor of his petition; but the Prince Regent has, as yet, not acted, although his attention has been frequently solicited. I feel armed, on this subject, with the views, opinions, and arguments so well and forcibly expressed in the instructions of the President. I cannot doubt of the ultimate success. To accomplish this end, I will devote most faithfully my time and abilities.

I have the honor to be, &c., &c., &c.,

JOSEPH A. WRIGHT.

Hon. LEWIS CASS, *Secretary of State.*

Mr. Wright to Mr. Cass.

[Extract.]

No. 81.] LEGATION OF THE UNITED STATES,
Berlin, June 25, 1859.

SIR: * * * * * * * *

It is impossible to engage the attention of the government of Prussia, at the present time, upon the subject mentioned in your dispatch No. 18, dated May 12, 1859.

I have the honor to be, &c., &c., &c.,

JOSEPH A. WRIGHT.

Hon. LEWIS CASS, *Secretary of State.*

Mr. Cass to Mr. Wright.

No. 20.] DEPARTMENT OF STATE,
Washington, July 8, 1859.

SIR: I am directed by the President to call your immediate attention to the case of Christian Ernst, a naturalized American citizen, who is said to have been recently forced into the service of the King of Hanover, and to be now performing military duty in his army. According to the representations of his friends, Mr. Ernst is a native of Hanover, but left that country some eight or ten years ago, and came to the United States, where he declared his intention to become an American citizen, and where he was legally naturalized on the 24th of February, A. D. 1859. His oath of allegiance to this government was administered in the court of common pleas for Scioto county, Ohio, and nearly all his relatives reside in that State. They allege that at the time of his departure from Hanover, he was neither in actual service in the Hanoverian army nor had been drafted to serve in it, and that consequently he was under no military obligation to that kingdom. Under these circumstances, having occasion to visit Germany, he obtained a passport from this department on the 24th of March last, and in the following April he proceeded to his destination. Soon after his arrival there, he is said to have been arrested by the authorities of Hanover, and compelled to do military service in the Hanoverian army. If the facts thus stated by his friends are correct, there is reason to believe that a great wrong has been done to an American citizen, which requires the prompt intervention of this government.

Inasmuch as in discussing this case with the government of Hanover the rights of our naturalized citizens may be drawn in question, and you may find it necessary to maintain them, I am instructed by the President to present to you the following as his views upon this important subject:

The right of expatriation cannot at this day be doubted or denied in the United States. The idea has been repudiated ever since the origin of our government, that a man is bound to remain forever in the country of his birth, and that he has no right to exercise his free will and consult his own happiness by selecting a new home. The most eminent writers on public law recognize the right of expatriation. This can only be contested by those who, in the nineteenth century, are still devoted to the ancient feudal law with all its oppression. The doctrine of perpetual allegiance is a relic of barbarism which has been gradually disappearing from Christendom during the last century.

The Constitution of the United States recognizes the natural right of expatriation by conferring upon Congress the power "to establish an uniform rule for naturalization." Indeed, it was one of the grievances alleged against the British King, in the Declaration of Independence, that he had "endeavored to prevent the population of these States, for that purpose obstructing the laws of naturalization of foreigners, refusing to pass others to encourage their migration hither," &c., &c. The Constitution thus clearly recognizes the principle of expatriation in the strongest manner. It would have been inconsistent in itself, and unworthy of the character of the authors of that instrument, to hold out inducements to foreigners to abandon their native land, to renounce their allegiance to their native government, and to become citizens of the United States, if they had not been convinced of the absolute and unconditional right of expatriation. Congress have uniformly acted upon this principle ever since the commencement of the federal government. They established "a uniform rule of naturalization" nearly seventy years ago. There has since been no period in our history when laws for this purpose did not exist, though their provisions have undergone successive changes. The alien, in order to become a citizen, must declare on oath or affirmation that he will support the Constitution of the United States, and at the same time he is required to "absolutely and entirely renounce and abjure all allegiance and fidelity to every foreign prince, potentate, State, or, sovereignty whatever, and particularly, by name, the prince, potentate, State or sovereignty whereof he was before a citizen."

The exercise of the right of naturalization, and the consequent recognition of the principle of expatriation, are not confined to the government of the United States. There is not a country in Europe, I believe, at the present moment, where the law does not authorize the naturalization of foreigners in one form or other. Indeed, in some of these countries this law is more liberal than our own towards foreigners.

The question then arises, what rights do our laws confer upon a foreigner by granting him naturalization? I answer: All the rights, privileges, and immunities, which belong to a native-born citizen, in their full extent, with the single qualification that, under the Constitution, "no person, except a natural-born citizen, is eligible to the office of President." With this exception, the naturalized citizen, from and after the date of his naturalization, both at home and abroad, is placed upon the very same footing with the native citizen. He is neither in a better nor a worse condition. If a native citizen chooses to take up his residence in a foreign country for the purpose of advancing his fortune, or promoting his happiness, he is, whilst there, bound to obey its municipal laws equally with those who have lived in it all their lives. He goes abroad with his eyes open, and, if these laws be arbitrary and unjust, he has chosen to abide by the consequences. If they are administered in an equal spirit towards himself and towards native subjects, this government have no right to interfere authoritatively in his behalf. To do this, would be to violate the right of an independent nation to legislate within its own territories. If this government were to undertake such a task, we might soon be involved in trouble with nearly the whole world. To protect our citizens against the application of this principle of universal law, in its full extent, we have treaties with several nations securing exemption to American citizens, when residing abroad, from some of the onerous duties required from their own subjects. Where no such treaty exists, and an American citizen has committed a crime, or incurred a penalty, for violating any municipal law whatever of the country of his temporary residence, he is just as liable to be tried and punished for his offense as though he had resided in it from the day of his birth. If this has not been done before his departure, and he should voluntarily return under the same jurisdiction, he may be tried and punished for the offense upon principles of universal law. Under such circumstances, no person would think of contending that an intermediate residence in his own country for years would deprive the government whose laws he had violated of the power to enforce their execution. The very same principle, and no other, is applicable to the case of a naturalized citizen, should he choose to return to his native country. In that case, if he had committed an offense against the law before his departure, he is responsible for it in the same manner as the native American citizen, to whom I have referred. In the language of the late Mr. Marcy, in his letter of the 10th January, 1854, to Mr. Jackson, then our chargé d'affaires to Vienna, when speaking of Tousig's case, "every nation, whenever its laws are violated by any one owing obedience to them, whether he be a citizen or a stranger, has a right to inflict the penalties incurred upon the transgressor, if found within its jurisdiction."

This principle is too well established to admit of serious controversy. If one of our native or naturalized citizens were to expose himself to punishment by the commission of an offense against any of our laws, State or national, and afterwards become a naturalized subject of a foreign country, he would not have the hardihood to contend, upon voluntarily returning within our jurisdiction, that his naturalization relieved him from the punishment due to his crime. Much less could he appeal to the government of his adopted country to protect him against his responsibility to the United States or any of the States. This government would not for a moment listen to such an appeal.

Whilst these principles cannot be contested, great care should be taken in their application, especially to our naturalized citizens. The moment a foreigner becomes naturalized his allegiance to his native country is severed forever. He experiences a new political birth. A broad and impassable line separates him from his native country. He is no more responsible for anything he may say or do, or omit to say or do, after assuming his new character than if he had been born in the United States. Should he return to his native country, he returns as an American citizen, and in no other character. In order to entitle his original government to punish him for an offense this must have been committed while he was a subject and owed allegiance to that government. The offense must have been complete before his expatriation. It must have been of such a character that he might have been tried and punished for it at the moment of his departure. A future liability to serve in the army will not be sufficient; because before the time can arrive for such service he has changed his allegiance and has become a citizen of the United States. It would be quite absurd to contend that a boy brought to this country from a foreign country, with his father's family, when but twelve years of age, and naturalized here, who should afterwards visit the country of his birth when he had become a man, might then be seized and compelled to perform military service, because if he had remained there throughout the intervening years, and his life had been spared, he would have been bound to perform military service. To submit to such a principle would be to make an odious distinction between our naturalized and native citizens.

In my letter to Mr. Hofer of the 14th ultimo, I confine the foreign jurisdiction in regard to our naturalized citizens to such of them as "were in the army or actually called into it" at the time they left Prussia; that is, to the case of actual desertion or a refusal to enter the army after having been regularly drafted and called into it by the government to which at the time they owed allegiance. It is presumed that neither of these cases presents any difficulty in point of principle. If a soldier or a sailor were to desert from our army or navy, for which offense he is liable to a severe punishment, and after having become a naturalized subject of another country, should return to the United States, it would be a singular defense for him to make that he was absolved from his crime because after its commission he had become a subject of another government. It would be still more strange were that government to interpose in his behalf for any such reason. Again, during the last war with Great Britain, in several of the States, I might mention Pennsylvania in particular, the militiaman who was drafted and called into the service was exposed to a severe penalty if he did not obey the draft and muster himself into the service, or in default thereof procure a substitute. Suppose such an individual, after having incurred this penalty, had gone to a foreign country and become naturalized there, and then returned to Pennsylvania, is it possible to imagine that for this reason the arm of the State authorities would be paralyzed, and that they could not exact the penalty? I state these examples to show more clearly both the extent and the limitation of rightful Hanoverian jurisdiction in such cases. It is impossible to foresee all the varying circumstances which may attend cases as they may arise; but it is believed that the principles laid down may generally be sufficient to guide your conduct.

It is to be deeply regretted that the German governments evince so much tenacity on this subject. It would be better, far better for them, considering the comparatively small number of their native subjects who return to their dominions after being naturalized in this country, not to attempt to exact military service from them. They will prove to be most reluctant soldiers. If they violate any law of their native country during their visit, they are, of course, amenable like other American citizens. It would be a sad misfortune if, for the sake of an advantage so trifling to such governments, they should involve themselves in serious difficulties with a country so desirous as we are of maintaining with them the most friendly relations. It is fortunate that serious difficulties of this kind are mainly confined to the German States; and especially that the laws of Great Britain do not authorize any compulsory military service whatever. From these views it will be seen, that if the case of Mr. Ernst has been correctly stated by his friends, he has been deeply wronged by the authorities of Hanover, and is entitled to the most prompt redress. You will lose no time, therefore, in bringing the subject to the attention of the minister of Hanover at Berlin, and will request him to present it at the earliest possible moment to his government, in order that full justice may be done to Mr. Ernst without unnecessary delay. This government has no desire to interfere in the slightest degree with the domestic affairs of Hanover, or to excuse its citizens who visit that kingdom, for any crime which they may commit against its peace and order. It only demands, as it surely may rightfully do, that when its citizens who go there, submit themselves in good faith to its laws, and conduct themselves in a peaceable and orderly manner, they shall be protected in their persons and property, and shall be permitted to enter and leave the kingdom without molestation. To this protection they are clearly entitled by our treaty with Hanover of November, 1840, which is still in force. The first article of this treaty provides that "there shall be between the territories of the high contracting parties, a reciprocal liberty of commerce and navigation;" that "the inhabitants of their respective states shall mutually have liberty to enter * * * the territories of each party where foreign commerce is admitted;" and that "they shall be permitted to sojourn and reside in all parts whatsoever of said territories, in order to attend to their affairs * * * provided they submit to the laws, as well general as special, relative to the right of residing and trading." Even in the absence of this treaty, or of any treaty between the parties, for the government of either to seize a citizen of the other, whom it might find sojourning peaceably within its territories, and force him to do duty in its army, would be regarded as not only an unfriendly act to the government of that citizen, but as inconsistent, also, with the civilization of the present day. Under the provisions, however, to which I have just referred, such an act would be unquestionably an act, also, of bad faith. By this treaty, every inhabitant of the United States has a right to visit Hanover and sojourn there in the prosecution of his business, without any let or hindrance whatever, so long as he submits to the laws. No distinction is made in this respect between a native citizen and a naturalized citizen of the United States, nor could this government have ever consented to a treaty in which such a distinction was embraced. But every "inhabitant," whether belonging to one or the other of these classes, is entitled to all the benefits of the treaty, while he obeys the laws. If he fails to comply with this condition, he forfeits the protection which he might otherwise claim, and becomes liable to suffer the penalty of the law which he has broken; but if, without such forfeiture, he is unjustly wronged in his person or his property, he is entitled to full redress for such wrongs, by whomsoever committed. This is the rule which the President expects to be applied in the case of Mr. Ernst, and you will accordingly demand his immediate discharge from his compulsory service, and full reparation for whatever injury he has suffered either in person or property. It is due, also, to the friendly relations which exist between Hanover and the United States that an occurrence like this should be rendered, by such wise provisions as may be found necessary for the purpose, impossible in the future, and that thus the harmony and good understanding which now happily subsist between them may not be disturbed hereafter by any similar cause.

Mr. Ernst is represented to be now serving at Nordesheim, in the third regiment of Hanoverian infantry. I inclose the description of his person, which accompanied his application for a passport.

I am, sir, your obedient servant,

LEWIS CASS.

JOSEPH A. WRIGHT, Esq., *&c., &c., &c., Berlin.*

Mr. Wright to Mr. Cass.

[Extract.]

No. 88.] LEGATION OF THE UNITED STATES,
Berlin, August 6, 1859.

SIR:

* * * * * *

The minister of foreign affairs has advised me, to-day, that the Prince Regent has granted a full pardon to Francis A. Hoffmann, as contemplated by my dispatch No. 66. Mr. Hoffmann left this country without performing his military duty, after he was twenty years of age, and settled in Illinois. Since then he has been a member of the legislature and a candidate for lieutenant governor of the said State. He returned to Prussia, and spent several days, during this year, in Berlin, and in the place of his birth, yet he was not disturbed, and now he receives a full pardon.

It is evident that this government does not wish to have any difficulty with the United States on the question of military service, and is disposed to yield in individual cases; but it will make great opposition to surrendering the principle involved.

In my opinion, the prompt stand taken by the President in the case of Christian Ernst, upon the principle involved in his case, will triumph. I should be pleased to receive a copy of the unanswerable opinion of the Attorney General in the case of Christian Ernst.

I have the honor to be, &c., &c., &c.,

JOSEPH A. WRIGHT.

Mr. Wright to Mr. Cass.

No. 89.]

LEGATION OF THE UNITED STATES,
Berlin, August 10, 1859.

SIR: I have the honor to forward herewith copies of the correspondence with Baron Reitzenstein, the chargé d'affaires of his Majesty the King of Hanover at this court, during the absence of the minister plenipotentiary of Hanover, in reference to the release of Christian Ernst from the Hanoverian army.

Mr. Butler, of his own accord, and at his own expense, has visited Ernst, at Nordheim, notwithstanding that Baron Reitzenstein and the minister of foreign affairs of Prussia endeavored to dissuade him from what they considered "a dangerous errand."

The details which he then obtained, being found important in the treatment of this case, they have been set forth in the communication which is dated the 9th. I am now momentarily expecting the chargé's reply.

It is not true, as stated by many of the American newspapers, that "there are several American citizens in the Prussian army." I know of none. John Statz's case, reported by my predecessor, was the last, and it is believed that he is now released.

I have the honor to be, very respectfully, your obedient servant,

JOSEPH A. WRIGHT.

Hon. LEWIS CASS,
Secretary of State.

Mr. Wright to Baron Reitzenstein, the Chargé d'Affaires pro tempore of his Majesty the King of Hanover, at the Court of Berlin.

A.] LEGATION OF THE UNITED STATES,
Berlin, August 6, 1859.

MONSIEUR LE BARON: Having had the honor to read to you upon yesterday, the 5th instant, the dispatch from my government concerning the case of Christian Ernst, a citizen of the United States, who is now being forced to serve in the army of his Majesty the King of Hanover, and to request that you will apply immediately to your government for full powers to treat this case with me, I being now authorized by my government, I have the honor to comply with your request to furnish you with a copy of said dispatch, herewith annexed, and to beg that you will call the immediate attention of your government to its matter.

I seize this occasion, Monsieur le Baron, to assure you of my distinguished consideration.

J. A. WRIGHT.

B.] LEGATION OF THE UNITED STATES,
Berlin, August 11, 1859.

MONSIEUR LE BARON: Since my several interviews with you in reference to the discharge of Christian Ernst from the Hanoverian army, I have been made acquainted with additional facts connected with his arrest and treatment through so authoritative a source that I feel it my duty to submit them to your government, through you, for their immediate consideration.

I am advised that at the time of the arrest of Christian Ernst, at the town of Peine, in the Kingdom of Hanover, he was rudely deprived of his passport, and of some of one hundred and sixty rix-thalers, which he had about his person; also, that he was placed in the common prison, during from two to three days each, of the towns of Peine, Hanover, and Nordheim, where he was made to eat the food and keep the company of criminals, until he was forced by four men to put on the uniform of the Hanoverian infantry. Christian Ernst left Hanover when nineteen years of age, before he had ever received an intimation of any duty to serve in its army. He left his native country, having committed no offense against its laws, and without any debts, and sought in the United States a future home—an undoubted right in the nineteenth century. Therefore, on his return to his native land, Christian Ernst visits Hanover, as an American citizen, and in no other character.

In submitting to you, Monsieur le Baron, a copy of the dispatch from the government of the United States in reference to Christian Ernst, as well as during the several conversations which we have had on the subject, I have flattered myself with the belief that the government of his Majesty the King of Hanover would at once see the propriety of complying with the views expressed in said dispatch, and with its demand for Ernst's immediate release, since said demands are dictated on the grounds of international comity and of strict justice. Now, I am convinced that your government will perceive the propriety of an immediate and favorable reply. In demanding the immediate discharge of Ernst, with full reparation for the injuries he has sustained in person and property, I am not only expressing the language of the government of the United States in the dispatch before you, but the sentiments of the people of every nation which protects its citizens when abroad.

I need not assure you, Monsieur le Baron, that a determination to press into the military service of Hanover American naturalized citizens, under such circumstances as are presented by the case of Christian Ernst, cannot but lead to the most serious difficulties between the United States and the kingdom of Hanover.

This legation desires to do all in its power to preserve the kind feelings and respect which so happily exist at present between the said countries.

While obeying my instructions in placing plainly and frankly these facts before the government of his Majesty the King of Hanover, I take this occasion to renew to you, Monsieur le Baron, assurances of my highest consideration.

J. A. WRIGHT.

Monsieur le BARON DE REITZENSTEIN,
Chargé d'Affaires of his Majesty the King of Hanover, &c.

Mr. Wright to Mr. Cass.

[Extract.]

No. 90.] LEGATION OF THE UNITED STATES,
Berlin, August 13, 1859.

SIR: * * * * * * *

I have the honor to forward herewith a copy of the only note received from the Hanoverian chargé d'affaires at this court in the case of Christian Ernst.

Desiring to extend the utmost courtesy to the government of Hanover, knowing such to be the desire of the President in treating all diplomatic negotiations, I have concluded to wait a few days before replying to this note. The department shall be promptly advised of every step taken in the case.

I have the honor to be, very respectfully, your obedient servant,

JOSEPH A. WRIGHT.

Hon. LEWIS CASS,
Secretary of State.

Baron Reitzenstein to Mr. Wright.

[Translation.]

A.] BERLIN, *August* 11, 1859.

SIR: In reply to the notes of your excellency, of the 6th and 9th of this month, I have the honor to say temporarily that I am directed by my government to announce to your excellency that, in conformity to your wish, the affair of Mr. Christian Ernst will be prosecuted with all possible promptitude. But it will be impossible for me to give your excellency a precise answer in regard to this affair at a very early period, inasmuch as my government is not sufficiently informed as to what relates to the person of Mr. Christian Ernst, and as to the period at which he left his country to go to America. The minister of war will therefore be under the necessity of communicating in the first place with several Hanoverian officers, in order to assure himself in regard to these points, and to be able to report the affair for the decision of his Majesty the King, who is at this time at Norden. As soon as I am notified of the result of these inquiries, I shall have the honor of communicating it to your excellency.

Accept, meanwhile, the assurances of my very distinguished consideration.

REITZENSTEIN.

His Excellency Mr. WRIGHT,
Envoy Extraordinary and Minister Plenipotentiary, &c., &c., &c.

Mr. Wright to Mr. Cass.

No. 91.] UNITED STATES LEGATION,
Berlin, August 20, 1859.

SIR: Baron Reitzenstein, chargé d'affaires for Hanover, has this moment advised me of the receipt of a dispatch from his government, informing him of the discharge of Christian Ernst from the Hanoverian army.

By next mail I shall be able to furnish the department a copy of the dispatch received by Baron Reitzenstein, as the baron cannot furnish me the same in time for this day's mail.

I have the honor to be, very respectfully, your obedient servant,

JOSEPH A. WRIGHT.

Hon. LEWIS CASS,
Secretary of State.

Mr. Wright to Mr. Cass.

UNITED STATES LEGATION,
Berlin, August 24, 1859.

SIR: I have the honor to inclose two dispatches of Baron Reitzenstein, of the date of the 16th and 20th instant. Knowing the interest the President takes in this case, I have forwarded the original dispatch of August the 20th, also an English translation of the same, made out by an excellent scholar.

Expecting additional information as to the arrest and treatment of Mr. Ernst, I shall be able in a few days to make a reply on the subject of satisfaction and compensation, undoubtedly *his right*, and to the other matters mentioned in said dispatch.

I have the honor to be, most respectfully, your obedient servant,
JOSEPH A. WRIGHT.

Hon. LEWIS CASS,
Secretary of State, Washington City.

[Translation.]

BERLIN, *August* 16, 1859.

Having reference to my note of the 11th of this month, I have the honor to inform your excellency that the minister for foreign affairs of Hanover immediately communicated to his colleague, the minister of war, the dispatches you were pleased to remit to me, with your note relating to the affair of Mr. Christian Ernst.

The minister of war has now replied, that by these communications alone has he received information of the fact, that Mr. Ernst is enrolled in the royal army of Hanover. The minister has called for a prompt report from the prefect of Hildesheim on the case in question, but does not believe that he will be able to pass upon the affair until the receipt of this official report.

My government is further of opinion, that Mr. Ernst should at once have asked protection and defense from the superior authorities of the country in the particular in which he believes his rights are violated, and thinks that in case Mr. Ernst had complained to the minister at war of Hanover, he would probably have succored him before his complaint could have reached the government of the United States of America.

Be pleased to accept, sir, the assurance of my very distinguished consideration.

REITZENSTEIN,
The chargé d'affaires of Hanover.

His Excellency Mr. WRIGHT,
Envoy Extraordinary, &c., of the United States of America.

[Translation.]

BERLIN, *August* 20, 1859.

The undersigned feels great pleasure in being able to make to his excellency the minister of the United States, Mr. Wright, the follow-communication *in re* Christian Ernst, of Portsmouth, which has just reached him from his government.

John Henry *Christian* Ernst was born on the 22d October, 1831, at Handorf, in the district of Peine. He went to the United States about Easter, 1850, leaving his parents behind, and without having given notice to the magistrate of his intention of emigrating. He wrote to his relations once after the lapse of one year, when during several years he gave no further news about himself. After having entered, in 1852, the age when he became liable to military service, he was summoned to appear, like every other citizen liable to serve in the army; at his non-appearance he was once more invited through the public papers to return; and, finally, on the 19th February, 1855, he was condemned as a military absentee by the criminal court at Hildesheim, in pursuance of the Hanoverian legislation on the subject.

On the 11th February, 1854, the appointed guardians of said Ernst, whose father died on the 26th May, 1852, delivered a notarial act, issued on the 27th December, 1853, at Evansville, Vanderburg county, Indiana, to the purport of obtaining his liberation from his allegiance to the Hanoverian government. However, at the then state of the affair, that petition could not be taken into consideration.

The legal sentence has been published, put into execution as far as possible, and the name of said Ernst inscribed at his native place on the black-board (hue and cry) as a deserter.

On the 4th May of the present year the magistrate of Peine got notice that said Ernst had come back to his native place. The high bailiff of Hildesheim having been consulted, ordered the magistrate to produce said Ernst for the subsequent fulfillment of his military duties. The latter was induced, on the 18th May, to put said Ernst under provisional arrest, after his having received a sum of money from his guardians, and after his having given to understand that he intended to leave the country immediately, in order to avoid irremediable annoyances. On the 20th May he was sent under escort to Nordheim, where he was incorporated, on the 22d of the same month, into the 2d battalion of the 3d regiment of infantry, and where he is in actual service.

Such is the exact state of things.

Now, in passing to the contents of the dispatch addressed on the 8th July, of the present year, by the under Secretary of State of the United States, at Washington, to his excellency the minister at Berlin, the following arguments may be humbly submitted:

The naturalization in general exists in the kingdom of Hanover and in the other States of the German Confederation just as in the United States. The same may be said of the permission granted to subjects for emigrating; which, in fact, is guarantied by section 43 of the Hanoverian constitution, under the condition of a due observance of the legal formalities on the subject.

The naturalization of foreigners commonly depends upon certain suppositions. Now the citizenship of a country implying both rights and *obligations* for the citizens, the freedom of emigration is subject to certain limitations until said obligations have been fulfilled or dispensed with.

The laws concerning citizenship vary in the different countries, nor can they be expected to be uniform since the peculiarities of every individual State require different considerations according to its internal constitution. Thus it may happen that immigrants into Hanover from a certain State are considered as Hanoverian subjects, according to the Hanoverian law, whilst in their native country they are still legally considered as subjects of that country, and although being citizens of a foreign State, and still liable to fulfill civic obligations in their native country.

The promulgation of laws and regulations respecting naturalization and emigration is undoubtedly the own (or domestic) affair of the respective governments; and, considering the diversity that exists between the laws on that subject, the intention of putting a foreign law in force in another country without taking notice of the legislation of that same country, must be looked at as an encroachment upon the rights of every individual State.

The principles adopted in Hanover with regard to emigration may be said to be the most liberal of all the States of the German Confederation. They may be resumed in the following few words:

The freedom of emigration, (with the exception of crimes, &c., committed, and not yet punished,) is subject to certain restrictions with respect to the male population in consequence of the general military obligations to which every subject is liable. The fulfillment of military duty is not required from sons emigrating with their fathers before they enter the age of conscription, (twenty-first year,) nor from natural children emigrating with their mother. Those who want to emigrate without their parents, before having fulfilled their military duties, require the permission of a magistrate, (a certificate of emigration,) which is granted without difficulty up to the year preceding the year when the conscription takes place, and which, even in that very same year is not refused, provided it be shown that the interested party finds a better provision for the future abroad. Said grant is not to be eluded by the simple reason because it serves to distinguish honest emigrants from those who evade their military duties by flight. When within the age of military conscription, (from twenty-first to twenty-seventh year,) those subjects are alone allowed to emigrate, who, having not yet entered the military service, do not, by their departure, endanger the rights of other parties liable to serve in the army. Even those subjects to whom, under such circumstances, said permission might be refused, may obtain the same, after having procured a substitute, nay, after having giving a sufficient security for finding a substitute, in case the young men should be called out for military service.

In applying the above principles to the present case, the following result is obtained:

Christian Ernst, born in 1831, left the Hanoverian territory about Easter, in 1850, leaving his father behind; therefore, if he intended to give up his rights as a Hanoverian subject, and to settle in the United States, he required a certificate of emigration, which, up to the 1st January, 1852, would not have been withheld. That intention, however, not having been evinced, the certificate was not granted; consequently, the said Ernst could but be condemned, like every other refractory absentee, as a deserter, and at his return be treated as such.

The sentence having been brought to public notice, his name having besides, been inscribed on the black-board, (hue and cry,) said Ernst could well know by himself or others what he might expect in the kingdom of Hanover. He therefore must attribute to himself alone the disagreeable consequences arising therefrom for him.

If the government of the United States would not consent to naturalize a foreigner before his having shown that he duly fulfilled his *obligations* to his native country—as generally done, under terms of reciprocity, by the different governments of Europe—a naturalized American citizen at his return to his native country could never happen to be claimed for not having fulfilled his duties at home.

Now, according to the contents of said dispatch, the right of the foreign State of admonishing naturalized American citizens returning to their native country to fulfill obligations preceding the time of their emigration to the United States, is generally recognized. This, however, is done with certain restrictions, based upon considerations of laws existing in the United States, but not in the respective foreign State. Thus said dispatch, with respect to the violation of the military duty, uses an argument which is entirely contrary to the Hanoverian principles, viz: it says that such a violation is only committed by him who leaves the country after having entered the military service, or after having been duly summoned to enter the same. From that argument, the inference is drawn that said Ernst, who acquired the American citizenship only *on the 24th February of the present year*, thus being up to that period only a Hanoverian subject, sojourning in the United States, has illegally been forced to enter the military service.

The natural relation between independent States seems to require that the State granting letters of naturalization to the subject of another State can only do this, provided those obligations, the military duties included, which the interested party has yet to fulfill in his native country, according to its laws, should continue, and that the said State should consequently not try to prevent naturalized American citizens from being required to fulfill those obligations at their voluntary return to their native country.

Consequently, the proceedings of the Hanoverian authorities against said Christian Ernst are quite legal, and the demand of the government of the United States to liberate said Ernst from the military service might, according to the state of things, be considered as an encroachment upon the internal affairs of the Hanoverian government, a supposition against which the said dispatch itself protests.

Nevertheless, the royal Hanoverian government, anxious to show the greatest possible compliance with the wishes of a friendly power united by so many ties with Hanover, is most ready to come to an agreement with the government of the United States for the purpose of preventing the frequent complications of a similar nature. Should the royal government, as done before, render the liberation from the military service dependent on his finding a substitute, such a course would be equivalent to a refusal to pardon, since the price of substitutes in the present unsettled political state of things has reached such a height as to bring such a sum without the reach of said Ernst. The royal Hanoverian government, therefore, does not hesitate *to remit at once the penalty incurred by said Ernst*, BY GRANTING HIM A FULL PARDON, *and to cause him to be dismissed from the military service.* The necessary *measures have been taken for that purpose.*

The recurrence, however, of similar conflicts can only be prevented by the government of the United States renouncing to its own views on the subject, which do not agree with international relations, or by arriving at a certain agreement, the above representation offering certain openings which it must be left to the initiative of the government of the United States to make the proper use of.

Finally, concerning the pretended ill treatment of said Ernst, the explanations required from the various authorities have not yet entirely come in; as far, however, as they go, it appears that all the proceedings against said Ernst have been entirely legal, and that said Ernst has no reason to complain of an unfair treatment.

The undersigned having the honor to deliver, most respectfully, the present communication to his excellency the minister, Mr. Wright, avails himself of this opportunity of renewing to his excellency the assurance of his most distinguished consideration.

The Hanoverian chargé d'affaires:

W. REITZENSTEIN.

Mr. Wright to Mr. Cass.

No. 93.]

UNITED STATES LEGATION,
Berlin, August 31, 1859.

SIR: The promised reply of the minister of foreign affairs of Hanover, on the subject of the treatment, arrest, and satisfaction to Mr. Ernst, has not come to hand.

I have written to Mr. Ernst for information, and received no reply.

As the dispatch from the Hanoverian government surrendering Mr. Ernst alludes to the settlement of this vexed question, and says the initiative must come from the United States, I would respectfully suggest to the consideration of the President the following propositions:

1. The abandonment of all military service where their subjects have been absent for five years from the land of their birth, and have become citizens of the United States.

2. The suspension of all judicial proceedings against those residing in the United States for any neglect of military duty.

3. No citizen of the United States to be ordered out of the country

without personal notice and trial in a court of record, with the right of appeal to the highest tribunals of the land.

4. Total exemption of citizens of the United States residing in Hanover, Prussia, &c., from liability to support in any manner soldiers, officers, and those connected with the military service of the country.

I hope by next mail to send the department a copy of my reply to the Hanoverian minister on the subject of the satisfaction due Mr. Ernst, &c.

I have the honor to be, most respectfully, your obedient servant,

JOSEPH A. WRIGHT.

Hon. LEWIS CASS, *Secretary of State.*

Mr. Cass to Mr. Wright.

No. 23.]

DEPARTMENT OF STATE,
Washington, September 15, 1859.

SIR: I have the honor to acknowledge the receipt of your dispatch of August 24, 1854, (No. 92,) announcing the discharge of Christian Ernst.

The President has received this intelligence with great satisfaction, and approves the promptitude and energy with which you presented the case for the consideration of the Hanoverian government. While he appreciates, also, the comity and good will towards the United States, which were manifested in the pardon and discharge of Ernst, and are expressed in the communication of Baron Reitzenstein, he regrets that the views of the government of Hanover on the subject of expatriation are not more fully in accordance with those of this government. It is hoped that upon a further consideration of the subject, it may be led so far to modify its present opinions, as to prevent any future disagreement between the two governments in respect to the rights and privileges of American citizens.

In reference to the arrest and treatment of Mr. Ernst, as soon as you shall have transmitted to the department the further information which you anticipate, such additional instructions will be sent to you as the case may seem to require.

I am, sir, your obedient servant,

LEWIS CASS.

JOSEPH A. WRIGHT, Esq., *&c., &c., &c., Berlin.*

Mr. Cass to Mr. Wright.

No. 26.]

DEPARTMENT OF STATE,
Washington, December 9, 1859.

SIR: Your dispatch, dated October 12, announcing the closing of your correspondence with the Hanoverian government has been received at the department, and it affords me pleasure to inform you that your course in this matter is fully approved. And I have to express equal gratification at the manner in which you have urged upon the Prussian government our views respecting the rights of American citizens, and am confident you will lose no proper opportunity to impress upon it the importance which the United States attach to this matter, and their firm persuasion that the Prussian government will afford to their citizens, while in Prussia, the protection to which we maintain they are entitled, as well by the law of nations as by treaty stipulations. In this view of the subject, any additional treaty with reference to it, seems by no means indispensable, since what we claim for our naturalized citizens is not a concession on the part of Prussia, but only the recognition of their unquestionable rights. The principles we maintain, and the rights which they insure, are clearly laid down in your instructions, and need not be recapitulated. We trust they will be recognized, and faithfully observed by Prussia, and that no case in violation of them will be permitted to arise hereafter within the Prussian territories.

I have not failed to observe the suggestion of the Hanoverian minister, reported in your No. 93, that in the settlement of this vexed question of military service the initiative must come from the United States; and your own views of what might well be proposed as the basis of negotiation, if this initiative should be undertaken, have also been considered. It is hoped, however, that after the full deliberation which recent events have naturally led the German powers to bestow on this, it can no longer be regarded as a "vexed question," but that practically, at least, it will cease to disturb in any way our relations with those powers. As I have already said, the claim which we urge in behalf of our naturalized fellow-citizens, is a claim not of favor but of right, and except for the regulation of details or modes of proceeding it is not perceived that anything more is necessary than that these citizens when they visit Germany, should be allowed to remain there without hindrance and depart in peace. The question raised in your first proposition of the length of time they may have been absent from the land of their birth, does not appear to this department to have any important bearing upon the *status* which they are entitled to occupy after their temporary return. If they are citizens of the United States, they are entitled to all the rights of citizens, whether they have been absent ten years, or five years, or one year. And if they have thus become citizens of this country, it is difficult to understand why any special exemption should be claimed for them in respect to judicial proceedings, as mentioned in your proposition No. 2. The liability of a citizen of the United States before the courts of Hanover cannot depend upon the question whether he is a native or naturalized citizen, but upon the question only whether he has committed any offense against Hanoverian law. Expatiation, as you have been already instructed is no such offense, and we cannot permit an unreasonable distinction to be made between different classes of our citizens.

Your third and fourth propositions are not necessarily connected with this subject. It is certainly desirable, however, that no American citizen should be ordered out of a German State, without the notice and trial to which you refer; and should this be done, without good cause to justify the summary proceeding, it might well be regarded as an unfriendly act. Our existing treaty with Hanover, you are aware, permits the free residence of our citizens there, and grants them free access to the judicial tribunals. It is quite possible that these privileges may be extended with advantage, and if so, the opportunity should not be lost. The trial of German citizens in this country is always public, and such should be the trial of our citizens in Germany. We should be glad, also, to secure for them a right of appeal. Of course we have no disposition to interfere with the domestic affairs of other States, or to dictate to them their modes of judicial proceeding. A friendly representation, however, on this subject, cannot be regarded as in any way objectionable, and may avoid unpleasant complications hereafter. Whenever one of our citizens is secretly tried and punished, the proceding necessarily creates complaint, and always requires explanation. It is better to avoid the opportunity of complaint by avoiding the secrecy which leads to it.

In respect to your fourth proposition for the "total exemption of the citizens of the United States, residing in Hanover and Prussia, from liability to support in any manner soldiers, officers, and those connected with the military service of the country," I do not understand precisely the nature and extent of the existing obligations to which you refer; and before instructing you on this subject I shall be glad to hear from you again. Certainly the relinquishment of any tax imposed upon our citizens in Germany would be highly acceptable to this government; but we do not wish to urge such an exemption to the extent of an interference with the just rights of the German States. We would, of course, ask nothing from other governments in behalf of our citizens, which we would not be willing, in like cases, to concede to them.

Having thus placed you fully in possession of the views of your government, I have only to repeat the instruction already given you, to urge them, by all proper means, upon those governments with whose representatives you may be brought in connection at Berlin. In this way, it is hoped that such a friendly understanding may be reached on this whole subject as will make it impossible for any new case to arise, in reference to it, requiring the intervention of this government.

I am, sir, your obedient servant,

LEWIS CASS.

JOSEPH A. WRIGHT, Esq., *&c., &c., Berlin.*

Mr. Cass to Mr. Wright.

No. 27.]

DEPARTMENT OF STATE,
Washington, December 17, 1859.

SIR: Herewith I transmit the copy of a letter of the 18th October, addressed to this department by Isidor Dandson, a resident of California, in relation to the enforced military service now being performed in Prussia by his brother, Simon Dandson, whom he represents to be a citizen of the United States. You will investigate the circumstances connected with this case, and take such measures as, under the instructions already given you by the department respecting similar cases, you shall think proper, should the representations of Mr. Dandson prove to be correct.

I am, sir, your obedient servant,

LEWIS CASS.

JOSEPH A. WRIGHT, Esq.,
&c., &c., &c., Berlin.

Mr. Wright to Mr. Cass.

[Extract.]

No. 119.] LEGATION OF THE UNITED STATES,
Berlin, March 7, 1860.

SIR: I have the honor to forward herewith copies of the correspondence with the minister of foreign affairs in the case of Darnston, or Dandson, or *Davidson,* mentioned in your dispatch No. 27, dated December 19, 1859. It appears that he, Davidson, was discharged from military service long since. His conduct is in keeping with that of a great many other naturalized citizens. It seems that he exhibited no passport, and did not state to any person that he was an American citizen.

* * * * *

I have the honor to be, very respectfully, your obedient servant,

JOSEPH A. WRIGHT.

Hon. LEWIS CASS,
Secretary of State.

Mr. Wright to Baron de Schleinitz.

LEGATION OF THE UNITED STATES,
Berlin, January 17, 1860.

MONSIEUR LE BARON: A dispatch from my government, just received, incloses the complaint of Isidor D., that his brother, Simon Darntson, (or Dandson,) formerly a subject of his majesty the King of Prussia, but now a citizen of the United States, left the State of California, one of the United States, to visit his parents, in Prussia, on the 20th of September, 1858, with a passport from the government of the United States; and that upon his reaching Prussia, he has been forced to do military service in one of the regiments of its army stationed at Grandenz. As such complaints of wrong annoy the government of the United States greatly, I have to pray your excellency to have this complaint investigated immediately, and to communicate to me the result as soon as possible.

Your excellency will please permit me to renew assurances of my distinguished consideration.

J. A. WRIGHT.

His Excellency the Baron de SCHLEINITZ,
Minister of Foreign Affairs, &c.

[Translation.]

Baron Von Schleinitz to Mr. Wright.

BERLIN, *March* 3, 1860.

SIR: I made it my duty, on the reception of your letter of the 17th January last, to inform the minister of war of the reclamation of Mr. Isidor Darnston, or Dandson, citizen of the United States, who complains that his brother Simon, on the occasion of a visit made to his parents, in Prussia, was compelled to enter the ranks of the army.

I send you the result of a report which General de Roon demanded upon this subject from the competent military authority. Simon Darntson, or Dandson, is apparently the same who figures in the list of young people of the circle of Strasburg for the year 1852, under the name of Simon Davidson. This individual, born 6th May, 1831, at Strasburg, where his parents still live, is undoubtedly a Prussian by origin. The 2d July, 1852, the provincial councilor of the circle caused a passport to be issued to him, *available for one year*, which authorized him to go to America, for which, in effect, he placed himself *en route* in the month of March, 1853. Simon Davidson only returned to his native country towards the end of the year 1858. Not having obtained, meantime, a permit of emigration, and not having been able to obtain one, because he had not yet satisfied his military duties, he was first enrolled in a battalion of the third brigade of infantry, and on the 11th August, 1859, in the third battalion of the fourth regiment of the landwehr, in garrison at Grandenz. Soon found to be unfit for military service, he was set at large 22d November last, and since then has settled at Thorn.

You will convince yourself by this exposé, sir, that the proceedings taken in regard to the said Simon Davidson have been in strict conformity to law. For the rest, this person has never pretended, at any examination he has undergone since his return to Prussia, that he was a citizen of the United States and provided with an American passport.

Accept, sir, I pray you, the assurance of my high consideration.

SCHLEINITZ.

Mr. WRIGHT, &c., &c., &c.

MESSAGE

OF THE

PRESIDENT OF THE UNITED STATES,

COMMUNICATING,

In compliance with a resolution of the Senate, all correspondence not heretofore called for, relating to the claim of any foreign government to the military services of naturalized American citizens.

APRIL, 17, 1860.—Read and ordered to lie on the table.

To the Senate of the United States:

In compliance with the resolution of the Senate of the 4th instant, requesting information not heretofore called for relating to the claim of any foreign government to the military services of naturalized American citizens, I transmit a report from the Secretary of State and the documents by which it was accompanied.

JAMES BUCHANAN.

WASHINGTON, *April* 16, 1860.

DEPARTMENT OF STATE, *Washington, April* 16, 1860.

The Secretary of State, to whom was referred the resolution of the Senate of the 4th instant, requesting the President, "if, in his opinion, not inconsistent with the public interest, to furnish to the Senate copies of all correspondence not heretofore called for relating to the claim of any foreign government to the military services of naturalized American citizens," has the honor to lay before the President a copy of the papers specified in the subjoined list.

Respectfully submitted.

LEWIS CASS.

The PRESIDENT.

List of accompanying documents.

Mr. Bancroft to Mr. Buchanan, 8th December, 1848, with inclosures.
Same to same, 12th January, 1849—extracts.
Same to same, 26th January, 1849—extract—with inclosure.
Mr. Bancroft to Mr. Clayton, 21st August, 1849, with inclosure.

Mr. Bromberg to Mr. Clayton, 25th June, 1850—extract—with inclosures.

Same to same, 2d July, 1850—extract.

Mr. Hodge to Mr. Everett, 16th November, 1852—extract—with inclosures.

Same to same, 22d November, 1852—extracts—with inclosures.

Same to same, 31st December, 1852—extract.

Mr. Everett to Mr. Hodge, 3d March, 1853—extract.

Mr. Hodge to Mr. Marcy, 12th April, 1853—extract.

Mr. Marcy to Mr. Campbell, 8th September, 1854.

Mr. Schleiden to Mr. Cass, 23d October, 1858.

Mr. Appleton to Mr. Ten Brook, 12th March, 1859.

Mr. Schleiden to Mr. Cass, 16th March, 1859.

Mr. Cass to Mr. Schleiden, 9th April, 1859.

Mr. Ten Brook to Mr. Appleton, 18th April, 1859.

Mr. Cass to Mr. Mason, 27th June, 1859.

Mr. Mason to Mr. Cass, 2d August, 1859, with inclosure.

Mr. Buchanan to Mr. Cass, 24th September, 1859, with inclosures.

Same to same, 30th September, 1859, with inclosures.

Mr. Appleton to Mr. Ten Brook, 4th October, 1859.

Mr. Buchanan to Mr. Cass, 7th October, 1859.

Mr. Cass to Mr. Buchanan, 21st October, 1859.

Mr. Buchanan to Mr. Cass, 30th October, 1859, with inclosures.

Mr. Schleiden to Mr. Cass, 28th November, 1859.

Mr. Calhoun to Mr. Cass, 6th December, 1859, with inclosure.

Mr. Cass to Mr. Calhoun, 31st December, 1859.

Mr. Ricker to Mr. Cass, 4th January, 1860—extract—with inclosures.

Mr. Doering to Mr. Appleton, 12th January, 1860—extract.

Mr. Ricker to Mr. Cass, 19th January, 1860—extract—with inclosure.

Mr. Cass to Mr. Schleiden, 26th January, 1860.

Mr. Cass to Mr. Buchanan, 4th February, 1860.

Mr. Ricker to Mr. Cass, 14th February, 1860—extract—with inclosure.

Mr. Helm to Mr. Cass, 22d February, 1860, with inclosures.

Mr. Cass to Mr. Helm, 3d March, 1860.

Mr. Helm to Mr. Cass, 28th February, 1860, with inclosures.

Mr. Appleton to Mr. Helm, 8th March, 1860.

Mr. Ricker to Mr. Cass, 23d February, 1860.

Mr. Buchanan to Mr. Cass, 26th February, 1860—extract.

Same to same, 29th February, 1860—extract.

Mr. Cass to Mr. Preston, 1st March, 1860.

Mr. Cass to Mr. Ten Brook, 7th March, 1860, with inclosure.

Mr. Cass to Mr. Preston, 8th March, 1860.

Mr. Ricker to Mr. Cass, 9th March, 1860.

Mr. Appleton to Mr. Ten Brook, 18th March, 1860.

Mr. Cass to Mr. Wright, 30th March, 1860.

Mr. Appleton to Mr. Ricker, 5th April, 1860.

Mr. Bancroft to Mr. Buchanan.

No. 105.]

AMERICAN LEGATION,
London, December 8, 1848.

SIR: I have this day received a note from Lord Palmerston, informing me officially of the liberation of Messrs. Bergen and Ryan, and inclosing a communication from Sir William Somerville on their arrest and liberation. I inclose copies of these papers, which appear to me to require no further attention.

I remain, sincerely yours,

GEORGE BANCROFT.

JAMES BUCHANAN, Esq.,
Secretary of State.

NOTE.—For the previous correspondence on this part of the subject see Ex. Doc. No. 19, second session, Thirtieth Congress.

FOREIGN OFFICE, *December* 7, 1848.

SIR: I have the honor to inform you that I have referred to Sir George Grey, her Majesty's secretary of state for the home department, the observations contained in the letter which you addressed to me on the 10th ultimo, in reply to my note of the 30th of September, respecting the imprisonment in Dublin of Mr. James Bergen and Mr. Richard Ryan, and respecting the orders which were issued in August last to the Irish police, with reference to persons arriving in Ireland from America.

I now beg leave to transmit to you a copy of a statement upon those matters, which Sir George Grey has received from the government in Ireland, containing a further explanation of the grounds upon which the Irish government found it necessary to order the adoption of those measures of precaution.

You will, however, learn from the inclosed statement that the Irish government had given directions for the liberation of Mr. Bergen and Mr. Ryan.

I have the honor to be, with high consideration, sir, your most obedient, humble servant,

PALMERSTON.

GEORGE BANCROFT, Esq., *&c.*, *&c.*, *&c.*

DUBLIN CASTLE, *November* 28, 1848.

SIR: I am directed by the lords justices to acknowledge the receipt of your letter of the 20th instant, with its inclosures, relative to the arrest in Ireland of certain persons coming from America; and I am desired by their excellencies to state, for the information of Secretary Sir George Grey, that the reply of Mr. Bancroft to Lord Palmerston's letter of the 30th of September complains of the detention without trial in this country of Mr. James Bergen and Mr. R. F. Ryan, stated to be American citizens; and also, of a certain order, issued in the month of August last, with reference to natives of America visiting Ireland.

With reference to the first-named gentleman, the American minister states it to be the opinion of persons on whose integrity he can rely, and who had good opportunity for observation, that Mr. Bergen was not a political agent. It has been already stated, in a former letter of the 19th September, that the lord lieutenant had reason to come to a different conclusion.

As regards Mr. R. F. Ryan, it will be observed that Mr. Bancroft does not convey any similar assurance.

With respect, however, to the detention of these gentlemen, although the act of last session applying to aliens may be naturally appealed to by Mr. Bancroft, who regards the gentlemen referred to as American citizens, and owing allegiance to the United States alone, yet the lords justices must observe that it is a mistake to suppose that the 11 Victoria, cap. 20, alone of the two exceptional acts of the last session refers to aliens; persons who are charged in this country with being suspected of treasonable practices may, whether aliens or not, be detained under the habeas corpus suspension act without trial or bail until the privy council may make an order to that effect; and the *treasonable* acts of those parties, if really such, may be charged against them, whether committed within the realms of her Majesty or without; and the right to arrest and detain persons suspected of high treason or treasonable practices, whether aliens or not, and detaining them under the provisions of 11 Victoria, cap. 35, cannot, it is presumed, be legitimately questioned.

But, supposing Mr. Bergen not to have committed a crime in uttering his opinions on Irish affairs in America, yet, when he proclaims not only his hostility to the British government, but his intentions to act offensively against it in Ireland, and actually arrives in Ireland as soon as possible after the announcement of his intentions, the government would indeed have been unmindful of its duty and indifferent to the public tranquillity, seriously threatened at that time, if it acted upon the presumption that Mr. Bergen was merely a braggart, and that he had come all the way from the United States to Dublin to improve his means in paternal solicitude for his family. His discreet conduct on board the ship, and his abstinence from public meetings when he arrived in Ireland, were precisely what was to be expected from one fit to perform the particular duties for which he had been selected.

Mr. R. F. Ryan arrived in Ireland notoriously for the purpose of aiding in a revolution which was to overthrow her Majesty's authority and dominion in this part of the United Kingdom. He visited the residence of one of the leading rebels in arms against the sovereign, (Mr. Doheny,) who is now a refugee in France. He was arrested on suspicion of treasonable practices, and papers found in his possession abundantly proved that the accusation was well founded. He is known to be a native of this country, and it would indeed be a strange perversion of the accepted law of nations if a subject of her Majesty, born in Ireland, and living in his native country, could go to the

United States, be admitted a citizen there, return to Ireland, use his utmost efforts to promote rebellion and overthrow the government, and then claim immunity from the British laws against which he had offended, on the ground that he owed allegiance to the United States alone. The government of the United States is even more interested than that of her Majesty in protesting against such a doctrine, because the facility with which the rights of citizenship are there obtained would be little else than protection to every foreign malefactor, and might thus cause the United States to be viewed as the enemy and the disturber of every other country.

With respect to the order issued in August last, it is to be observed that the plan publicly announced in America for promoting civil war in Ireland was, that American citizens, as they were styled, but who were at the same time Irishmen recently arrived in the United States, should go over in parties of twenty and thirty, and that each should repair to the locality with which he was acquainted and endeavor to excite the people with promises of active support from the United States—promises which the meetings, the speeches, and the subscriptions throughout the United States fully justified these emissaries in giving and the ignorant people of Ireland in believing.

No attention was at first paid to these threats by the Irish government; but when information was received from America that persons were about to embark at New York on this mission, when they actually arrived in Liverpool, and subsequently in Ireland, where they lost not a moment at the port of disembarkation, but spread themselves over the country for the very objects that had been previously announced, it became the duty of the government to take precautions for the public tranquillity, and persons coming from America were, therefore, ordered to be arrested and detained for further examination, until a communication had been made to the government. This order only called upon the authorities to be vigilant in the execution of the law in regard to persons coming from that country, where a conspiracy against the Queen's authority was openly carried on; and it was in fact fully justified by the 50 Geo. III, cap. 102, sec. 7, under which strangers, whether subjects of her Majesty or otherwise, may be arrested and detained in any district. Any unreasonable detention of parties so arrested, whether American or British subjects, would not be justifiable; and their excellencies are not aware of such having taken place. It was a matter of sincere regret to the Irish government that the stringent enforcement of this law, (at a moment when a general insurrection appeared imminent,) should have subjected some American gentlemen to inconvenience. The circumstances were fully explained, and this regret expressed by Mr. Redington in the only instance where grounds for complaint existed.

The gentlemen were also relieved from arrest immediately on the facts being brought under notice, and before twenty-four hours had elapsed, though the detention had taken place upwards of eighty miles from the seat of government.

The lords justices feel satisfied that her Majesty's government would be far from complaining that freedom of speech, in private and in public, should be protected in the United States. It is so in the United

Kingdom, where, as in the United States, sympathy with any political movement in a foreign land is no offense; but, with reference to Mr. Bancroft's allusion to Poland, it may be observed that, if tumultuous assemblages of Poles were suddenly to take place in every part of the United Kingdom upon the occasion of an anticipated rebellion in Prussia, Austria, or Russia; if English subjects had taken an active part at such meetings; if the most unmeasured abuse and the foulest calumnies against any of those governments had been there put forth, and received with enthusiasm; if large subscriptions had been obtained; if plans had been announced and organized, and partly carried into execution, for promoting rebellion, and had only been stopped by its suppression; and if, during all that time the British government had neither manifested its disapprobation nor its inclination to interfere, it is much to be doubted whether, as Mr. Bancroft supposes, its friendly relations with the powers in question would not have been in danger of serious interruption.

It is perfectly true, as Mr. Bancroft observes, that "all human affairs come before the tribunal of public opinion, and the formation or expression of a judgment by the public opinion of a people is not an act of hostility;" but experience shows that it is impossible to submit the feelings of governments, or the interests of nations, to the rigid guidance of axioms; and, if when the United States declared war upon Mexico the lively sympathies of the British people had been manifested in favor of the latter country; if meetings had been held at which the conduct of the American government had been denounced in the vilest terms of reprobation; if immense subscriptions had been collected; if men and arms had been promised to the Mexicans; and, if privateers had been fitted out against American merchantmen, it is to be feared that the American government would hardly have regarded this as the formation or expression of public opinion, nor would they have refrained from remonstrating upon it with the British government; while the natural feelings of hostility it must have engendered in the minds of the American people would have led to the interruption of friendly relations between the two countries.

If demonstrations of this kind had occurred, it must be frankly admitted that the American government would have been justified in their remonstrance, and in intimating that such a state of things was not "compatible with a continuance of friendly relations between the two governments."

As far as the Irish government is concerned, it would not appear conducive to any good end further to protract this discussion, heartily agreeing, as the lords justices do, with Mr. Bancroft, that the judgment, the interests, and the well-considered policy of the two countries, as well as their ratified treaties, guaranty the maintenance of their friendly relations; and, in conclusion, Mr. Bancroft may be informed that the Irish government, in the exercise of the extraordinary power confided to them by Parliament, have been guided by a spirit of moderation, both as respects British subjects and foreigners, who have sought to disturb the tranquillity of the United Kingdom; and as it appeared that the release of Messrs. Bergen and Ryan would not now be dangerous to the public peace, it had been determined to take measures for their liberation even before the receipt of Mr. Bancroft's note, in Dublin, where it had been transmitted for the observations of their excellencies.

I have, &c.,

WM. M. SOMERVILLE.

G. CORNEWALL LEWIS, Esq., *&c., &c., &c.*

Mr. Bancroft to Mr. Buchanan.

[Extracts.]

No. 112.]

UNITED STATES LEGATION,
London, January 12, 1849.

SIR: * * * * * * *

I have received your dispatch No. 44, of 18th December, directing me to enter a protest against the orders of the police department in Ireland, of August last. It would be somewhat late to do it now. The orders have long since been inoperative, and the laws under which they were issued are already a dead letter, and will expire in a few weeks. But happily, knowing well what the President's views must be, I protested at the time; protested continuously; protested formally, in a note to Lord Palmerston of 10th of November, of which I fear the full significance has escaped the President's attention, (for otherwise I trust he must have directed an unqualified approval of it,) and repeated my protests in every one of many interviews with different branches of the government, till the arrests ceased. Apologies were offered for the arrest of those against whom no grounds of suspicion existed; and the release from prison was effected, even of those of our citizens, whether native or adopted, against whom it was pretended suspicions existed.

* * * * * * * *

After turning over many books, both of American and English jurists, and ancient and recent writers on public law, and considering the bearing of many British statutes, and particularly investigating the usages of the continental powers, I took the ground of the clear and absolute right of any native of the United Kingdom, in the present age and under existing laws, to change his allegiance. This I showed from the usage of the Greek and Roman republics, which are the fountains of our law; from the abolition of all feudal servitudes; from the example of France; from the published declaration of united Germany; from a succession of British statutes, authorizing naturalization in the colonies; from the very nature of emigration, as authorized by British laws, and as fostered and encouraged, as I know, by the public voice of this country, and specially by members of the present British government. These and many more considerations have been urged in conversation, and I inferred from them that no difference should be made in this kingdom, any more than in America, between native and naturalized American citizens. In this line of argument

I persevered till Mr. Ryan was released. Had he not been liberated, they would have been presented fully in a note. On his liberation, I thought the discussion, so far as the Irish government is concerned, might, on our part, cease or be suspended, till some case should arise requiring a renewal of it. None such is likely to arise; but should it prove otherwise, the President will find me as ready as I have ever been to vindicate firmly the rights of our adopted and of our native citizens.

I trust the course I have pursued will meet the unqualified approbation of the President. Should he think that a further protest is necessary, since nothing is now doing under the orders, the protest will be as seasonable a month hence as now.

* * * * * * * * *

I am, sir, sincerely yours,

GEORGE BANCROFT.

JAMES BUCHANAN, Esq.,
Secretary of State, Washington, D. C.

Mr. Bancroft to Mr. Buchanan.

[Extract]

No. 114.]

UNITED STATES LEGATION,
London, January 26, 1849.

SIR: After maturely considering your dispatch of the 18th of December, perceiving that you, in one paragraph, speak not only of protesting, but of "remonstrating," against any distinction between native and naturalized citizens of the United States; observing also that you make your dispatch my "general" guide, and are good enough to leave the form and language of the protest to my own discretion, I have believed that it was intended to give me full power to frame the paper to be addressed to the British government according to what might remain in question at the time of presenting it. Instead, therefore, of entering a protest, as such, against orders which are now obsolete, I have written rather a remonstrance or declaration of representation on the principles involved in those orders, and have embodied in it the substance of your dispatch, in a general form. I am very anxious to know if this paper, of which I inclose a copy, meets the approval of the President.

* * * * * * * * *

I am, sir, sincerely yours,

GEORGE BANCROFT.

JAMES BUCHANAN, Esq.,
Secretary of State.

UNITED STATES LEGATION,
London, January 26, 1849.

The undersigned, envoy extraordinary and minister plenipotentiary of the United States of America, has been specially directed by the President of the United States to make to her Majesty's government, through Viscount Palmerston, her Majesty's principal secretary of state for foreign affairs, a representation growing out of the orders recently issued in Ireland affecting the personal liberty and rights of American citizens. Not only were the unfortunate objects of government suspicion deprived even of the small protection against unjust imprisonment which a previous *ex parte* accusation, under oath or affirmation, would have afforded; not only was the duty of exercising a calm discretion in the execution of the law dispensed with by commanding in advance the arrest of "all persons coming from America;" not only was an invidious and arbitrary distinction made between citizens of the United States and citizens or subjects of other nations, (all of which, if persisted in, must have formed the subject of a most earnest protest;) but throughout the period of the disturbances, in an order of the 18th of August last, and on other occasions, her Majesty's government have made a distinction between native and naturalized American citizens. The faith and honor of the United States are pledged alike for the protection of both.

On this subject the undersigned has been instructed to employ, in the most solemn and earnest manner, the strongest terms of remonstrance. There can be no stronger language than that of reason, justice, and humanity; and if this language is employed on the present occasion, will it not secure the respectful attention and assent of her Majesty's constitutional advisers?

The sufferings of Europe, from an excess of population, combined with other causes, have led to an annual emigration from Europe to the United States of about one quarter of a million souls; and this emigration appears to be increasing. Of this vast number, the islands composing the United Kingdom alone furnish at least one hundred and fifty thousand persons. In the past quarter of a century a million of the natives of these islands may have gone to America; in the next seven years another million of them may be added to her population. The condition of these people, when received into America, is certainly a question of the gravest magnitude—fit to be dispassionately considered, and definitively settled.

If her Majesty desires to retain in her dominions all her natural-born subjects, America will make no complaint. If, with the consent of her Majesty, this expatriation takes place, America, which receives them, should certainly be recognized as having the right so to regulate their condition as may most conduce to the well being of the emigrants, and the safety of the commonwealth.

It is certain that misery, or the fear of misery, want of employment, or the apprehension of want, despair, and hope, are among the causes which crowd the principal British havens with multitudes of emigrants. To America they are especially attracted by the opportunity of becoming freeholders. "You would be surprised," writes an unprejudiced friend of the undersigned from New York, "to know a fact which has been brought particularly to my notice as a conveyancing lawyer—the mania of the Irish for the possession of the soil. In all the suburbs of this city, Brooklyn, Williamsburg, and elsewhere, great numbers of cheap lots are held by Irish laborers. When one of them has saved up a hundred dollars or so, he buys a lot, pays part of the price down, gives his mortgage for the rest, and never ceases till he has paid it off. They are the most punctual of debtors."

That the emigrants are not unmindful to send relief to their kindred who remain in the Queen's allegiance, appears from a fact which came to light during the discussion of the late international post office arrangements. The number of drafts from the United States on one single British house, for sums varying from one pound to fifteen pounds, was for one year £8,233. And this house was but one of many in one of the many rich and populous towns of this kingdom.

If Great Britain is relieved of the charges of burdensome people, if good is returned to its subjects from the steady influence of those affections which are not extinguished by the voyage across the Atlantic, then her Majesty's government, instead of making of this emigration a cause of discord between the two countries, doubly owes America good will.

Have these emigrants a natural right to expatriate themselves? The Roman law is the fountain of modern jurisprudence. *Ne quis invitus civitate mutetur: neve in civitate maneat invitus. Haec sunt enim fundamenta firmissima nostrae libertatis, sui quemque juris et retinendi et dimittendi esse dominum.* This right of every reasonable being to seek a new country, Cicero, the great Roman advocate, describes as the very foundation of liberty. Truth is the same in all places and in all ages. It is not one thing in the presence of a Roman prætor, and another in the court of queen's bench. It is not one thing on the banks of the Thames, and another on those of the Main, the Spree, the Tiber, or the Hudson. In enumerating the undoubted rights of all Germans, the first German parliament at Frankfort, speaking for the German people and princes, insists on the right of expatriation as a natural right. Nor did the hour of revolution first engender this doctrine. Prussia had before avowed it, and acted upon it. The sovereign of Prussia, willing to promote the happiness of all who are born in his dominions, recognizes their right to emigrate and choose for themselves a country. Even if military service is due, he freely remits the military service, and bids the emigrant God speed on his way to a new world and an adopted land. With France the United States have no difference on this subject. France, like the United States, values its citizenship too much to insist that it shall be retained by a native after he has transferred his allegiance. One of her eloquent sons, now a fellow-citizen of the undersigned, was recently elected to the Senate of the United States. France does not hold that Senator to be a French citizen. She recognizes his renunciation of his first allegiance, and takes pride and satisfaction at his commanding respect in his new home. One of the predecessors of the undersigned at this court was a naturalized American citizen.

Great Britain, Great Britain alone, claims as her subjects those of her children who, finding no place spread for them at the too full table of their native land, seek hospitality, home, and a country under another sky.

But the undersigned begs leave to assert that naturalized American citizens are not subjects of Great Britain. Whatever difference of opinion may exist in America on the desirableness of so vast an influx of men born and educated under other institutions, the government and people of America have but one conviction as to the duty of giving full protection to those whom they receive as citizens. The naturalized citizens themselves, in the face of heaven and their adopted country, repudiate all other allegiance. When this country claims them as subjects it makes them rebels.

Nor does the acquisition of American citizenship give the means of plotting the overthrow of any part of the British government with impunity. The American government never interferes in the internal affairs of other countries; not from a want of sympathy with the nations, but from the full trust in that overruling Providence which leaves no country free from the guiding power of the intelligence of the age. By the principle of the revolution of 1688, which sanctioned the right of resistance, a British subject may consider what acts of government will justify resistance. The foreigner who becomes an American citizen has divested himself of all responsibility for political events in the land of his nativity. American citizenship is a hostage of neutality in foreign affairs.

Yet Great Britan would consider all her expatriated sons to be "subjects" still. But allegiance in this continuing sense is servitude. Are the people of this island still in a state of imperfect emancipation? Does the badge of servitude still cling to every one born in this kingdom?

Further: this feudal notion of perpetual allegiance implies the social hierarchy of superiors and subordinates from the throne through a succession of ranks, and the right to exact military or other services, imposed through all the degrees, the correlative duty of support. Does the owner of the soil desire to retain the services of all who are born upon his domains? Is the owner of the soil willing to employ and support all that are found upon it? Assuredly, his unwillingness to do so is notorious. In proof of this, witness the continuing efforts of kind-hearted landlords, by large expenditures of money, to assist the emigration of men thus dependent on their care. Witness the process of "evictions," which became of such a nature, and so frequent, as to attract the serious attention of the imperial legislature. Witness the rule which many landlords have adopted, of never permitting a new house to be built on land over which their power extends, except on the demolition of another; a rule which drives away the increase of population. Witness the determined and inexorable policy which removes from all parts of these islands, from the sparsely-settled highlands of Scotland to the rich plains of Ireland, all the population which is deemed superfluous. Witness the English language itself, as spoken in this island, where usage has added a new meaning to a word, and "*clearing*," which, in the old English tongue, as spoken in America, means the subduing the forest to purposes of fertility, has come to signify the removing of children, women, and men from an estate.

These references are not made invidiously; for it is only that America exceeds in land, and this kingdom exceeds in inhabitants. But it is plain that the claim to service derived from the old feudal subordination is given up by the landed proprietors themselves, who refuse to their subordinates shelter, or drive them from the soil by process of law, or assist their expatriation by generous contributions.

Nor is this expatriation permitted, encouraged, and enforced by the landed proprietors alone. Public opinion demands it. A most respectable quarterly journal, whose pages have been adorned by the writings of men participating in the government of this country, censures the insufficiency of the present emigration, enormous as it is, and demands its large increase for many successive years as essential to the peace and prosperity of this kingdom.

The emigrants themselves, then, the landlords, the intelligent press, the public judgment, all coincide in representing the vast expatriation which is going on as beneficial and desirable. Nor is this all. The laws of this kingdom sanction it; acts of parliament regulate it. Not a clearance is given, at Liverpool or Dublin, to a passenger ship openly laden with emigrants, but it virtually contains the assent of the Queen to their solemn and final separation from their native country.

The United States, when they receive a man to citizenship, require of him a renunciation of all other allegiance. They would as soon tolerate a man with two wives as a man with two countries; as soon bear with polygamy as that state of double allegiance which common sense so repudiates that it has not even coined a word to express it. A slave cannot have two masters; nor a freeman two lieges. In the United States, the adopted citizen becomes "*a natural born.*"

And is it right that England should question the propriety of this course on the part of the United States? The United States have, on this subject, as on so many others, adopted, or rather inherited, British legislation. The principle of making adopted citizens "natural born," and requiring of them true allegiance, is derived from a British statute, which was the law of all British America prior to the independence of the United States, and has been continued to this time by those States, without one essential modification. Reference is not now made to that British act which naturalizes foreign Protestants serving two years in a royal regiment; nor to that which naturalizes every foreign seaman who in time of war serves two years on board an English ship; nor to that which gives the rights of the natural born to all sailors who for three years serve in whaling ships; the undersigned refers to the 13 Geo. II., cap. 7, of which the preamble and enacting clause are in these words:

"Whereas the increase of people is a means of advancing the wealth and strength of any nation or country; and whereas many foreigners and strangers, from the lenity of our government, the purity of our religion, the benefit of our laws, the advantages of our trade, and the security of our property, might be induced to come and settle in some of his Majesty's colonies in America, if they were made partakers of the advantages and privileges which the natural-born subjects of this realm do enjoy:

"*Be it therefore enacted, &c.*, That from and after the 1st of June,

1740, all persons born out of the legiance of his Majesty, who have inhabited or resided, or shall inhabit or reside, for the space of seven years or more, in any of his Majesty's colonies in America, and shall not have been absent out of some of the said colonies for a longer space than two months at any one time during the said seven years, and shall take and subscribe the oaths, and make, repeat, and subscribe the declaration in the act, [1 Geo. I., cap. 13,] and also make and subscribe the profession of his Christian belief, prescribed by the act, [1 Will. & Mary, cap. 18,] before the chief judge or other judge of the colony wherein such persons respectively have so inhabited and resided, or shall so inhabit and reside, shall be deemed, adjudged, and taken to be, his Majesty's natural-born subjects of this kingdom, to all intents, constructions, and purposes, as if they and every of them had been or were born within this kingdom."

And to-day, in like manner, America in its turn advances her wealth and strength by the unexampled increase of her people; and many, even hundreds of thousands, of "foreigners and strangers" are moved by the sweet attraction "of the lenity of her government," "the purity of her religion," where religion is not the handmaiden of political institutions, the benefits of equal laws, the advantages of open trade, and the security of property, in a land where the people love the laws and institutions which they themselves have made, to come and settle in the clime which once was filled with colonies of Great Britain, France, and Spain, and now with independent States. The British Parliament in those days enacted that the foreigner "becomes, by virtue *of this act, a natural-born subject* of this kingdom;" and the United States, under nearly similar circumstances, efface the traces of his origin and adopt him as "a natural born" freeman of the American republic.

Let not Great Britain dissent from what is but the reflection and the continuance of its own policy, kept up in its colonies even to the present day, and sanctioned again with respect to its colonies by an act of Parliament passed even since the undersigned has had the honor of being accredited to this government.

Thus then, by Roman law, by the law of France and of Germany, by the law of the civilized world, by the policy adopted by Great Britain itself in its colonies, foreigners become on naturalization as "*natural born.*"

The United States cannot consent to a denial of this accepted doctrine of ancient and modern nations. Once naturalized, the persons adopted by America are no longer Bavarians, nor Prussians, nor Frenchmen, nor Englishmen; they are Americans. Wherever they are found, in whatever pursuit they are engaged, on land or on board ship, at home or abroad, everywhere they are Americans. This the United States have promised; this their faith and honor are pledged to make good.

But suppose for a moment the principle to be true, that an adopted American citizen is still a subject of his former sovereign. Last year, in the whirlwind of revolutions, language was made a guide to establish political nationality. Shall the millions in the United States of

German descent constitute a member of the new German Confederation?

Of the natives of these islands it has already been said that perhaps a million are already in America, and another million, as it were, on the wing. Are these millions to remain subjects of her Britannic Majesty, bound to obey the voice of this country? In the midst of the American republic are they to seat themselves as the vassals of monarchy, owing fealty to an hereditary sovereign? Is England sending among the United States, not only people to be provided for by sharing in the opportunities of industry, but sending "subjects" who may get arms and still serve her Majesty? Is England planting garrisons in all our towns, and in all our territories? The good faith of the British government forbids the supposition, that England is seeking either to make war on our republican institutions, or to fill our country with men still bound to her service. And as a consequence, good faith requires that Great Britain should renounce all claim to allegiance from naturalized American citizens.

And how would the doctrine, if true, affect the emigrant himself? He that owes allegiance to her Britannic Majesty cannot hold land in the United States. He that owes allegiance to her Britannic Majesty cannot serve in the government. Now, when men quit these islands because they cannot find in them bread, when in tears and sorrow they transfer their allegiance and homes, will the sovereign of these realms follow them to the new world with a doctrine which would stifle their aspirations and destroy all their hopeful prospects? Shall English obligations go with them where those obligations only arrest their career of prosperity, and blight their happiness? If this were so, emigrants to the new world would be as much insulated in America as the Jews were in Europe in the middle ages. And if America consents not to exclude forever the foreign emigrant from franchises, shall such perpetual disfranchisement be the act of the country from which he sprung? Humanity forbids it. Humanity so revolts at it, that it cannot even image to itself the dreadful consequences that would follow from the doctrine of perpetual allegiance. The doctrine that natives of the United Kingdom remain subjects of her Majesty even after expatriation and naturalization in the United States, is altogether, at all times, in all places, and at all hazards, inadmissible.

For centuries, the King of England wore the title of "King of France." Good sense at last renounced the title. Yet the sovereign of England was as truly sovereign over France as now sovereign over adopted American citizens.

It is quite time that the two nations should come to an understanding on this subject. If the United Kingdom really wishes to retain as subjects all the natives of this realm, let the United Kingdom forbid the emigration of its sons. But if their emigration is permitted, and even stimulated, the land which accepts the anxious responsibility of receiving them must take full power of regulating their political condition.

The undersigned avails himself of this occasion to renew to Viscount Palmerston the assurance of his most distinguished consideration.

GEORGE BANCROFT.

Mr. Bancroft to Mr. Clayton.

No. 141.] UNITED STATES LEGATION,
London, August 21, 1849.

SIR: I annex a copy of a paper just received from Lord Palmerston in reply to my note of 26th January last.

I take this occasion to say that, comparing the passage in No. 48 from the department, beginning at "*but he*" (the President) "*still entertains*" * * to the end of the dispatch, with the first part of my note to Lord Palmerston of 26th January, I confess myself unable to perceive the difference between the opinion of the President as expressed on the 17th of February, regarding what should be done by me, and what I had actually done. I have in that note, as you will perceive, protested specifically against the two orders of the 2d and 18th of August last, and on the very grounds on which the President wished it done. It is true, I called the paper, on one occasion, "a remonstrance," and on another, "a representation," but it was also none the less a *protest*, which is "*a solemn declaration* of opinion."

The British government has never been left in doubt as to the opinion which the American government entertained of the character of the orders of the 2d and the 18th of August last.

I am, sir, sincerely yours,

GEORGE BANCROFT.

Hon. JOHN M. CLAYTON,
Secretary of State, Washington, D. C.

Lord Palmerston to Mr. Bancroft.

FOREIGN OFFICE, *August* 16, 1849.

The undersigned, her Majesty's principal secretary of state for foreign affairs, has the honor to acknowledge the receipt of the note which Mr. Bancroft, envoy extraordinary and minister plenipotentiary of the United States of America at this court, addressed to him on the 26th of January last, referring to the imprisonment in Ireland of some American citizens, who were arrested in that country in August, 1848, under the act 11 and 12 Vict. cap., 35, and remonstrating against the consequences of the doctrine which Mr. Bancroft assumes to be maintained in this country in regard to the allegiance due to the Queen from her Majesty's natural-born subjects.

In reply, the undersigned begs to state, that he apprehends that the remonstrance contained in Mr. Bancroft's note has originated in a mistaken notion as to the doctrine held by her Majesty's government upon this matter; because Mr. Bancroft states that one consequence of the British doctrine of natural allegiance is, that Great Britain denies to the United States the right of regulating the condition of emigrants from Great Britain in such manner "as may most conduce to the well-being of the emigrants and the safety of the (American) commonwealth." Now, although by the law of England natural allegiance is a tie which cannot be severed or altered by anything but the "united concurrence of the legislature," and although it is true (as observed by Mr. Justice Story, an eminent American authority) that "every nation has hitherto assumed it as clear, that its laws extend to and bind natural-born subjects at all times and in all places," yet her Majesty's government do not dissent from the opinion of the same learned judge, that "in speaking of the right of a state to bind its own native subjects everywhere, we speak only of its own claim and exercise of sovereignty over them, and not of its rights to compel or require obedience to such laws, on the part of other nations;" and her Majesty's government concur with Mr. Justice Story, in maintaining that "*every nation has an exclusive right to regulate persons and things within its own territory according to its own sovereign will and polity.*"

The undersigned considers the above exposition of public law to be perfectly correct, and it appears to him to meet the objections to the doctrine of her Majesty's government which have been raised in Mr. Bancroft's note.

With reference to those observations of Mr. Bancroft, from which it would appear that he assumes that her Majesty's government is disposed to doubt whether the poorer classes of emigrants who have come from Great Britain to the United States have a natural right to expatriate themselves, the undersigned begs to observe that it has never been denied by the British government that those persons leave this country by virtue of that right, which is asserted by Mr. Bancroft to be the foundation of all liberty, namely, "the right of every reasonable being to seek a new country;" and it is well known that by the laws of Great Britain no restraint can, except in very special cases, be placed upon the perfect liberty of every British subject to leave the realm, when and for whatever period of time he chooses. It does not appear, however, that the passage quoted by Mr. Bancroft from Cicero sanctions expatriation, in the sense of a voluntary abjuration of natural allegiance, without the assent of the sovereign power; nor does an emigrant's departure from Great Britain debar him from returning thereto, at any subsequent time, as a natural-born subject. So long as the emigrant remains in the United States, or in any other country, he is amenable to the laws of the country in which he resides; and it cannot therefore be said, as suggested in Mr. Bancroft's note, that the British crown, by permitting its subjects to emigrate to the United States, is sending among the United States not only people to be provided for by sharing in the opportunities for industry, but "subjects" who may get arms and still serve her Majesty, or that England is planting garrisons in all the territories of the Union.

The undersigned has also to observe that Mr. Bancroft has referred generally to the orders issued in Ireland last year for the arrest of suspected persons, and has alluded to the distinction drawn by her Majesty's government between native and naturalized American citizens; and, although Mr. Bancroft's argument does not bear specifically upon that point, the undersigned begs leave to repeat what he has stated in his previous correspondence with Mr. Bancroft respecting this matter, namely: that natural-born subjects of Great Britain, who may have become naturalized in a foreign country, but who return to the United Kingdom, are as amenable as any other of her Majesty's subjects to any laws which may be in force, either of a permanent or of a temporary nature; and the maxim, "*ignorantia legis non excusat*," must apply to them as well as to those who may be permanently resident within the United Kingdom.

The undersigned begs, in conclusion, further to remark, that the Stat. 13 Geo. II, c. 7, to which Mr. Bancroft has adverted, has no bearing upon the *status* of a native of Great Britain naturalized in the United States. That statute applies only to persons not being subjects of Great Britain, who settled in America before the declaration of American independence. And it never has been contended by Great Britain that that statute would affect in the slightest degree the "*status*" of the foreign settler as a subject of the country of his origin, if he should think proper to return to such country.

The undersigned has the honor to renew to Mr. Bancroft the assurances of his high consideration.

PALMERSTON.

George Bancroft, Esq., *&c.*, *&c.*, *&c.*

Mr. Bromberg to Mr. Clayton.

[Extract.]

No. 5.] Consulate of the United States of America,
Hamburg, June 25, 1850.

Sir: I had the honor to address you on the 23d of last month. I now take the liberty of communicating to you a case in reference to a citizen of the United States, which I deem it my duty to lay before you, although no final decision has been made by the authorities here in reference thereto.

An individual named Theodore C. Schuster, born here, in 1826, left when fourteen years of age; he had been duly naturalized in the United States district court for Massachusetts, and besides, had a mariner's protection issued at the Boston custom-house. Said Schuster arrived here on the 10th of May last, in the brig Czarina, of New Orleans; his mother residing here, he was desirous to remain in Hamburg for a short time. Before leaving the Czarina, he received a notice from the committee on arming, (bewaffnung's committee,) to to appear before them, being liable to do military duty, as being born here. The notice was left on board the Czarina by the police; but, on Schuster's promising to come to the committee's office after seeing the United States consul, they left. Mr. Schuster being undecided how long he might remain here, I deemed it best to go with him to the chief of the arming committee, Dr. Kleinworth, and, at the said Dr. Kleinworth's request, I not only produced the proofs of Mr. Schuster being a United States citizen, but left his papers with Dr.

Kleinworth, by him to be laid before the committee. After a lapse of several days, I received the papers back, and on the 31st of last month I received from Dr. Kleinworth a note. (Translation hereby inclosed marked letter A.) Thereupon, I addressed a note (copy hereby inclosed marked letter B) to Syndicus Merck, in charge of foreign affairs, and, on the 19th instant, I received from the syndicus a note. (Translation and original, I deemed it best to send it, herewith transmitted, marked letter C.) I replied by note, (copy herewith transmitted marked letter D,) and from the tenor of Syndicus Merck's, note, I should not be surprised if an attempt was made to compel said Mr. Schuster to do military duty, or, in default thereof, imprison him. I have deemed it my duty to protect said Mr. Schuster as far as lay in my power. In the present state of Germany, when every one is made to serve in the army, these attempts to oblige adopted citizens to do military duty, will be frequent, and your instructions how to act, would relieve me of a great responsibility.

I would also call your attention to the case of John Gottfried Heyne, an affiliated citizen of the United States, to whom permission was refused to work here, even for a short time, at his profession as a mechanician, by the police authorities; and the person wishing to employ him, prohibited from employing said Heyne. The affidavit of Mr. J. G. Heyne, (marked letter E,) which I hereby transmit, shows the whole case; and letter F (inclosed herewith) is a copy of a note I addressed to Syndicus Merck on the subject; but, as sixteen days elapsed before the senate decided in the first case, I do not know how long it may be before I hear more of this matter; in the mean time, the man dare not work, and has hardly the means to live without doing so. In this case of Mr. Heyne, I believe, that being only an affiliated citizen, if he resides out of the United States, he cannot, I think, acquire the right of citizenship; but being abroad, after having renounced allegiance to his former sovereign, where could he look for protection? If I had doubts in this case, I deemed it best to try to protect him as far as I could, but must, in these cases as in all others, best be guided by your instructions. * * * * * *

Finally, I would remark that the Hon. W. Forward, during his short sojourn here, on being made acquainted by me with Mr. Schuster's case, advised me to persevere in the course taken.

I remain very respectfully, your obedient servant,

SAMUEL BROMBERG.

Hon. JOHN M. CLAYTON,
Secretary of State, Washington, D. C.

[Translation.]

A.] BUREAU OF THE ARMING COMMITTEE,
Hamburg, May 31, 1850.

The undersigned has laid the papers relating to J. C. Schuster, which you did me the honor to hand before the arming committee; and the committee regrets that in their position they cannot grant the request to release him from his liabilities to do military service, as there is legally nothing before them which might exonerate him therefrom; and I am requested, sir, to notify you, that any further steps you may deem requisite you must appeal to the high senate who alone are competent to decide further, in this case.

With assurances, &c.,

KLEINWORTH, Dr.,
First Official.

S. Bromberg, *Consul &c.*,

B.] Consulate of the United States of America,
Hamburg, June 3, 1850.

Sir: The undersigned begs leave to address you in reference to one Theodore C. Schuster, a naturalized citizen of the United States of America, who came to this city as a mariner on board the brig Czarina, of New Orleans. Shortly after his arrival here, the said Schuster received a notice to appear before the bewaffnung's committee of this place. Mr. Schuster called on me, and producing his proof of being a United States citizen, I called (said Schuster not knowing how long he might remain here) on Dr. Kleinworth, to explain to him how said Schuster could not be liable to do military duty here, or elsewhere, except in the United States of America, being a citizen thereof. At the request of Dr. Kleinworth, I left the documents proving said Schuster to be a United States citizen, with him, said Dr. Kleinworth, and on receiving, on the 31st of last month, a note from the bureau of the Bewaffnung's committee informing me "that there was no lawful proof of said Schuster not being liable to do military duty here," I can only suppose that my application at the bewaffnung committee was wrong, and I ought at once have applied to you, sir; for I cannot suppose a citizen of the United States of America (either native or naturalized) can be liable to do military duty in the city of Hamburg.

Permit me, sir, in conclusion, to remark, that my applying to the bureau of the bewaffnung's commission arose from no want of due respect towards you; but only from a desire, as said Schuster might shortly leave, to expedite the proving of his not being liable to do military duty, deeming the proof thereof so good I did not want to intrude myself on you.

With assurances, &c.,

SAMUEL BROMBERG,
Consul United States of America.

His Magnificence Syndicus Merck.

[Translation.]

C.] Hamburg, *June* 18, 1850.

The undersigned, syndicus, has the honor to reply to the kind favor of the 3d instant of the United States consul, S. Bromberg, as follows:

Theodore C. Schuster was born at Hamburg, in 1826, and according to the laws of this State, liable to do military duty in 1847. Therefore, in 1847, his name was put in the wheel and a number drawn for him, by which drawing he became obligated to do military service in our contingent. Being absent, no proceedings could be had against him until he returned, a few weeks since, on board of an American vessel.

Should you, sir, take it for granted that said Schuster, by becoming a citizen of the United States, has been released from his previous existing liabilities towards the State of Hamburg, I am sorry to say I cannot coincide in this view.

Considering all legal grounds, the Hamburg government may rely and appeal to reciprocity, for the United States would never consent to let any individual belonging to them by birth and nationality evade the duties arising therefrom.

As little (so wenig) as the United States will acknowledge as legal a right of citizenship acquired in another State, and as little will consent that a citizen by birth, being obligated to defend his country, may withdraw himself from this duty by entering in another States union, the less can they dare (dürfen) demand this from the State of Hamburg.

Moreover, the laws of Hamburg make the discharge (austritt) out of the nexus,* which is to be done on certain conditions, expressedly dependent on the consent of the government; therefore, said Theodore C. Schuster could not legally enter into the States Union of the United States, for he must, moreover, on this side, be considered so long as belonging to the State of Hamburg, until his release has been legally pronounced by the government of Hamburg, and this could only be done when he had fulfilled his military duty, either in person or by substitute, or had been expressly released from them by said government.

The subscriber doubts not that the recapitulation of these simple facts and legal maxims will prove satisfactory, and may prove to convince the consul, &c., that the committee on arming has only done what was right of them, by requiring said Schuster, as a native-born Hamburger, to fulfill his duty by serving in the military, and takes this occasion to assure you, sir, &c.,

MERCK, Dr.

S. Bromberg, &c.,
Consul United States of America.

D.] Consulate of the United States,
Hamburg, June 21, 1850.

The undersigned, United States consul, has the honor to acknowledge the receipt of your favor of the 18th instant, and would hereby take the liberty to make a few remarks only, not being desirous of provoking a controversy, which must eventually be decided by the govern-

---

* Nexus is a law bureau, where by going through certain forms and paying certain moneys, an individual is proclaimed to be discharged therefrom; being then no more regarded as a Hamburg citizen.

ment he has the honor to represent, and to whom he will without delay submit the case in question.

The undersigned can hardly consent to go back to the time when said Theodore C. Schuster has been liable to military duty in this city; said Schuster left when a minor, (1840,) and whilst acquiring the right to become a citizen of the United States, he could not at the same time be liable for or in another State to any duty or fealty.

The United States government has always upheld the doctrine, and in defence thereof, poured out their blood and treasure, that those that became citizens of the United States by adoption were entitled to their full protection, and no power or potentate could under pretense or claim of former allegiance, impress or force them into service.

Further, to adopt the doctrine that no person may become a United States citizen, without the consent of the State or potentate to whom he owed fealty, would strike at the very root of our naturalization laws. Those desirous of being admitted to the rights of citizenship are required to swear, even when declaring their intentions to become citizens, "that they have entirely renounced and abjured all allegiance and fidelity to every prince, power, or potentate; and in being obliged to take this oath, the person so doing, can certainly not continue to owe fealty or service to any other State, nor can the right and privilege of becoming a citizen of the United States ever be made dependent on the consent or approval of any power or potentate.

There is no law in force in the United States taking cognizance of the absence of any citizen, if becoming a subject or citizen of a foreign power, he loses his privileges of citizenship; but the United States would never compel a reluctant service from any one desirous to expatriate himself.

The undersigned can, therefore, till the decision of his government is known to him, only protest, and does hereby protest, against the said Theodore C. Schuster being molested in any way, manner, or shape, during his stay or sojourn in the city of Hamburg.

And the undersigned takes this occasion to renew to you, sir, the tender of his highest esteem and consideration,

SAMUEL BROMBERG.

His Magnificence Syndicus MERCK.

E.] CONSULATE OF THE UNITED STATES OF AMERICA,
Hamburg, June 21, 1850.

I, John Gottfried Heyne, being duly sworn, do depose and say, that I am born at Muserburg, Kingdom of Prussia; that on the 16th day of May last, after having resided in the United States for eighteen months, I declared my intention, in the superior court of the city of New York, to become a citizen of the United States; that I procured a certified copy of said declaration, and also an instrument dated New York, May 20, 1850, and signed by J. B. Nones, a sworn notary public of said city of New York, certifying my being an affiliated citizen of the United States, and entitled to its protection; that I arrived at Hamburg, per ship North America, from New York, on or about the 17th instant; that I called at the office of the United States consul at Hamburg, who indorsed his visé on my papers; that being obliged by the state of my health to remain at Hamburg some time, I found work at my profession as a mechanican, and was advised to apply at the police bureau for a permit to remain here for some time; that on calling at said police bureau, (on the 19th instant,) and after producing my papers to the persons employed therein, I was informed I had better not remain at Hamburg; that the police bureau might grant me a card to permit me to remain here for a few days, but that under any circumstances I could never be permitted to work here, for the police bureau would not grant me permission to do so, and the person I engaged with could not employ me without such permit; and this I was told by said person he dare not do, being liable thereby to a heavy fine; that I then again called on the United States consul, who volunteered to go himself to see the police authorities, but on account of the crowd in said police bureau, could not procure a hearing; that said consul then wrote a letter to the police authorities, which I took sealed to said bureau; that said police authorities, after reading said letter, told me that I might remain at Hamburg for a short time, but must not think of working here; that I should attend next day, as they would lay the consul's letter before the chief of the police bureau, called a senator; that I attended as requested, on the 20th, when I was told by the chief of the bureau, after many questions being put to me, (to all of which I declared of considering myself entitled to the protection of the United States, and as such ought to be permitted to work here for my support during my stay here,) that I should not, and could not be allowed to work here; that I had better return to the United States, or to Prussia, where I originally belonged, and the letter of our consul was returned to me opened amongst my papers. And further deponent saith not.

JOHANN GOTTFRIED HEYNE.

CONSULATE OF THE UNITED STATES OF AMERICA AT HAMBURG.

Sworn to before me, the day and year above written.

SAMUEL BROMBERG,
Consul, U. S. A.

F.] CONSULATE OF THE UNITED STATES OF AMERICA,
Hamburg, June 22, 1850.

The undersigned, consul of the United States, feels sorry to trespass again on your valuable time, but feels himself constrained to call your attention to a case wherein an individual named John Gottfried Heyne, an affiliated citizen of the United States, has been refused even the right of following in this city his profession as a mechanican; said Heyne arrived here on or about the 17th instant, from New York, and produced to the undersigned his papers, proving him to be an affiliated citizen of said United States.

The said Heyne, being obliged by circumstances, not material to the point at issue, to remain here some time, found employment at a respectable shop; with the proofs thereof he called at the bureau of the police administration for his permit (aufenthalts-karte) to remain here, but said Heyne was informed he could not be permitted to work here. Heyne then applied to the undersigned, who, thereupon, addressed a few lines to the police administration, stating said Heyne's case, and informing them of said Heyne being entitled to the protection of the United States.

The said Heyne, attending at the bureau of police administration yesterday, as per request, he was again informed by the chief of said bureau that under any circumstances could he [be] allowed to work in this city, and had better return to the United States, and the lines which the undersigned took the liberty to address to the police administration were returned to him, the said Heyne, and by him to the undersigned, who will not comment on these facts, being ignorant of any law whereby an individual owing allegiance to a friendly power may be prevented to follow, peacefully and unmolested, his vocation in the Hamburg State or territories.

And the undersigned takes again this occasion to assure you, sir, of his highest esteem and regard.

SAMUEL BROMBERG.

His Magnificence Syndicus MERCK.

CONSULATE OF THE UNITED STATES OF AMERICA,
Hamburg, June 19, 1850.

John Gottfried Heyne, who, by his papers, is entitled to the protection of the United States of America, has called at this office and reports that the police authorities of this city have refused him a card of permission to work here at his trade as a mechanician. If such be the case, I can only suppose this originated in some error, knowing that said J. G. Heyne, being an affiliated citizen of the United States, should not be prevented from following his lawful vocation, and therefore trust no obstacles will be thrown in said Heyne's way so to do.

With assurances of my highest esteem and regard,

SAMUEL BROMBERG,
Consul United States of America.

EIN HOCH LOBLICHT,
Polizey Administration.

Mr. Bromberg to Mr. Clayton.

[Extract.]

No. 6.] CONSULATE OF THE UNITED STATES OF AMERICA,
Hamburg, July 2, 1850.

SIR: I had the honor of addressing you on the 24th of last month, inclosing documents in reference to several cases at issue with the

Hamburg government. Nothing new has occurred in the case of Schuster, who yet remains here. Mr. Heyne has not received permission to work here, and, being prevented from doing so, he has not the chance of earning enough to join his family in Prussia, previous to removing them to the United States. The syndicus has not replied to my note in relation to Heyne's case, nor explained why a communication sent to a component part of the Hamburg authorities, under the seal of the consulate, had been returned (or rather handed) open to a third party. The Hamburg government either have dropped these cases or have carried them to your department for a decision, and I must await your favors before I could deem it advisable to agitate these matters further.

* * * * * * * *

I remain, very respectfully, your obedient servant,

SAMUEL BROMBERG.

Hon. JOHN M. CLAYTON,
Secretary of State, Washington, D. C.

Mr. Hodge to Mr. Everett.

[Extract.]

No. 15.] MARSEILLES, *November* 16, 1852.

SIR: * * * * * * * *

I have an unpleasant affair in my charge. It is the *detention of an American citizen*, Mr. Allibert, of New Orleans, as an "*insoumis.*" He is well known to the Hon. Pierre Soulé, United States Senator from Louisiana. He left this city in 1839; went to New Orleans; applied in 1841 to be naturalized; received his papers of naturalization on 10th July, 1846; came here in August, 1852; arriving at Digne, Basses Alpes, his native village, was arrested as an "*insoumis*;" after long detention, was tried by a "*conseil de guerre*," and, in opposition to the orders of the honorable minister of war, he was condemned to a month's imprisonment. Monsieur Carpentin, "*commissaire du gouvernment*," called to inform me of the decision, and that Mr. Allibert was detained in the Fort St. Nicholas. I expressed myself in such decided terms as regarded this national insult, this violation of all national law, this gross outrage of the sacred rights of an American citizen, and the course my government would take, that he was released after three hours' detention, and he is now "on parole." On the following day, 16th October, I wrote a full, detailed account of the affair to General Hecquet, commander-in-chief of this ninth military division of the empire. I protested in the most decided manner against this violation of the law of nations; and "I protest against this military decision as violating the sacred rights of an American citizen, guaranteed by an act of Congress and confirmed by the unanimous voice of the American people; I protest against it as in opposition to the code of the great Napoleon, chap. 2; I protest against it," &c.

The answer from General Hecquet was received on 22d October. On 25th same I sent copies of the documents to the Hon. William C. Rives, minister plenipotentiary, envoy extraordinary, &c., at Paris, observing, (in addition to full details): "To your superior judgment I transfer it, well satisfied that an American citizen, whether born on the soil or adopted, we know no difference, will meet that protection which the law of the land and the unanimous voice of the nation guaranty." He has not replied to me, which leaves me at a loss to conjecture how he views this affair. He may think it not entitled to his attention, or disposed to let me act on my own responsibility. If I knew such to be the case, "*coûte que coûte*," I should neither shrink nor hesitate. Mr. Allibert is an adopted citizen, entitled to the same protection as if born on the soil, and in this consulate all such shall have it. He has been detained *since August;* his commercial business in New Orleans suffers very much owing to this detention. By the next steamer copies of the correspondence, documents, &c., shall be forwarded to the honorable Secretary of State, and I solicit to be informed how I am to act if another instance occurs, of which I have no doubt, as I was told it would be to an *honorable* senator of the United States, if he visited France, and were an "*insoumis.*" This is the second appeal I have made to the department, (first, see dispatch No. 1, 3d March, 1850,) as the honorable minister resident at Paris declined replying, or did not, to my letters of 16th January and 23d Febuary, 1850, of which copies were forwarded to the department. The Hon. John M. Clayton, at that time Secretary, in his dispatch, 9th May, 1850, says that the course pursued by me "meets the approbation of the department," which I flatter myself will be the same on this great national question. I am fully aware of my limited powers, only a commercial consul, but "the consul" of one of the greatest powers. * * * * * * * *

I have the honor to be, with great respect, sir, your very obedient servant,

JOHN L. HODGE,
United States Consul at Marseilles.

The Hon. SECRETARY OF STATE, *Washington.*

Document No. 2.

[Translation.]

NINTH MILITARY DIVISION, GENERAL OF DIVISION, THIRD BUREAU, NO. 1743.

MARSEILLES, *October* 22, 1852.

MR. CONSUL: I have received the letter which you did me the honor to address to me on the subject of Mr. Allibert, the insubmissive young soldier of the department of the Lower Alps, and, since his insubmission, a naturalized citizen (*sujet*) of the United States of America.

In bringing before a court-martial this individual, charged with an offense which, according to our French laws, admits of no plea of limitation, and which was committed by him before his naturalization as an American citizen, I have only complied with the law, with established jurisprudence, and with a special instruction from the minister of war, to whom I had applied in the particular case of Mr. Allibert.

The court-martial having pronounced against him the penalty of imprisonment, I took it upon myself, through consideration for the government of the United States, to suspend the execution of the sentence, and I immediately made a report of this to the minister of war. I also sent him your letter, which I am now answering.

You will understand, Mr. Consul, that I have neither the power to violate or omit the formalities of justice, nor the right to amend the judgments rendered by it. The power is merely conferred on me to suspend in certain cases the execution of those decrees, and I have used it in favor of Mr. Allibert. This is all which it was possible for me to do; the rest is within the competency of the government alone. I do not doubt of a prompt disposition on its part to intervene.

Be so good, Mr. Consul, as to accept the assurance of my high consideration.

HECQUET,
Gen. of Division, Com'dg the 9th Military Division.

The Consul of the United States of America, *Marseilles.*

No. 3.

[Translation.]

Ninth Military Division.—Post of Marseilles.—Court-Martial, Public Prosecutor's Office.

Marseilles, *October* 29, 1852.

Mr. Consul: I have written, by mail, to Mr. Lucian Allibert, at Puymoisson, for the purpose of informing him that, on the appeal drawn up by me against the judgment which condemns him to a month's imprisonment for insubmission, the council of revision has broken that decision, and sends him back before the court-martial at Toulon.

In case Mr. Allibert should not receive my letter, I have the honor to request you to be so good as to cause the one which is herein inclosed to reach him.

Be so good, Mr. Consul, as to accept the assurance of my high consideration.

A. CARPENTIN,
Commissioner of the Government, near the Court-Martial.

The Consul of the United States, *Marseilles.*

Document No. 6.

MARSEILLES, *November* 20, 1852.

The present will be handed to you by Mr. Allibert, an American citizen, who goes to your city, having been arrested as an "*insoumis*," which I in no way admit. I have protected him, shall continue to do so as a naturalized citizen, being the same in the United States as if born on the soil. You will do all in your power to aid, assist, and protect him in this extraordinary trial before a military court in violation of national law, of that of the United States, and of the Code Napoleon. I will write you more fully on this subject, as the present is merely, as Mr. Allibert goes off at once, to make him known to you.

Your obedient servant,

J. L. HODGE.

Mons. TROUCHET,
United States Vice-Consul at Toulon.

Document No. 4.

[Translation.]

NINTH MILITARY DIVISION, THIRD BUREAU, NO. 1588.

MARSEILLES, *September* 18, 1852.

In a dispatch of the 15th of this month, the minister of war orders me as follows:

The commissioner of the government near the court-martial, in your division, calls my attention to the affair of the man named Allibert, (Lucian,) who has been arraigned on a charge of insubmission as a young soldier, of the class 1839, of the department of the Lower Alps.

This officer makes known to me that Allibert, who embarked in 1838 for New Orleans, where he caused himself to be naturalized as a citizen of the United States on the 10th of January, 1846, entrenches himself now behind his act of naturalization, as having released him from all prosecution as an insubmissive, and moreover from the obligation to serve.

This claim of Allibert is founded on right, if it is really sustained by an act of naturalization dated the 10th of January, 1846. This man, by the fact of his naturalization, has lost the quality of a Frenchman, and is consequently incapable of serving among the French troops in the terms of article 2 of the law of the 21st of March, 1832.

As to the offense of insubmission which he has committed, it could not certainly be blotted out by the fact alone of his naturalization; but it must be acknowledged that he is now covered by the limitation of three years, (article 638 of the Code of Criminal Prosecution,) which period commenced on the day in which Allibert became a citizen of the United States, lost his quality of Frenchman, and ceased to be liable to serve.

If it were otherwise—that is to say, if the three years established for the duration of the limitation had not lapsed at the time of the arrest of Allibert—it is certain that this man, notwithstanding his new quality of citizenship of the United States, would have to answer for an offense which he had committed against the French law when he was a Frenchman.

Every judgment of condemnation which could at that time have been rendered against him would, beyond any doubt, have had to be carried into effect; only, at the expiration of his penalty, instead of being incorporated into a regiment, he would have had to be set at liberty.

In the present state of things, if Allibert brings proof of an act of naturalization, dated the 10th of January, 1846, the court-martial must make this act and article 638 of the Code of Criminal Prosecution, the basis of its action, and simply acquit him on the charges made against him.

Be so good, in what concerns you, as to conform to the foregoing directions.

By the general of division commanding the ninth military division.

By order:

The Colonel of the Staff.

A true copy.

The Commissioner of the Government near the Court-Martial of the General Military Division.

Signed: SERSY.

Mr. Hodge to Mr. Everett.

[Extracts.]

No. 16.] Marseilles, *November* 22, 1852.

Sir: I regret that I have to intrude such voluminous documents on the valuable time of the honorable Secretary of State, so soon after his installation into office. They relate to the affair—a national question—noticed in my last dispatch, No. 15, of the 16th instant: the rights of an adopted citizen, Mr. Allibert, of New Orleans, who was arrested early in August as an "*insoumis,*" tried on the 15th of October by a petty "*conseil de guerre,*" and condemned to a month's imprisonment.

Document No. 1.—My letter to General Hacquet, commander-in-chief of this ninth military division of the empire, which will fully explain the details of this extraordinary affair. I requested Mr. Allibert not to appeal; if done, it would be acknowledging the right of a petty military court to try an American citizen. The court of revision at Paris (see Document No. 3) annulled the decision of a month's prison, and gave orders for a new trial at Toulon. It has been intimated to me from a high source, "it has been so decided to have Mr. Allibert liberated." He left here last evening for Toulon, in the expectation that the new trial would take place this week.

Document No. 2.—General Hacquet's letter to me in reply to mine of the 16th of October. If it had depended on the general, no trial would have taken place, as he remarked to me on the 15th of August: "Comme une preuve de la confiance et de l'estime qui j'ai pour vous, je suis charmé d'avoir l'occasion de vous en donner une preuve et je donnerai l'ordre que Monsieur Allibert soit mis en liberté sans caution, ni sans être tenue de fournir un remplacement, mais seulement en sa qualité de citoyen des Etats-Unis." [As an evidence of the confidence and esteem which I have for you—and I am pleased at having an opportunity of affording you evidence thereof—I shall give orders that Monsieur Allibert be set at liberty, without security and without being required to furnish a substitute, but merely in his character as a citizen of the United States."] Unfortunately, the prefect of the Basses Alpes had sent the affair to Paris, and no action could be taken except from that quarter, which has caused this affair to linger in so strange a manner.

Document No. 3.—Letter from Mr. Carpentin, *commissaire du gouvernement.*

Document No. 4.—Letter from Colonel Count de Sercey, chef d'etat-major, of 18th September, handing extracts of the minister of war's instructions of 15th, same, in regard to this affair, which positively state that Mr. Allibert should be released if the proofs were as represented; all which was fully justified—admitted by the "*conseil de guerre*" to be correct. Notwithstanding these orders, this tribunal condemned him! The *commissaire du gouvernement*, some days after the decision, told me if an honorable Senator of the United States Senate should visit this country, and it were proved that he was an "insoumis," he would be arrested by the gens d'armes.

Document No. 5.—My letter to the Hon. William C. Rives, minister plenipotentiary, envoy extraordinary, &c., &c., at Paris. I saw that this affair would train, consume great time, expense, and be ruinous to Mr. Allibert's business in New Orleans. Knowing it could instantly be decided at Paris, *there only*, I wrote to the honorable minister; otherwise I should not have done so, but, on my own responsibility, brought it to a close. For reasons unknown to me, the honorable minister appears not to have taken notice of it, as he has not replied to me in the cause of a suffering countryman. His motives may be judicious—a dread to come in contact with the imperial government, as it might interfere with other views. It would, however, have been a satisfaction to me if the honorable minister had replied to me.

Document No. 6.—A few introductory lines, for Mr. Allibert, to the United States vice-consul at Toulon, which I gave to show that I continue to act with a firm determination to protect an American citizen.

Mr. Allibert has been treated with such crying injustice, as well as gross insult also to our country, that I think an "*amende honorable*" is not only due, but that he should be compensated for his heavy expenses, wanton loss of time, and the disgrace of imprisonment.

Unacquainted with the law of nations on this subject, so familiar to the honorable Secretary, I respectfully touch on this delicate question.

I have a voluminous correspondence, which I do not send, as the above documents will fully explain the nature of the affair.

* * * * * * * * *

I noticed in the French papers that a similar call lately took place in another quarter of France. The "*insoumis*" had been naturalized in the United States; he was tried, condemned, and obliged to serve in the French army. I should be pleased to have decided instructions, as I am nothing but a consul—no diplomatic powers. I will, however, carry out, to the full extent, whatever I may be ordered by the honorable Secretary of State.

I have the honor to be, with great respect, sir, your very obedient servant,

JOHN L. HODGE,
United States Consul at Marseilles.

The Hon. SECRETARY OF STATE.

Document No. 1.

CONSULATE OF THE UNITED STATES OF AMERICA,
Marseilles, October 16, 1852.

SIR: As general-in-chief of this ninth military division, which distinguished command you have filled in so honorable a manner to yourself and country, so universally esteemed have you been, owing to your course of strict justice, that I feel a confidence in addressing you, and placing before you the details of the arrest, trial, and condemnation by a "*conseil de guerre*," as it is called, of an American citizen, on the plea that he is an "*insoumis*," and subject to the laws of France.

Mr. L. Allibert, a native of the Basses Alpes, embarked, in 1838, at Marseilles for the United States, a youth under eighteen years of age, fully authorized, having a passport from the mayor of this city. In 1841, he applied to the United States district court, sitting in New Orleans, to become a citizen, renouncing all allegiance to the then reigning monarch, Louis Philippe. After the usual term, as prescribed by law, five years' residence, proof of good conduct, &c., he was admitted to the rights of an American citizen. Absent from this country fourteen years, little intercourse with his family, anxious to see his venerable father, he left New Orleans, with a regular passport, French consul's visé, also the *original certificate of naturalization*, dated July 10, 1846. As a citizen of the United States he did not anticipate any molestation in France. He passed through this city. On arriving at his father's residence, Basses Alpes, he was immediately arrested as an *insoumis* of 1839. Since *August* 16 *he has been in charge of gens d'armes*, or having his father, a wealthy *propriétaire*, as security that he would not quit France, but be forthcoming at his trial. This security I as consul had previously declined giving, knowing him to be a citizen of the United States, and as such entitled to protection while on the soil of a friendly nation. Orders were given to bring him to trial. On the 6th instant he was fully interrogated before the *juge d'instruction*, I being present. After the examination, as the proofs were so clear of his being an American citizen, in addition to which was presented a letter from the honorable secretary of war, dated Paris, September 15, 1852, saying: "This man, by the fact of his naturalization, has lost the quality of a Frenchman, and is consequently incapable of serving among the French troops." Again: "that he is now covered by the limitation of three years, (article 638 of the Code of Criminal Prosecution,) which period commenced on the day in which Allibert, becoming a citizen of the United States, lost his quality of Frenchman, and ceased to be liable to the obligation to serve. In the present state of things, if Allibert brings proof of an act of naturalization, dated the 10th of January, 1846, the court-martial (*conseil de guerre*) must make this act and article 638 of the Code of Criminal Prosecution the basis of its action, and simply acquit him of the charges made against him." All which were fully *justifié*, and no attention paid thereto. I was also told, at the first meeting, by the *juge d'instruction, that no further difficulties* would *present;* not necessary for me to appear before *le conseil de guerre*, to sit on the 15th instant. Yesterday, however, I accompanied Mr. Allibert, being the day designated, and was informed, before the opening of the court, by Monsieur Carpentin, *commissaire du gouvernement*, that it was useless for the consul to remain in the court, seeing that the affair of Mr. Allibert was quite plain; that he would be acquitted of the charges against him. I consequently left the Fort St. Nicholas under the full belief that it was a mere form to be observed, and that Monsieur Allibert would be immediately restored to liberty. Late in the afternoon, Monsieur Carpentin called at the consulate, informed me that Monsieur Allibert had been tried and condemned to a months' imprisonment; that he had the privilege of an appeal to another *conseil du guerre*, "which, if it confirmed the sentence of the first court, he could carry the appeal to the courts of revision and of cassation," giving to him three years time. I observed to Monsieur Carpentin, the condemnation and imprisonment of an American citizen as an "*insoumis*," admitting, as this military court did, that he was an American citizen, would be viewed by my government in an unfriendly light; could not fail to call forth a grave national question; that when we were in our infancy as a nation, without an ally, as combined Europe was encamped in France, we waged war with the mighty Britain for the rights of our adopted citizens; that this powerful nation had abandoned the vaunted right, "that born a British subject, always so," and liable to the laws of the mother country; and never again would that great empire presume to enforce such pretensions, as this right of naturalization was so strongly ingrafted on the minds of our people that it would not be renounced if united Europe armed against us. After a long interview, Monsieur Carpentin observed that he would do all in his power to have Monsieur Allibert liberated; that three or four hours' detention could not be considered as being in prison. Soon after, Monsieur Allibert, being released, made his appearance; told me he had been incarcerated in a filthy *caserne;* that Monsieur Carpentin, *commissaire du gouvernement*, who had informed me that my presence at the *conseil du guerre* would not be required, as it was so simple an affair, was the person decidedly opposed to him. In stating to me the terms of the appeal, I requested him not to accept them—as a citizen of the United States, as he was in France—to abide by any forced constructions a military tribunal might please to decree; to trust to the protection of his adopted country, as he was the same, in the eye of the law, as if born on the soil. As Mr. Allibert had been ordered to return to the fort St. Nicholas at 9 o'clock in the morning, I accompanied him. He declined, in compliance with my request, to sign the papers prepared for the appeal, as I would not admit that such a tribunal had the right to judge an American citizen. We were told by Monsieur Carpentin that the judgment, &c., would be sent to Paris, and no further steps taken before orders were received from the minister of war. And I, as consul of the United States of America, in the name of my government, in the most decided manner, do protest against this decision of a military court, being in violation of the law of nations which admits of naturalization. I protest against this military decision as violating the sacred rights of an American citizen, guarantied by an act of Congress, and confirmed by the unanimous voice of the American people. I protest against it as in opposition to the code of the great Napoleon, chap. 2. "The quality of a Frenchman is lost, 1st, by naturalization acquired in a foreign country; 2d, by the acceptance, not authorized by the Emperor, of public functions conferred by a foreign government; and 3d and last, by any settlement in a foreign country without intention of returning." I protest against it as violating the sacred rights of hospitality towards an American citizen, which this very decision admits him to be, at the same time condemns him to an ignominious imprisonment for having separated himself from the land of his birth. After thus disgracing him, he is to have the privilege, granted by this military court, to embark for the United States with the full rights of an American citizen, not again to be molested if he should return to France. I beg leave to place before you, as it is applicable in the present affair, extracts of a correspondence I had with the legal authorities residing in this city, in regard to an American citizen arrested two years ago, under a similar charge. "Monsieur Bellarger, *chef du service de l'arrondissement maratime de Marseille*," appears to think the United States have no right of naturalizing French citizens so as to prevent the mother country claiming their services. In the United States a naturalized citizen is the same in the eyes of the law, decidedly so in the feelings of the country, as if born on the soil. The present Secretary of State, the Hon. Daniel Webster, one of the first jurisconsults of the present age, declared, on the 20th May, 1851, alluding to the correspondence with Lord Ashburton, English embassador, who negotiated the late treaty between the two countries: "On that occasion it was decided that every man on board of an American vessel, whether mercantile or naval, was protected by the flag of America, no matter what brogue was on his tongue; if the stars and stripes were over him, he was for that purpose an American citizen, and from that day to this we have heard of no pretensions on the part of the British government that it could send an officer on board of an American ship and take from her any human being whatsoever, and never shall."

Lord Ashburton stated: "I must admit that, when a British subject—Irish, English, or Welsh—becomes an American, and claims no longer the protection of his country, his own country has no right to call him a subject, and put him in a position to make war on his adopted country.''

I hand the full extracts to show how a naturalized citizen is the same as a native. In the Senate of the United States we have two Senators of foreign birth, the Hon. Pierre Soulé, a native of France, and Hon. Patrick Shields, a native of Ireland. Has France or England any claim on these citizens? No more than on the immortal ashes of George Washington, the father of his country. Dear and sacred as are these sleeping ashes to the people of the United States, they are not more so than the rights of an adopted citizen, if an attempt were made to violate. By the Code Napoleon, France permits her citizens to be naturalized by other nations; she also naturalizes—witness the leading mercantile houses of Marseilles, the Greeks, Swiss, Italians, and others—and, without doubt, she would protect them. As the person alluded to was released, I presume, owing to the advice of that distinguished lawyer, Mons. Dufour, who was at that time *procureur de la république*, I made no mention of it to my government. In this affair, owing to the extraordinary powers assumed by a military court, in judging and condemning an American citizen as if he were a Frenchman, it becomes my duty to place all the details before the government at Washington, which I shall do in a frank manner.

I have the honor to be, with great respect, sir, your very obedient servant,

JOHN L. HODGE,
United States Consul at Marseilles.

General HECQUET,
General of Division Com'g the Ninth Military Division,
Grand Cross of the Legion of Honor, &c., at Marseilles.

Document No. 5.

CONSULATE OF THE UNITED STATES OF AMERICA,
Marseilles, October 25, 1852.

SIR: Permit me to place before you the inclosed documents. No. 1, my letter of the 16th instant to Gen. Hecquet, commandant de 9*me division militaire*. I regret it is so long. Being a grave national question, the arrest, trial, and condemnation of an American citizen, Mr. Allibert, of New Orleans, as an ''*insoumis*,'' to me it appeared advisable to state all the details, his departure from this country with a French passport, his naturalization in the United States, residence of fourteen years, his return to France, arrest, trial, and condemnation by a *conseil de guerre*, which acknowledges that he is a citizen of the United States, at the same time punishes him as an ''*insoumis*:'' my decided protest against the proceedings, giving my reasons for so doing, expressing the opinion of the people of the United States in regard to our adopted citizens, as I wished to show how strongly ingrafted this sacred right is on the minds of our people. Being a great national question is my apology for the long document to so high a functionary as the commander-in-chief of this department. I cannot avoid requesting your kind indulgence in my sending to you the rough document, as I have not the time to write a fair copy. It is, however, with trifling corrections, the same as the original.

No. 2. Gen. Hecquet's letter of the 22d instant, in reply.

No. 3. Letter from Mons. Carpentin, *le commissaire du gouvernement pres le conseil de guerre*, which advises that the *conseil de revision* annuls the decision, refers the affair to another *conseil de guerre* to be held at Toulon. In an interview this afternoon with Mr. Carpentin and the colonel, Count de Sersey, *chef d'état-major*, they intimated to me that they thought it was done to have a favorable decision. This, however, in no way alters the assumed right to try an American citizen in France. In the course of conversation I mentioned that the honorable Pierre Soulé, an United States Senator, I understood, was in the same position, an "*insoumis.*" Both asserted, if he came here, he would be arrested by the *gens d'armes*. I could not but express my feelings on the subject, as to me it appeared more audacious than when Britain dared to impress our seamen, and shows the necessity of proving to France, as we have to England, that we will protect our citizens, "*coûte que coûte.*" As this affair has been so long in suspense, a prospect of its continuance, I hand the documents to enable you to demand justice at headquarters, as the proceedings are so extraordinary; violating the law of nations, the sacred rights of an American citizen; also, so *injurious* to Mr. Allibert as a merchant, *whose business* at *New Orleans* is *now suffering*, *owing to his* forcible detention in this country. I was led to believe, from what Gen. Hecquet told to me on 15th August, that Mr. Allibert would immediately be released. It appears that the affair had then been sent to Paris, and was no longer under his control. When the letter from the honorable secretary of war was received, no doubt remained on my mind, confirmed by what Mons. Carpentin, *commissaire*, told to me. In opposition to all these strong appearances the business is again postponed, and to your superior judgment I transfer it, well satisfied that an American citizen, whether born on the soil or adopted, we know no difference, will meet that protection which the law of the land and the unanimous voice of the people guaranty.

I have had a long correspondence with Mr. Allibert, letters from the authorities, &c., in regard to this affair, which I do not send to you, as I think my letter of 16th instant so clear, and will enable you to act as you may judge proper.

I have the honor to be, with great respect, sir, your very obedient servant,

JOHN L. HODGE,
United States Consul.

Hon. WILLIAM C. RIVES,
Minister Plenipotentiary, Envoy Extraordinary, &c., &c., from the United States, at Paris.

Mr. Hodge to Mr. Everett.

[Extract.]

No. 17.] CONSULATE OF THE UNITED STATES OF AMERICA,
Marseilles, December 31, 1852.

SIR: In my dispatch, No. 16, of the 22d ultimo, I gave full details of the arrest, &c., of Mr. Allibert, an American citizen. I have now the satisfaction to inform the department that on the second trial before "*le conseil de guerre à Toulon,*" he was *unanimously acquitted*, which I attribute to the decided stand I early took in this usurped attempt on the part of a French tribunal to judge an American citizen as an "*insoumis.*" If Mr. Allibert had found no protection, as occurred in a similar case in another quarter of France, he would have been condemned, and no appeal, also forced to enter the army or to have found a substitute; such was the judgment with the above-mentioned "*insoumis.*" So certain did Mr. Allibert appear to view his own fate, that he proposed to find the substitute, which I would not permit. My protest was sent to Paris, as General Hecquet, commander-in-chief of this division of the empire, wrote to me. The imperial government clearly saw if Mr. Allibert were condemned it would cause a grave national question, the one so dear to the American people. Under this belief, I have no doubt, orders were sent to the *conseil de guerre* to release him, *which now* and *forever* establishes *the right of a Frenchman*, even an *insoumis*, to be *naturalized* in the United States. This affair I engaged in, carried on, finally succeeded, on my own responsibility, as the envoy extraordinary, minister, &c., at Paris, did not reply to my letters on the subject. My friends of the consular corps and of the high imperial authorities, known to be very friendly to me, all advised me not to embark in it; said France will never abandon the right over her citizens, certainly not with those who come under the conscription, as it would encourage parents having means to send their sons to the United States to be naturalized, consequently deprive the country of the services of the educated, injure the high standing, talents, discipline, and pride of the army; that I would be mortified by certain defeat. I told them that my country did not know the word defeat. If I, as a commercial consul, were not able to protect him, the United States would do so "*coûte que coûte.*" I hope that my conduct in this affair will meet the [approbation] of my government. I have acted from the best of my judgment, in the firm belief it was my duty, as certainly my feelings dictated, to protect an American citizen.

* * * * * * * *

I have the honor to be, with great respect, sir, your very obedient servant,

JOHN L. HODGE,
United States Consul at Marseilles.

Hon. EDWARD EVERETT,
Secretary of State, Washington, D. C.

Mr. Everett to Mr. Hodge.

[Extract.]

DEPARTMENT OF STATE,
Washington, March 3, 1853.

SIR: * * * * * * *

The department is gratified to learn that Mr. Allibert, whose arrest and imprisonment as an "*insoumis*," although a naturalized citizen of the United States, was mentioned in your communication, has been released. This is undoubtedly due to the firm and decided stand, maintained throughout the long controversy, in your official correspondence with the local authorities on the subject.

It is much to be desired that this case may be considered a precedent, as you intimate, and that hereafter naturalized citizens of the United States may visit France without danger of arrest for military service. In this event a fruitful source of irritation and unfriendly feeling will be avoided.

* * * * * * * *

I am, sir, your obedient servant,

EDWARD EVERETT.

JOHN L. HODGE,
United States Consul, Marseilles, France.

Mr. Hodge to Mr. Marcy.

[Extract.]

No. 19.] MARSEILLES, *April* 12, 1853.

SIR: I was highly gratified on the reception of the letter of 2d March, addressed to me by the ex-Secretary of State, the honorable Edward Everett, as he approved of the manner I had conducted the "Allibert affair." I should be much flattered if the present distinguished head of the State Department would give it a bird's-eye perusal. In this city the favorable termination gave great satisfaction to the consular corps, as no one anticipated such a result; at the same time, great mortification to the "imperial dignitaries," as it yielded so important a right to permit even an "*insoumis*" to expatriate himself, to become a citizen of the United States, and thus escape conscription. It proved, as all proclaimed, *the great desire of France to cultivate the friendship of the United States.* Such an acquittal would not have been tolerated, in the first trial of this important question, to any other power; now it has been acknowledged, and all intend to claim it. If this decision were made known in the United States, it would perhaps enable many naturalized citizens, who are in the same position, "*insoumis*," to visit this country, now under the dread, if they come here, of arrest and being sent to the army. The right of claiming "*insoumis*" was so fully ingrafted in the minds of Frenchmen that the "*juge d'in-*

struction," the "*conseil de guerre,*" and "*Mons. le commissaire du gouvernement,*" as Mons. Allibert had mentioned that the Hon. Pierre Soulé, Senator of the United States, was an "*insoumis,*" told me if he came to France that he would be arrested by the *gens d'armes.* I could not but express my opinion very freely in reply to this vaporing threat of these usurped lawgivers, as I did during the long and tedious affair, from August to the last of December, as I, individually, felt assured my government and the people would support me "*coûte que coûte.*"

* * * * * * * *

I have the honor to be, with great respect, sir, your obedient servant,

JOHN L. HODGE,
United States Consul at Marseilles.

Hon. WILLIAM L. MARCY,
Secretary of State, &c., Washington, D. C.

Mr. Marcy to Mr. Campbell.

DEPARTMENT OF STATE,
Washington, September 8, 1854.

SIR: I transmit a copy of a letter of the 5th instant, addressed to this department by John J. Wendell, a highly respectable gentleman, of Albany, New York, expressing apprehensions that Mr. Johannes Van Beuren, a son of a naturalized citizen of the United States, and who has himself become naturalized by the act of Congress of the 14th of April, 1802, may be impressed into the Dutch army or navy. It is desirable that, if possible, this should be prevented, and as Johannes is supposed to be at Rotterdam, or in its vicinity, you will do anything which you properly can for that purpose. It is not deemed necessary to raise or discuss the question of the right of the Dutch government to the services of Johannes, notwithstanding his naturalization in this country. The expediency of exercising this right, if not the existence of the right, even in a time of war, has heretofore been zealously disputed by this government. If, however, for argument's sake only, the right in the abstract were to be acknowledged, it is deemed unadvisable to enforce or to assert it when Holland is at peace with all the world. You will consequently make these circumstances known to the Dutch authorities, and, if necessary, you will communicate with Mr. Belmont on the subject, transmitting to him a copy of this letter. You will also send Johannes to the United States, if he should be willing to return, and if you can take that course without interfering with his engagements or without any other charge to the government than that authorized by law.

I am, sir, your obedient servant,

W. L. MARCY.

WILLIAM S. CAMPBELL, Esq.,
United States Consul, Rotterdam.

Mr. Schleiden to Mr. Cass.

BREMEN LEGATION,
New York, 5 University Place, October 23, 1858.

Most of the German States require of all their subjects a certain amount of military service, and each State is bound by a convention, concluded in Frankfort-on-the-Main on the 10th of February, 1831, to arrest and surrender any deserter from such military service when found within its boundaries and claimed by his government. In a similar way there exist conventions for the mutual delivery of fugitives from justice between all the German States.

During the last years cases have occurred more than once that such deserters or fugitives from justice, who in the mean time had become naturalized citizens of the United States, have been indiscreet enough to return to Germany without having beforehand obtained a pardon from the government of their native country, and have in passing through Bremen on their way to the interior of Germany, or on their return to the United States, been claimed by the government of their native State, from the laws of which they had escaped.

Demands of this kind put the government of Bremen in the disagreeable position, either to be suspected by its German confederates of not complying with the treaty stipulations in regard to the delivery of deserters and fugitives from justice, or to surrender a naturalized citizen of the United States to another government notwithstanding its friendly feelings for the great sister republic and the earnest remonstrations of the American consul. The Bremen government must of course reserve to itself the right of deciding such cases according to their merits, and would not more hesitate to surrender a naturalized American citizen than the citizen of any other country, where the circumstances justify such a course. Anxious, however, to avoid if possible even the appearance of disregarding the rights of American citizens, the Bremen Senate has deemed it proper to direct its undersigned minister resident to call the attention of the honorable Secretary of State of the United States to this subject, and to submit the following observations to his consideration:

It is believed to be the acknowledged policy of the United States government not to interfere in behalf of any naturalized citizen who, having left his native country without permission, as a deserter from military service or as a fugitive from justice, afterwards returns to the same, and thereby renders himself amenable to the laws he had violated before becoming a citizen of the United States. If this be the adopted policy of the United States, it seems to be only a simple consequence of the said principle, that it would also not be competent for this government to protect its naturalized citizens from the operation of the laws of their native country in case they should go to another foreign country which by treaty is bound to surrender them, on application, to their native State as deserters or fugitives from justice.

The Bremen government is confident that these are the views taken by the United States government in regard to immigrants who have declared their intention to become citizens of the United States, or who really have been naturalized as such, and who afterwards bid defiance to the laws of their native country. The principles here laid down have, however, for aught known, never been embodied in any law of the United States, or any published general regulations of the State Department. The present, as well as former American consuls at Bremen, have, therefore, in cases like those mentioned above, sought to extend their protection to naturalized fellow-citizens of theirs, a demand for the surrender of whom had been made by some other German government. Though the Bremen Senate has, out of courtesy, never hesitated to answer any representations made in a courteous manner in behalf of such American citizens, and though in all cases which hitherto have occurred, it has been able to decline for some reason or other the surrender of any American citizen claimed as a deserter or fugitive from justice, it wishes to avoid entering into any discussion with the American consul in regard to so delicate a matter, or even justifying to any one but the honorable Secretary of State himself its action, in case it should feel itself under the obligation of surrendering an American citizen to one of its German confederates. The undersigned has, therefore, in the name of his government, to request the honorable Secretary of State of the United States that he may be pleased to inform him whether the views taken in this communication in regard to the protection which naturalized American citizens, deserters, or fugitives from justice from their native country, can claim in foreign countries, are these of the United States government, and if so, to instruct the American representatives abroad, particularly the United States consul at Bremen, accordingly.

The undersigned avails himself of this occasion to offer to the honorable General Lewis Cass renewed assurances of his high consideration.

R. SCHLEIDEN.

Hon. General Lewis Cass,
Secretary of State of the United States, Washington, D. C.

Mr. Appleton to Mr. Ten Brook.

Department of State,
Washington, March 12, 1859.

Sir: I transmit herewith a copy of a communication addressed to Hon. J. H. Jewett, a representative in the Thirty-fifth Congress from the State of Kentucky, by A. Whittleshofer, in which he states that he emigrated from Bavaria to the United States in 1846, and subsequently took the requisite steps to become an American citizen. He now desires to revisit Bavaria for the purpose of seeing his aged mother, and wishes to obtain permission from the Bavarian authorities for that purpose without exposing himself to the danger of being impressed into the military service of his native country.

You are requested to make a representation of the facts to the proper authorities, and endeavor to obtain, if not incompatible with the laws and usages of Bavaria, the permission which is requested by Mr. Whittleshofer.

I am, sir, your obedient servant,

JOHN APPLETON,
Assistant Secretary.

A. Ten Brook, Esq.,
U. S. Consul, Munich, Bavaria.

Mr. Schleiden to Mr. Cass.

Bremen Legation,
Washington, D. C., March 16, 1859.

Sir: On the 23d of October last I had the honor of calling your attention to the conventions concluded between all the German States in regard to the mutual surrender of deserters from military service, and of criminals, fugitives from justice. I explained on that occasion that these conventions admit of no exceptions in favor of persons who, after having in the meantime become naturalized citizens of the United States, are indiscreet enough to return to Germany and to bid defiance to the laws of their native country. I informed you that my government, although reluctantly, would not more hesitate to surrender a naturalized American citizen than a citizen of any other country, whenever the circumstances justify such a course, and that it did not doubt that the United States government would recognize that Bremen is fully justified in doing so, it being not competent for the United States to protect its naturalized citizens from the operation of the laws of their native country in case they should go to another foreign country which by treaty is bound to surrender them, on application, to their native State as deserters or fugitives from justice. I finally requested you, in the name of my government, to inform me whether these views meet with your assent, and, if so, to instruct the American representatives abroad, particularly the United States consul at Bremen, accordingly.

The pressing business which soon after devolved upon you and your department in consequence of the meeting of Congress has, I suppose, prevented you from taking this matter into earlier consideration, and though my government has, in its communications to this legation, repeatedly expressed its wish to avoid discussions likely to arise in future, in case of its finding itself under the obligation of surrendering a naturalized American citizen, by coming beforehand to a full understanding in regard to the principle argued in my note of October 23d last, I have until now refrained from urging a speedy answer to my said communication. Congress having now adjourned, a dispatch of my government just received makes it, however, my duty to call again your attention to the subject in question.

It is understood that your predecessors in office have repeatedly declared that if a subject of any foreign country, lying under a legal obligation in that country to perform a certain amount of military duty, leaves his native land without performing that duty or obtaining the permission to emigrate, comes to the United States and is naturalized, and afterwards, for any purposes whatever, goes back to his native country, it is not competent for the United States to protect him from the operation of the law of his native land. This doctrine being considered to be still that of the United States government, the only question remaining is, whether it does not follow from this doctrine, as a necessary consequence, that the United States government is also not competent to interfere in behalf of such a naturalized citizen, who, instead of returning to his native State, goes to a third foreign State which by treaty is bound to surrender him to his native country. This question having already been argued in my note of the 23d of October last, I beg leave simply to refer to the same and to submit here only another point of view to your consideration, which, as far as the relations between Bremen and the United States are concerned, will prove still more the justice and equity of the wish of my government to have the principle in question fully recognized by the United States government.

The preamble of the Constitution of the United States mentions among its principal objects, "*to insure domestic tranquillity and to provide for the common defense,*" and according to article 1, section 8, page 15, Congress has power, "*to provide for calling forth the militia to execute the laws of the Union, suppress insurrections, and repel invasions.*" In the same manner, the organic act of the Germanic Confederation defines (article 2) its object as consisting in "*preserving the external and internal safety of Germany, and the independence and inviolability of the several German States.*" Article 2 of the additional organic act of 1820, ("Wiener Schluss, Acte vorn 15 Mai, 1820,") makes it the duty of the German Diet to organize the military system of the Confederation and to provide for the common defense, and in pursuance of this article a *military constitution* of the Germanic Confederation was resolved upon, and, on the 9th of April, 1826, declared an organic law of the Confederation. The convention for the mutual surrender of deserters from military service, concluded between all the German States, at Frankfort-on-the-Main, on the 10th of February, 1831, and mentioned in my note of 23d of October last, is only one of several acts made for the purpose of insuring the objects of the Confederation. A deserter from the military service of Prussia, or of Hanover, or of Bavaria, or of any other German State, is not only a deserter from the military service of his native State, but from the united army of the Germanic Confederation, the military forces of all the German States forming only parts of this united army. He weakens, by his escape, not only the power of defense of one German State, but that of all, of Bremen as well as of Prussia, Hanover, or of whatever other State he may be a subject. The obligation of Bremen to surrender such a deserter, when found within her territory, to his native State is, therefore, not only an obligation imposed by express treaty stipulations, but also an obligation clearly in the own interest of Bremen. Taking this view, every State of the Germanic Confederation to which a deserter from the military service of any of them may return, after having, in the meantime, been naturalized in America, is to be considered in the same light as if he had returned to his native country; and if the United States recognize, as they do, that a naturalized American citizen who has left Prussia, or any other German State, without having performed his military service, and without leave, remains liable to the claims of his native country to such service whenever he return thither, it cannot be doubted that they will also recognize the right of any other State of the Germanic Confederation to enforce such claim against such a deserter from the German army, when he is indiscreet enough to venture himself into any German State. If a soldier or sailor, enlisted in the United States army or navy, should desert the service, become a naturalized citizen of Bremen or any other German State, and afterwards return to any one of the States of this Union, he would no doubt be made amenable to the military law, and representations made in his behalf by the government of his adopted country would not be listened to by the United States government. This case is virtually the same as that of a deserter from the military service of any German State, who, after having been naturalized in the United States, returns to any one of the German States. For, though the military forces of the several States of the Germanic Confederation are, in time of peace, under the sole command of the chief executive of each State, all of them form part of one united German army, the commander-in-chief of which, whenever called into active service, is appointed by the German Diet, to which he has to make oath of obedience as his only superior authority.

With reference to the foregoing observations, I renew my request, to inform me, at your earliest convenience, whether the United States government approves of the views expressed here, and in my note of October 23d last, in regard to the protection which naturalized American citizens, deserters, or fugitives from justice from their native country, may claim in foreign countries. The republic which I have the honor of representing, however anxious to preserve its happily existing most friendly relations with the United States, cannot allow that desire to prevent it from fulfilling its duties, or from maintaining its rights as one of the sovereign and independent States of the Germanic Confederation, and it will feel bound to surrender any naturalized American citizen to one of its confederates, whenever a fair construction of the special treaties alluded to, and of its duties as a member of the Confederation, should leave it without any other alternative. In making these views of my government known to you, I trust that no difference of opinion can exist between the two governments in regard to this subject, and that you will find it also in accordance with your own views to give the necessary instructions in this respect to the United States representatives abroad, and particularly to the United States consul at Bremen, for the purpose of avoiding any future discussions.

I avail myself of this occasion to renew to you the assurances of my high consideration.

R. SCHLEIDEN.

Hon. General LEWIS CASS,
Secretary of State of the United States, Washington, D. C.

Mr. Cass to Mr. Schleiden.

DEPARTMENT OF STATE,
Washington, April 9, 1859.

SIR: Your notes, of the 23d of October and 16th ultimo, relative to the surrender by Bremen to other German States of naturalized citizens of the United States, from whom military service may be claimed, were duly received, and have been taken into careful consideration. In reply, I am directed to inform you that, under ordinary circumstances, the President would not think it necessary to express an opinion with respect to suppositious cases. It is usually much safer to consider every case upon its own merits, and this is hardly practicable before the case has occurred. Since your communication, however, refers to a general principle, and is coupled, moreover, with an intimation that Bremen will feel itself free, in the absence of any disclaimer by the United States, to regard this government as acquiescing in the view of the subject which is presented in your letter, it is deemed expedient to make one or two observations in reply to your inquiry.

It is undoubtedly true that this government has acquiesced in the opinion expressed by Mr. Wheaton that, when a citizen who has been liable to military duty leaves his own country without permission, and without having performed this duty, and is naturalized in another country, he may be held to discharge his liability whenever he is found again in his native State. This opinion, however, is regarded by this government as applying not to cases of inchoate liability, but to cases only where the liability has become complete. To speak of a minor as liable to military service simply because, if he should live long enough in the country, he might become so, could not be fairly regarded as either appropriate or just. It is unnecessary, however, to discuss this distinction with reference to your letter, because your inquiry refers to a case of admitted liability, and you assert the right of Bremen to surrender a person thus liable to the country where he owes service. This right you assert in a special manner, whenever the demand is made by a German State.

It is not perceived that this latter consideration changes the duty of Bremen, or the character of the surrender. Bremen is a sovereign and independent State. She has her own authorities, and is represented abroad by her own diplomatic and consular agents. Her alliances are, therefore, within her own control, and in making conventions with one nation, she is not at liberty to disregard the duties which she owes to other nations. She is under obligations, for example, by solemn treaty stipulations, to give special protection to persons and property of citizens of the United States, of all occupations, who may be in her territories, either transient or dwelling therein. (Article 8, convention of December 20, 1827, with Hanseatic republics.) When a citizen of the United States visits Bremen, he has a right to rely upon this protection; but his reliance wholly fails, and the stipulation becomes of no effect, if he may be seized by the Bremen authorities and forcibly transferred to another State, which demands his surrender as a political refugee. In going to Bremen and temporarily residing there, he binds himself to respect the peace and order of that country, and to render obedience to its laws. While he does this, being a citizen of the United States, Bremen is bound to give him her protection. She can rightfully make no distinction, in cases of persons not natives of Bremen, between native citizens and naturalized citizens of the United States.

It is not her duty to inquire for the benefit of a third power into the circumstances of this citizenship, or of the expatriation which preceded it. It is enough that the person thus clothed with it, owes no allegiance to Bremen, has committed no breach of its laws, and is charged with no crime anywhere. If any political question is raised by a third power, as to the respective duties which he owes to that power and to the United States, it is respectfully submitted that this is a question with which Bremen has no concern, and she must leave it to be determined by the parties interested. She cannot rightfully decide it at the instance of one of these parties, without a hearing from the other, and then act upon her own decision by remanding the person claimed to the State which demands him. The practice of such a doctrine as this would be attended with numerous difficulties, and might lead to great injustice. While, therefore, this government has no wish to interfere with the proper jurisdiction of Bremen within its own territory, and would not withhold from it any one of its just rights as a sovereign and independent State, it cannot consent that it should first invite our citizens to reside within its borders by assuring them of its protection, and then violently seize them for no alleged crime, and transport them to another State with which their political relations are a subject of discussion between that State and the United States. The name and character of an American citizen must become less valuable than they now are, before this disregard of them can fail to be attended with the most serious consequences. It is earnestly hoped that no practical issue of this nature will ever occur to interrupt the cordial relations which now happily subsist between the United States and Bremen; and with the expression of this wish, I have the honor to be, with high consideration, your obedient servant,

LEWIS CASS.

RUDOLPH SCHLEIDEN, Esq., *&c.*, *&c.*, *&c.*

Mr. Ten Brook to Mr. Appleton.

No. 4.] CONSULATE OF THE UNITED STATES,
Munich, April 18, 1859.

SIR; I have the honor to acknowledge the receipt of your dispatch, dated March 12th, with its inclosure, in relation to the case of Aaron Whittleshofer. I proceed at once to make the preliminary inquiries in regard to the matter, and have just addressed a note in relation thereto to the department of state for foreign affairs of the government here. But without waiting for a reply, which may be for some time delayed, as the facts must be investigated at Mr. Whittleshofer's native place, in Franconia, I have deemed it better to state immediately how the case seems to me to stand, in order that Mr. Whittleshofer may continue or suspend his preparations as he shall deem the facts to justify.

The law applicable to the case is substantially as follows: Every young man is bound at the age of twenty years to draw for the military service. The number of men which each district must raise in a year is determined by the government. All who draw a *lower* number must serve, while those who draw a *higher* are free. All persons not charged with debt or crime can at any time obtain permission to emigrate, *except* able-bodied young [men] over the age of sixteen years, who shall not have drawn for the military service, and these *latter* can only obtain the permission by depositing securities sufficient to cover the expense of hiring a substitute in case they draw to *serve*, which are *returned* to them in case they draw *free*.

The above statement shows Mr. W's position in relation to the government of Bavaria. He stands partly as *criminal*, partly as *debtor*. In the *former* character, he might, in case of his return to Bavaria, be subjected to fine and imprisonment, in the *latter* to the payment of an amount sufficient to hire a substitute for the military service; and whether he return or not he is subjected to the loss of any inheritance which might be coming to him in Bavaria.

This, then, belongs to what are called *cases of grace*, which must go to the King in person. The two parties do not treat on equal terms—the one does not *demand* that which the other may *not* refuse, but presents a *petition* which *may* be *granted or not*.

As to the probable result, I can only say: 1st. The criminal features of the case will probably be remitted. 2d. As to the obligation to supply a substitute, I think it quite impossible that this should be entirely remitted, as no government will establish a precedent which destroys its own law, until it is ready to abandon the law itself. 3d. As the practice is not absolutely invariable, there may be some questions of fact to be decided. It having been known to the authorities that Mr. W. had left the country, it is a question whether his name was *dropped* from the lists of those who were to draw, or whether it was *retained*, and if the *latter*, whether he drew *free* or to *serve?* Three different suppositions are here presented, and the result of the application may be different according as the fact shall be found to correspond with one or another of them. In case it shall appear that the name was dropped, the most *unfavorable* result that is to be feared is, that he be deemed to have drawn for the service and made to hire a substitute, which every man is allowed to do for himself, and so may obtain one as cheap as an acceptable one can be obtained, which, however, is at present unusually high (1,000 florins—$400) in consequence of the prospect of a European war. The *mildest* result that could, on this supposition, be reasonably hoped, would be a commutation into a money payment, the amount being fixed by a calculation of the average results of the conscription, and the average price of substitutes: *e. g.*, if one half of the able-bodied young men must serve, and the average price of substitutes is 700 florins, 350 florins ($150) would be the commutation. As this may be thought to make the case of one who evades the law better than that of one who submits to it, it may not perhaps be obtained. If it shall be found that he drew to serve, the principles suggested above can be readily applied; and if he drew *free*, though this would not change the character of an attempt to evade the law, yet the case might be differently treated, and he *might even* freely obtain the desired permission.

I have had several interviews with the ministerial counselor, whose place it is to prepare such cases for presentation to his Majesty, and am assured that no effort will be spared to present the case in as favorable a light, and recommend as favorable action, as the preservation of the integrity of the law will allow. As proof that the preservation of the integrity of the law will be the only motive to limit the free permission to Mr. W. to visit his native country, I may mention that the ministerial counselor, to whom I have referred, *himself* suggested a way in which the visit could be made *without* the permission, viz: to come to the village in the borders of Wurtemberg nearest the home of his mother, (or any other place *out* of Bavaria,) and send for her to meet him there.

If Mr. W. desires to start immediately, he can do so, if he will send directions to this consulate as to where the result of his application shall meet him, (consulate at Frankfort, Leipsic, or Stutgard,) and it shall be there, and he can then take his choice between sending for his mother to meet him *out* of Bavaria, and accepting the conditions upon which he will be allowed to visit her at her home.

When the result shall be made known to me, I shall lose no time in communicating it to the State Department at Washington.

I have, sir, the honor to be, your obedient servant,

ANDREW TEN BROOK,
United States Consul.

Hon. John Appleton,
Assistant Secretary of State, Washington, D. C.

Mr. Cass to Mr. Mason.

No. 189.] Department of State,
Washington, June 27, 1859.

Sir: It is very desirable for this department to possess reliable information concerning the provisions of the French conscription laws relating to American naturalized citizens, born in France, who may at any time revisit their native country. You are therefore requested, as soon as you can conveniently, to procure and transmit such information. Does the French law, under any circumstances, and if so, under what circumstances, require a native-born citizen, naturalized in the United States, to serve in the army in case of his return to France? You are particularly desired to transmit the most precise information upon this point. You will see by the inclosed copy of a letter from this department to Mr. Hofer, that the condition of American naturalized citizens abroad has been brought to the attention of the government, and that its views have been distinctly stated. This government maintains the right of expatriation and naturalization, and maintains, also, that if a foreign-born citizen, naturalized here, returns to his native country, he is not liable to any military duty, except such as was actually due, and which he had been called upon to perform before his emigration. In any communication you may have with the minister of foreign affairs upon this subject, you will make known to him these views of the United States. Should any of our naturalized citizens be called upon to render military service, you will make yourself acquainted with the circumstances, and if the case comes within the principle I have stated, you will, in firm but temperate language, demand the release of the party; and I feel confident the demand will be complied with. If, however, the service is required because it was commenced before emigration, you will represent to the minister the hope of this government that the person may be discharged, as much ignorance prevails in this country respecting the operation of the French law in those cases, and they must be so rare that penal measures in relation to them cannot be of any importance.

I will thank you, also, to inform me whether, by the French law, naturalization in a foreign country is a right which a native born citizen of France may exercise at pleasure, without the authorization of the government.

I am, sir, respectfully, your obedient servant,

LEWIS CASS.

JOHN Y. MASON, Esq.,
&c., &c., &c.

Mr. Mason to Mr. Cass.

No. 407.]

UNITED STATES LEGATION,
Paris, August 2, 1859.

SIR: In executing your instruction contained in your No. 189, I have found it necessary to address the minister of foreign affairs a note, of which I herewith inclose a copy. It will probably be some time before I receive a reply; and therefore, it seems to me proper, without delay, to communicate the form in which I have made the inquiry. I cannot anticipate the answer; but there is no doubt that the French law recognizes the right of a Frenchman to lose his French nationality. This may be done by "naturalization in a foreign country." (See chapter 2, book 1, of the Fifty-seven Codes of 1856; title, "*de la privation des droits civils.*") I can express no confident opinion as to the acknowledgment of the right of expatriation, without authorization of the government. In practice, no such authority is required; but the government may not acknowledge the natural right. It is not in my power, in the absence of the minister's answer, to state authentically the present condition of the law. As soon as I am favored with a reply to my note to Count Walewski, I will lose no time in again addressing the department on the subject, which is deeply interesting.

I am, very respectfully, your obedient servant,

J. Y. MASON.

Hon. LEWIS CASS, *Secretary of State.*

LEGATION OF THE UNITED STATES,
Paris, July 27, 1859.

MONSIEUR LE MINISTRE: I am instructed by my government to obtain and communicate in an authentic form information on questions of much interest, and I know no more satisfactory mode of doing so than by invoking the aid of your excellency.

Since the discovery of the American continent, European settlement, either by colonization or emigration, has peopled that vast region.

In that portion of the continent within the limits and jurisdiction of the United States express provision was made in the federal Constitution giving power to Congress to pass uniform laws of naturalization. This grant of power, and the duty resulting from it, were founded on the fundamental doctrine of the natural right of man to expatriate himself from the country of his origin, relinquish the duty of allegiance which he owes it, and the right to its protection which a citizen or subject may rightfully claim from that government to which he owes allegiance. Laws for the naturalization of foreigners have been passed and executed in the United States from the beginning. In their practical administration the stranger is required to declare his intention to become a citizen of the United States, to renounce his duty of allegiance to any sovereign or State, and all the rights which may pertain to him from the government to which the accident of birth may have made him subject, and after the lapse of a prescribed term of years, he is permitted to consummate his right of naturalization formally and solemnly in a court of record. Thus assuming allegiance to the United States, he separates himself from the country of his origin, and becomes entitled to the rights of citizenship, and amongst them that of protection from the country of his adoption.

The vast exodus from the Old to the New World has, in the persons of emigrants and their descendants, added to the productive industry of the country, increased the number of good citizens, and swelled the population of the United States to a number probably little short of 30,000,000 inhabitants. It has necessarily raised questions of the gravest import. The United States, acting on the admission that man has an inherent right to change the domicil which nature gave him in the place of his birth, and to pursue elsewhere happiness and safety, has received with hospitality strangers who elected to cast their lot in the country and sought the rights of citizenship. But their policy has not been to entice away the people of other countries, or to protect them against responsibilities which in good faith attached to them. The change of residence and of allegiance necessarily involved delicate questions, and the attention of the federal government has been drawn to the subject with an earnest desire to discharge fully and justly its duty, as well to the adopted citizen as to the government of the country of his origin, at the same time to avoid controversy with foreign governments by guarding against any conflict of laws.

My government, with this honorable policy, has instructed me to obtain for its use authentic information as to the laws of France on this subject, especially in reference to the claim of military service exacted of one born in France who has become a naturalized citizen of the United States.

I respectfully request that your excellency will have the goodness to give me the desired information in reply to the following questions:

1. Does the French law recognize the right of a native-born citizen of France to exercise, without the authorization of his government, the right of becoming a naturalized citizen or subject of a foreign country?

2. If such a person shall have actually become naturalized in the United States, and shall revisit France without taking the steps prescribed in the French law to recover his lost nationality, and without the intention to remain permanently in France, does the French law, under these circumstances, authorize a claim that he shall be required to serve in the French army?

The government of the United States maintains the right of expatriation, and maintains also that if a foreign-born citizen, naturalized in the United States, returns to his native country without the intention of relinquishing his acquired nationality in the United States, he is not liable to military duty, except such as was actually due, and which he had been called upon to perform before his emigration.

I am aware that a native-born Frenchman may by law lose his French nationality by the act of naturalization in a foreign country. From this, it necessarily results that he may lawfully acquire the character of a naturalized citizen of such foreign country, if he shall not have recovered the French nationality which he may have thus lost.

3. Does the recruitment law of France make him on a casual return to France, liable to military service to the same extent as if he had not left the country of his birth and become naturalized abroad? If this liability continues at all, how far does it extend? If a French youth, under the recruitment law of France, shall have been called on before his actual immigration to enter the military service, and after this existing liability shall emigrate to the United States, become there a naturalized citizen, and return temporarily to France, the principle maintained by the United States will not protect him from fulfilling in good faith the duty thus attached, any more than to deny his submission to the French jurisdiction for trial and punishment of crime committed here, or to liability for pecuniary responsibility actually incurred.

The questions involved in the personal and civil condition of a naturalized foreigner, in respect to his old and new allegiance, are such that it is desirable to avoid any conflict of law between the United States and France. I sincerely hope that your excellency will give me such information in reply that my government will have no reason to anticipate any want of accord between the governments of France and the United States on the delicate and interesting questions involved.

I have much reason to express my thanks that during my residence in France, the imperial government has observed the most liberal conduct towards citizens of the United States, whether native or naturalized. There is no existing case here which gives cause of complaint. I make the inquiries suggested in this note with a purpose to secure accord in the future, and to avoid questions which probably would result from any conflict of law between the two countries on a subject peculiarly delicate.

With assurances of my high consideration, I am, very respectfully, your excellency's obedient servant,

J. Y. MASON.

His Excellency COUNT WALEWSKI,
Minister of Foreign Affairs.

Mr. Buchanan to Mr. Cass.

No. 21.] LEGATION OF THE UNITED STATES,
Copenhagen, September 24, 1859.

SIR: A few days ago, a gentleman by the name of Boie Smidt, a clergyman of the Methodist Church, called on me to complain that, being a regularly naturalized citizen of the United States, he had been illegally arrested and impressed into the naval service of his Majesty the King of Denmark, and to ask my assistance in having him discharged from his arrest. On examining the papers of Mr. Smidt, I found them regular and in proper form, and I determined at once to interfere in his behalf.

Supposing that the authorities having Mr. Smidt in charge would voluntarily release him, when they came to understand that he was in fact, and beyond dispute, a citizen of the United States, I put into his hands a note, a copy of which I now inclose to you, marked No. 1, and desired him to exhibit it to whatever authority might be claiming control over him. I also desired him to exhibit his papers of *naturalization* to such authority, and to communicate to me the result without loss of time. Mr. Smidt then left me, and in the course of an hour or two returned, informing me that he had complied with my directions, but that his discharge was refused. I immediately addressed the inclosed note, marked No. 2, to his excellency the minister of foreign affairs, to which note, as yet, I have received no reply.

I regret that I have no authentical copy of your dispatch of the 8th of July last to our minister at Berlin; but, understanding as I think I do, its tone and meaning, I will endeavor to act within its precepts.

Your obedient servant,

JAMES M. BUCHANAN.

Hon. LEWIS CASS, *&c.*

No. 1.] LEGATION OF THE UNITED STATES,
Copenhagen, September 21, 1859.

SIR: I have examined the papers which you have exhibited to me, and find them correct. You are a regularly naturalized citizen of the United States, and I feel assured that if you will present your papers to the authorities of whom you have spoken to me, you will be at once relieved from all trouble and uneasiness.

If I should be disappointed in this, I shall feel it my duty to demand your discharge in an official form.

With great respect,

JAMES M. BUCHANAN.

Mr. Boie Smidt.

No. 2.] Legation of the United States,
Copenhagen, September 21, 1859.

Sir: I beg to invite your attention to a matter which requires my immediate action. A gentleman by the name of Boie Smidt has called on me, to inform me that he is a regularly naturalized citizen of the United States of America, and he complains that he has been illegally arrested and impressed into the naval service of his Majesty the King of Denmark. I have required of him to exhibit to me the proper proofs of his being a naturalized citizen of the United States, and he has shown to me a certificate of the declaration of his intention to become a citizen of the United States, bearing date on the 18th day of April, 1850, and a certificate of his naturalization, bearing date on the 6th day of August, 1857. These certificates I find, after careful examination, to be regular and in due form; and I do not fail, therefore, in recognizing Mr. Boie Smidt as being, at this time, a naturalized citizen of the United States. I have thought proper to inquire of Mr. Smidt particularly, whether or not, up to the time of his leaving the kingdom of Denmark, he had been guilty of any infraction of the laws of Denmark, and he assures me he had not. After I had satisfied myself of the regularity of the naturalization of Mr. Smidt, I put into his hands a note, (a copy of which I now inclose,) addressed to him by me, which note I requested him to exhibit to the authorities having him in charge. This, Mr. Smidt informs me, he has done, but that the authorities refuse to discharge him.

With the information which I have now before me, supposing it to be correct, I cannot doubt but that Mr. Smidt is entitled to his discharge; and, with a view to that result, I must beg that your excellency will give to the investigation of the subject your prompt attention.

I avail myself of this opportunity to assure your excellency of my continued and very sincere regard.

JAMES M. BUCHANAN.

His Excellency C. Hall,
Minister of Foreign Affairs, &c., &c., &c.

Mr. Buchanan to Mr. Cass.

No. 23.] Legation of the United States,
Copenhagen, September 30, 1859.

Sir: I have the honor to inclose to you a note, which I have received from his excellency the minister of foreign affairs, in regard to the arrest and detention of Mr. Boie Smidt, a naturalized citizen of the United States. And I have also the honor to inclose to you my reply to the same, together with a translation of his excellency's note. I fear, if there be not some definitive understanding arrived at in regard to the rights of our naturalized citizens, when abroad, they will be often placed in positions of difficulty and embarrassment, if they should visit certain parts of Europe. And I would be glad if I might be permitted to know the views of my government on the subject in an authoritative form.

I have the honor to be, with great respect, your obedient servant,

JAMES M. BUCHANAN.

Hon. LEWIS CASS,
Secretary of State.

[Translation.]

COPENHAGEN, *September* 28, 1859.

SIR: I have had the honor to receive your dispatch of the 22d instant, in which you ask for my interference in behalf of a person of the name of Boie Smidt, who, after having been made a citizen of the United States, in 1857, has now been called upon to perform his military service as a Danish subject. I have lost no time in recommending this request to the special attention of the competent authorities; but I believe that I am in a position to inform you at present that, if it should turn out, upon an investigation of the affair, that the said Mr. Smidt, when he signified his intention to be naturalized in the United States, was, under the laws of the country, bound afterwards to perform his military service in his native country, then I do not presume that the laws now in force will enable the administration to release him now from the discharge of a duty which he owed to the State at the time when the above declaration was made.

Be pleased to accept, sir, the renewed assurance of my most distinguished consideration.

C. HALL.

Mr. BUCHANAN,
Minister Resident of the United States.

LEGATION OF THE UNITED STATES,
Copenhagen, September 29, 1859.

SIR: I have the honor to acknowledge the receipt of your note, bearing date on the 26th of this month, but which did not reach this legation until yesterday, the 28th, in reference to the note which I had the honor to address to you on the 21st of this month, in respect to the arrest and impressment into the naval service of his Majesty the King of Denmark, of a naturalized citizen of the United States, by the name of Boie Smidt; and, while I thank your excellency for the promptness with which you have acted in regard to the matter to which the note refers, I cannot forbear to express my regret, not to say my surprise, that the "competent authorities" having Mr. Smidt in charge should have declined to grant what, in my judgment, was a reasonable request—that is to say, a request for his immediate release.

I have reason to believe that, at the time of the arrest of Mr. Smidt, "the competent authorities" were fully aware of the fact that he was a naturalized citizen of the United States; and, I have no reason to suppose, that, at that time, or at any other time, the "competent authorities" alleged or claimed that Mr. Smidt, previous to his having left the Kingdom of Denmark, had incurred any penalty, violated any law, or assumed any duties under the government of Denmark.

The note of your excellency informs me "that, if it should turn out, upon an investigation of the affair, that the said Mr. Smidt, when he signified his intention to be naturalized in the United States, was, under the laws of the country, bound afterwards to perform his military service, in his native country, then I (you) do not presume that the laws now in force will enable the administration to release him," &c.

It would seem to me, to be only necessary for me, now to remark, while the investigation to which you allude is pending, if, on such investigation, it should so turn out that Mr. Boie Smidt had left his native country, Denmark, without having committed any offense against the law, before his departure, or without his being at the time of his departure in the army or navy of the government of Denmark, or actually called into the one or the other, then I should feel myself compelled to dispute the right of the government of Denmark to arrest and detain him.

It is the settled doctrine of the government which I have the honor here to represent, as I understand it, that a naturalized citizen of the United States, from and after the date of his naturalization, both at home and abroad, is placed on the very same footing with a native citizen, with the exception that none but a native citizen can occupy the office of Presidentor Vice-President of the United States; and the government will be disposed to extend to the one class of citizens the same protection which justly belongs to the other at all times and in all places.

I would remark to your excellency, that it seems to me irregular on the part of the "competent authorities" having Mr. Smidt in charge, to continue him in arrest, during the progress of the investigation which they propose to institute. Mr. Smidt exhibits his naturalization papers, duly authenticated. He shows himself to be an approved citizen of another government, and I may say of a government which has ever been on terms of amity with the government of Denmark. He establishes by all legal available means that he is, at least *prima facie*, entitled to his discharge, and yet he is deprived of his liberty, taken from his family, wounded in his feelings, and upon the mere allegation (based upon no perceptible evidence) that he has been guilty of the breach of some rule or law, yet to be investigated.

I trust it may be compatible with the sense of right of your excellency, to intercede for the discharge of Mr. Smidt, at least pending the investigation to which you have referred.

It remains for me only to say, that I shall loose no time in communicating to my government a copy of the note which you have been pleased to address to me. In the meanwhile, I beg to assure your excellency of my very sincere and high regard.

JAMES M. BUCHANAN.

His Excellency C. HALL,
Minister of Foreign Affairs, &c., &c., &c.

Mr. Appleton to Mr. Ten Brook.

DEPARTMENT OF STATE,
Washington, October 4, 1859.

SIR: Referring to your dispatch, No. 4, relating to the petition of Mr. Aaron Whittleshofer, for permission to revisit Bavaria, you are requested to report to the department what further proceediugs have taken place upon this subject, and to press the question to an early decision.

You will find the views of the department upon the rights of naturalized citizens of the United States embodied in a printed extract, herewith inclosed, from a dispatch addressed to the minister of the United States at Berlin.

I am, sir, your obedient servant,

JOHN APPLETON,
Assistant Secretary.

A. TEN BROOK, Esq.,
United States Consul, Munich.

Mr. Buchanan to Mr. Cass.

No. 24.]

LEGATION OF THE UNITED STATES,
Copenhagen, October 7, 1859.

SIR: Up to this time I have received no written reply to the note addressed by me to his excellency the minister of foreign affairs, on the 29th of September last, in regard to the arrest and detention of Mr. Boie Smidt, a naturalized citizen of the United States. But I deem it but proper to mention to you, that on last night I met the minister of foreign affairs at a dinner given by "his Royal Highness Prince Ferdinand" in honor of the birth-day of "his Majesty the King of Denmark." On that occasion the minister was particularly kind and civil in his deportment towards me, as I have on all former occasions found him to be. He at once (as soon as opportunity offered) introduced the subject of the case of Mr. Smidt, and in the course of conversation, he assured me that no difficulty or trouble should grow out of it. That it should be settled, and settled too in a manner which would be satisfactory. I expressed myself much gratified at this intelligence, and assured his excellency of the friendly disposition of our government towards the government of Denmark, and that it would have been extremely unpleasant if anything should have taken place calculated to weaken the ties of amity which now so cordially exist between the two governments.

I informed his excellency that the "subject of naturalization" was one which had occupied, and which still continued to occupy, much of the attention, care, and vigilance of the government of the United States, and that, as I understood the doctrine of the government on the subject, it was—that a *naturalized* citizen of the United States was *entitled* to the same protection from the government of the United States, both at home and abroad, as was a citizen of native birth. His excellency seemed well to understand this to be the doctrine of the government of the United States; but without entering into any particular discussion, yet he repeated that the case of Mr. Smidt should produce no estrangement between the governments.

I do not pretend to give all the conversation, but what I understand to have been the *substance* of it only. Whatever may be the result of the case of Mr. Smidt, I cannot help feeling assured that the minister of foreign affairs has every disposition to settle it in a manner which will be satisfactory to our government.

I have the honor to be, sir, with high respect and regard, your obedient servant,

JAMES M. BUCHANAN.

Hon. LEWIS CASS,
Secretary of State, &c., &c., &c.

Mr. Cass to Mr. Buchanan.

No. 11.]

DEPARTMENT OF STATE,
Washington, October 21, 1859.

SIR: Your dispatches, Nos. 21 and 23, on the subject of the arrest and detention of Mr. Boie Smidt, a naturalized citizen of the United States, have been received. Your course in promptly interceding in Mr. Smidt's behalf is fully approved, and it is hoped that he may already have been released. If he should still be detained, however, you will urge his release, pursuant to the views expressed in my dispatch to Mr. Wright, of the 8th of July last, in relation to the case of Christian Ernst, an extract from which is herewith inclosed.

I am, sir, your obedient servant,

LEWIS CASS.

JAMES M. BUCHANAN, Esq., *&c., &c.,*
Copenhagen.

Mr. Buchanan to Mr. Cass.

LEGATION OF THE UNITED STATES,
Copenhagen, October 30, 1859.

SIR: On the 26th of the present month I received the inclosed note from the minister of foreign affairs of Denmark, in reply to the note which I had written to him on the 27th of last month, concerning the case of Mr. Boie Smidt.

To the note of the minister I replied, as soon as I was able, after I had had an opportunity to converse with Mr. Smidt as to the true state of the facts in reference to his having *voluntarily* furnished (as was alleged) a "substitute."

The note of the minister, with a translation thereof, you will find within, marked No. 1, together with my note in reply thereto, marked No. 2. I have not yet had the honor to hear from my government in regard to this case of Mr. Smidt, but I am very well satisfied that, in a matter in which the rights of one of our naturalized citizens are so materially involved as are those of Mr. Smidt, it becomes my duty, as it is my wish, to act with promptitude.

I have, as yet, received no reply from the minister.

I have the honor to be, with great respect, your obedient servant,

JAMES M. BUCHANAN.

Hon. Lewis Cass,
Secretary of State.

P. S. In one of my dispatches I spoke of Mr. Smidt as a clergyman of the Methodist Episcopal church. I am informed by the Rev. C. Willerup that he is more particularly an "exhorter" in that church.

J. M. B.

[Translation.]

Copenhagen, *October* 25, 1859.

Sir: In writing you on the 26th ultimo respecting Mr. Böie Schmidt, I had an impression upon my mind that the competent authorities would experience some difficulty in complying with the demand contained in your dispatch to me of the 21st of the same month, yet the said authorities, by the minister for the Duchy of Sleswick, has nevertheless declared, with the view of acceding to my request to meet your wishes, that he was quite willing, by means of a special and exceptive measure, to remove the formal obstacles which had prevented the discharge of Mr. Schmidt.

It appears, however, from the inquiries which it was necessary to institute previous to the accomplishment of this object, that the interference of his Majesty's government in this matter has become superfluous, inasmuch as the minister for the Duchy of Sleswick has just informed me that the individual in question, whose real name is Boi Christianson Schmidt, on the 22d of September, being the day following that on which I received your first communication, and previous to my having got into possession of your letter of the 27th of the same month, had already presented himself before the committee of conscription, and having been permitted, in accordance with his own request, to provide a substitute for the performance of the military service, he has discharged himself from the obligation in question.

Finally, I beg to call your attention to the fact that B. C. Schmidt's stay within his Majesty's dominions has not been a short one, but that he rather seems to have taken up his residence in the Duchy of Sleswig.

Please accept, sir, the assurance of my most distinguished consideration,

C. HALL.

Mr. BUCHANAN,
Minister Resident of the United States of America.

LEGATION OF THE UNITED STATES,
Copenhagen, October 18, 1859.

SIR: I had the honor to receive, on the day before yesterday, your note of the 27th of last month, in reference to the case of Mr. Boie Smidt, a naturalized citizen of the United States. From the tenor of the note of your excellency, I am given to understand that "The competent authorities, namely, the minister for the Duchy of Sleswig, was quite willing, by means of a special and exceptive measure, to remove the formal obstacles which had prevented the discharge of Mr. Smidt," but that the interference of his Majesty's government had been rendered superfluous in the premises, inasmuch as the individual in question, Mr. Smidt, had thought proper, on the 23d of September last, to present himself before the committee of conscription, and ask permission to furnish a substitute; that the permission had been granted to Mr. Smidt to furnish a substitute; that he did furnish a substitute, and that by that act he had discharged himself from "the obligation" in question. It seems, then, that although Mr. Smidt is in person relieved from his arrest, he has not been so relieved from any act of the government of Denmark; but it is averred that he *has been relieved from his arrest* by means of his having procured of his own free will a substitute. I am very well satisfied that your excellency is not apprised of the whole state of the facts attending the furnishing of this substitute by Mr. Smidt; for if you were, I could not avoid the conclusion that your excellency would concur with myself in the opinion that the substitute should be at once discharged, and Mr. Smidt reimbursed by the government of Denmark the expense he has been subjected to in procuring the substitute. The facts as derived by me on yesterday from Mr. Smidt are substantially as follows:

Mr. Smidt is a naturalized citizen of the United States. A little more than two years ago he returned to Denmark, his native country, to visit his parents, intending to return again to the United States. Whilst here in Denmark, he was employed by the Rev. C. Willerup, a clergyman of the Methodist Episcopal church of the United States, as colporteur, to distribute books, tracts, &c., belonging to that denomination of Christians. In September last, when in Sleswig, engaged in the legitimate performance of his duties, he was arrested, and ordered to repair to Copenhagen, to be put into the naval service of his Majesty the King of Denmark. Mr. Smidt informed the "*cancel-*

ieraad" who had caused his arrest that he was a naturalized citizen of the United States.

He was told in reply, that that made no difference, and that if he did not repair at once to Copenhagen, and surrender himself to the authorities, he would be taken there by force. Under these circumstances Mr. Smidt made his appearance in Copenhagen.

He proceeded at once to the authorities, and explained to them that he was a naturalized citizen of the United States. This did not avail, and he was told he must enter on duty in the naval service of his Majesty the King; that he would either be put at work at the Three Crown Battery, or placed on board of a national vessel destined for the West Indies. This being the position in which Mr. Smidt found himself placed, and learning from the authorities that there was no hope of his being relieved, he asked as a necessity if he might be permitted to put some one in his place, protesting at the same time that the government of Denmark had no proper claim upon him. Permission was granted, and Mr. Smidt furnished a substitute at a cost far beyond his ability to bear. This substitute was furnished by Mr. Smidt *not* voluntarily, as has been suggested, but on compulsion.

He was under arrest, and he had no other alternative which he could then avail himself of. It is proper to mention that Mr. Smidt applied to me to ascertain from me what, in my judgment, his rights might be, and I informed him that, according to my understanding of the case, the government of Denmark had no claim upon him, and that any unauthorized act of his (Mr. Smidt) would not be considered by me as at all obligatory upon myself as the representative of the government of the United States at this court.

I am sure, from the facts I have narrated above, your excellency will agree with me that Mr. Smidt ought not to be held bound by any agreement he may have entered into whilst under arrest, and whilst surrounded by the circumstances adverted to. It is not necessary for me to remind your excellency that from my first communication with you in reference to this case of Mr. Smidt, I have been of opinion, and have so expressed it to you, after very careful examination of all the facts and circumstances, that neither at the time of the arrest of Mr. Smidt, nor subsequently thereto, had the government of Denmark any claim upon him whatsoever.

I hardly need say that I continue of that opinion up to this time, and mention it now only for the purpose of indicating that I do not consider the discharge of Mr. Smidt alone, in the manner in which it has been made, as satisfactory. In reference to the last paragraph in the note of your excellency, without perceiving its direct point, I am enabled to say, in reply, that Mr. Smidt is a resident, or rather a sojourner in Copenhagen, and has no idea whatever of locating permanently in any part of Denmark, or *elsewhere* than in the United States of America.

I beg to assure your excellency of my very sincere and high regard,

JAMES M. BUCHANAN.

His Excellency C. HALL,
Minister of Foreign Affairs, &c., &c., &c.

Mr. Schleiden to Mr. Cass.

BREMEN LEGATION,
Washington, D. C., November 28, 1859.

SIR: Your note of the 9th of April last, relative to the surrender by Bremen to other German States of naturalized citizens of the United States from whom military service is claimed, only came to hand after I had left Washington, and was on the eve of embarking for Europe. Under these circumstances I deemed it proper to abstain from replying to your note until I should have had an opportunity of laying the matter again before my government, and of ascertaining whether your observations would change its views as explained in my notes of October 23, 1858, and March 16 last. My sojourn at Bremen afforded the desired opportunity, and I am instructed to submit the following remarks to your consideration:

In your note of the 9th of April last you question the propriety of Bremen surrendering naturalized American citizens, deserters from the military service of their native State, on the ground that Bremen is bound by treaty (convention of December 20, 1827,) to give special protection to the persons and property of citizens of the United States, of all occupations, who may be in her territories, either transient or dwelling therein, as long as they have committed no breach of her laws nor are charged with crime anywhere, and on the further ground that Bremen has no concern with any political questions which may be raised by a third power as to the respective duties which such an American citizen owes to that power and to the United States.

Bremen fully acknowledges her obligation to give protection to all American citizens, of all occupations, without making any distinction between native and naturalized citizens of the United States. My government is, however, of the opinion that in claiming and exercising, in certain distinct cases, the right of surrendering a naturalized citizen of the United States to another German State, from the military service of which he had deserted, it does not violate this solemn obligation, construing, as it does, the treaty stipulation of 1827 in the same sense as the American government, by limiting the protection due to American citizens to such cases where those citizens have neither committed a breach of the Bremen laws nor are charged with crime anywhere. Neither of the two high contracting parties could, in promising protection to the citizens of the other party, intend or be willing to renounce the right belonging, according to international law, to every independent State, to surrender foreign criminals, fugitives from justice, to another State with which it might have concluded, or afterwards should conclude, extradition treaties, and to make its territory an asylum for such foreign criminals.

Applying this principle and this construction of the treaty of 1827 to the question at issue, it seems not to be doubtful that desertion from military service and the breach of the oath of fealty is not only according to the laws of Bremen and of every other German State, but also according to the laws of the United States, (see article 20 of war, of April 10, 1806, and act of Congress approved May 29, 1830,) regarded as a crime punishable with death or other severe punishment. But even if the United States should not view the act of desertion from their military service in the light of a crime justifying the demand of the extradition of the deserter, this would not make any difference, and not deprive Bremen of the right of concluding treaties with other States for the mutual delivery of deserters.

It is the object of all extradition treaties between different States to assist one another in having criminals brought to justice and not allowing them to escape punishment by fleeing to another country. In determining what crimes are to be deemed of sufficient gravity to make them a cause for the extradition of the perpetrator, every State has to consult its own interests, and if these interests should make the extradition advisable, no other State, the citizen of which the criminal may be, will, in the absence of express treaty stipulations, have a right to object, and still less to invoke special protection for such offender.

My government holds that desertion from the military service of any of the German States comes under that class of offenses (crimes) where, even without regard to the laws and regulations of the German Confederacy, the interest of Bremen itself may justify the surrender of the offender, (see my note of 16th March last,) and that no other State would have a right to complain of such surrender, on the ground that the deserter had, in the mean time, become its citizen. My government cannot consider a deserter from military service in the light of a political refugee, nor his act as a mere political offense. If the fact of desertion is proved it cannot make any difference that the individual (deserter) has afterwards, by deceiving the authorities of a foreign State in regard to his integrity and his *bona fide* expatriation, become the citizen of such foreign State; and it is the less expected that the United States government should ever claim special protection for a naturalized American citizen, a deserter from the military service of his native State, who has thus surreptitiously obtained the citizenship of the United States, as the difficult question of expatriation, though frequently discussed in the courts of the United States, has never been definitely settled there by judicial decision. Under such circumstances, it would be contrary to the well known sense of justice of this government, if it would not acknowledge the right of foreign governments to regulate the forms and modes of expatriation for their citizens as they may think proper.

According to most of the extradition treaties concluded by the United States, they do not hesitate to surrender even their own citizens, native as well as naturalized citizens, who, after having committed in a foreign country a crime warranting in their views such extradition, return to the States. They also would certainly not object against Bremen surrendering an American citizen charged with murder or arson, or robbery in any of the German States, and they would not expect Bremen to inquire into the natural or subsequent allegiance of such criminal, provided that the crime itself had been proved. Still less they would hesitate to surrender, in accordance with an extradition treaty with any foreign country, a Bremen citizen to such foreign country, notwithstanding the protection promised by the treaty of 1827, whenever he had there committed a crime, the parties being in all cases the judges as to the offenses (crimes) to be embraced in such treaties. This point of view will also hold good in the case of the crime charged being desertion, and may apply as well to native as to naturalized citizens. I may be permitted further to add, that in view of the large number of unnaturalized foreigners in the army and navy of the United States, it would scarcely be claimed that it is not competent for them to conclude an extradition treaty with a foreign nation for the delivery of any person who may have deserted from their service, to whatever nation such deserter may belong, and although he may never have been naturalized in the States.

It is a recognized rule of international law, recognized anew in your note of the 9th of April last, that a State to which allegiance has been transferred has not the right to protect the citizen against his former government, if by his voluntary act, he again places himself within its power, and as stated in my note of October 23, 1858, it is only a simple consequence of this principle that it would also not be competent for such State to protect its naturalized citizen from the operation of the laws of his native country, in case he should go to another foreign country, which by treaty, is bound to surrender him, on application to his native State, as a deserter or fugitive from justice. Far from interfering with any political question which may be raised, as to the respective duties which such an individual owes to his native State, and to his adopted country, the government of a third State to which he proceeds will, whenever his extradition as a deserter or fugitive from justice is demanded by his native State, only have to consult the facts of the crime charged, and the tenor of the treaties by which it is bound to surrender criminals in certain cases. In claiming, therefore, the right of surrendering an American citizen to another German State from the military service of which he had deserted, my government disavows any intention to decide his political relations, which may be the subject of discussion between that State and the United States.

I regret that a disregard of treaty obligations on the part of Bremen should ever have become the subject of our official correspondence as in the range of possibility, and anxious to avoid even the semblance of a want of regard for the rights of American citizens, my government has deemed it necessary to give this answer to your note of the 9th of April last.

Whatever the practical issue of the question may be, and whatever course the circumstances of the case may dictate to my government, I trust that it will never be difficult to justify such course as being in full conformity with the spirit of our treaties, and with the feelings of sincere friendship for the United States government, and a proper appreciation of the rights of its citizens, I avail myself of this occasion to offer to you renewed assurances of my high consideration,

R. SCHLEIDEN.

General Lewis Cass,
Secretary of State of the United States, Washington, D. C.

Mr. Calhoun to Mr. Cass.

No. 11.] LEGATION OF THE UNITED STATES,
Paris, December 6, 1859.

SIR: In your dispatch, No. 189, dated Washington, June 27, 1859, you instructed Mr. Mason to procure and transmit to the Department of State reliable information concerning the French conscription laws relating to American naturalized citizens born in France, who may at any time revisit their native country.

A copy of Mr. Mason's letter on this subject, addressed to his excellency Count Walewski, accompanied by his dispatch, No. 407, dated Paris, August 2, 1859.

I have the honor now to transmit a copy of the reply of the minister of foreign affairs to Mr. Mason's communication.

I have the honor to be, very respectfully, your obedient servant,
W. R. CALHOUN.

Hon. LEWIS CASS,
Secretary of State, Washington.

[Translation.]

Paris, November 25, 1859.

SIR: I have the honor to communicate to you the reply of the government of the Emperor to the questions which the deceased Mr. Mason had put to him in his letter of 27th July last, relative to Frenchmen emigrants to the United States who have there obtained letters of naturalization.

After having set forth the principles of the American law in the matter of naturalization, Mr. Mason reduced his inquiry to a formula, as follows:

First Question.—Does the French legislation recognize in individuals, French by birth, the right to cause themselves to be naturalized as subjects or citizens of a foreign country, without preliminary authorization from the government?

French legislation does not confer on a Frenchman the right to renounce his nationality, but he loses it by positive law (article 7, Code Napoleon,) through naturalization in a foreign country.

That naturalization, by the terms of the decree of August 26, 1811, may have grave consequences, provided for by that decree, when it has not been authorized by the government.

Even in cases in which such authorization has been accorded, it effectively disperses the prejudicial results of an unauthorized naturalization, but expressly maintains the loss of nationality.

Second Question.—Are Frenchmen by birth, but naturalized citizens of the United States, who return to France without having the intention to recover their nationality nor to establish themselves permanently, subject to the law of conscription?

The law of conscription imposes on every Frenchman the obligation of military service. It attaches to the fulfillment of this obligation a penal sanction.

Therefore, the Frenchman, who, before he had lost that quality, shall have emigrated, thus placing himself out of the way of the obligation of military service, would assuredly be punishable on his return to France, even although he should have obtained a foreign naturalization, and he may be prosecuted, whether as refractory, (Article 230, du Nouveau Code Militaire, loi du 9 Juin, 1859,) or as a deserter, (Articles 235, 236, 237, of same date.)

This, moreover, is recognized by the government of the United States, as it is a sequence from the letter of Mr. Mason, that it refuses its protection to the Frenchman become a stranger, in the two cases following:

1st. If the obligation of military service be anterior to the epoch of emigration.

2. If, before his emigration, the Frenchman had not satisfied the law of conscription. The question becomes more difficult when it treats of a man born abroad of French parents, and who, consequently, by the provisions of article 10 of Code Napoleon, is himself a Frenchman, and bound to military service, in conformity with article 6 of the law of March 21, 1832.

But if, in France, the quality of citizen is now actually acquired by parentage, yet, for a long time, nativity alone conferred it, and it may still be so in the United States. In such a case, it would be hard to subject to French law an individual who should have fulfilled similar obligations towards the country in which he was born.

Third question. Does the French law of conscription render the Frenchman, born and resident in a foreign country, subject to military service in the same degree as if he had not left the country of his birth, or as if he had not caused himself to be naturalized as a foreigner?

This question is disposed of by the solution which the federal government itself admits to the second.

If, in effect, the Frenchman, before emigrating and causing himself to be naturalized in a foreign country, has not satisfied the obligation of military service, evidently he may be prosecuted in France, in case of his return, even though the return should be only accidental. Besides, he might, during his absence, have been sentenced for contumacy, and his presence in France would impose, as well on the public authority as himself, the duty of clearing off this contumacy.

Such are the solutions which the three questions that the legation of the United States has presented to me can receive. It is difficult, moreover, to treat them theoretically, without knowledge of the circumstances which may have given birth to them, which often are of a nature to draw out modifications of the application of strict law.

I will add that all the points treated in the present dispatch present veritable questions of state, upon which the government of the Emperor can only express opinions, but the solutions belong exclusively to the courts.

Receive sir, the assurance of high consideration with which I have the honor to be, your very humble and obedient servant,

WALEWSKI.

Mr. CALHOUN,

Chargé d'Affaires of the United States at Paris.

Mr. Cass to Mr. Calhoun.

No. 7.]

DEPARTMENT OF STATE,
Washington, December 31, 1859.

SIR: Your dispatch No. 11, of the 6th instant, has been received. You are aware of the circumstances which make it important that we should have precise information in regard to those provisions of the French law which may affect naturalized citizens of the United States. The note of Mr. Mason to Count Walewski, of the 27th of July last, expresses the views which are maintained by the United States in regard to the exemption from involuntary military service due to their naturalized citizens in foreign countries, and is entirely approved by the President.

The principles of the French law, as explained by Count Walewski in his note to you of the 25th ultimo, might, if rigidly enforced, seriously affect the rights of American citizens, and we indulge the confident expectation that the French government will take such measures as may be necessary to prevent persons born in France and naturalized in the United States, when returning for temporary purposes to the land of their birth, from being held responsible for the non-performance of any military duty, unless they had actually been called upon to perform such duty previous to their emigration. There is a misapprehension upon this point in Count Walewski's note which it is important should be corrected, and you will embrace the first favorable opportunity for this purpose. It is not understood that under any circumstances is a returned Frenchman, naturalized in the United States, liable to be required to perform military service; but he is held criminally responsible, and subject to punishment, for having left France without fulfilling every duty which during life he would be held to render. Count Walewski supposes that this is a principle also recognized by the government of the United States. In this, however, there is a grave error. The note of Mr. Mason does not justify this inference. The minister of foreign affairs deduces from it the admission that the United States refuse their protection to the Frenchman become a naturalized citizen in the two following cases:

1. If the obligation of military service be anterior to the epoch of emigration.

2. If, before his emigration, the Frenchman had not satisfied the law of conscription.

These positions are not in accordance with the principles maintained by the United States, nor are they legitimate deductions from the views presented by Mr. Mason. On the contrary, his note states clearly and briefly our doctrine to be, that the naturalized emigrant cannot be made responsible, on his return, for any military duty, unless he had been actually required to perform it before his emigration, and had deserted from it. We do not recognize the binding obligation of contingent duties depending for their performance upon time and other future circumstances. Accompanying this, you will receive the copy of a letter of instructions, of the 8th of July last, to the minister of the United States at Berlin, respecting a case affecting an American citizen which recently occurred in the kingdom of Hanover. This dispatch, together with the letter to Mr. Hofer, of which you have a copy, contains the views of this government on the subject of the rights of naturalized American citizens returning to their native country. You will also receive, herewith, a copy of two other dispatches on the same subject, to our minister at Berlin. It is considered unnecessary to enter, at present, into any further consideration of the matter.

It is very desirable that an understanding should exist between this government and that of France, by which all danger of collision upon this important subject should be avoided. We cannot believe that the pretension to punish an American naturalized citizen for leaving France, when by so doing he violated no actual existing duty he was then required to perform, will be enforced in France. It is not expected you should urge this subject with undue haste, as there is no practical case now requiring action; but, as opportunity offers, you will present it to Count Walewski, explain to him precisely the position we occupy, and make known to him our wish that the French government should adopt such measures as will protect American citizens, under the circumstances stated, from being interfered with on their return to France.

There is one remark in the note of Count Walewski to you to which it may be well to advert. It is stated that, by the French code, a man born abroad of French parents is bound, on his return, to perform military service. But I understand it to be conceded by Count Walewski that this provision does not apply in cases where such person is born in a country which recognizes nativity as carrying with it the right of citizenship. That is an essential part of our political institution, and the soundness of the French position is, therefore, no subject for our consideration.

I am, sir, respectfully, your obedient servant,

LEWIS CASS.

W. R. Calhoun, Esq.,
&c., &c., &c.

Mr. Ricker to Mr. Cass.

[Extract.]

No. 4.] Consulate General of the United States of America,
Frankfort-on-the-Main, January 4, 1860.

Sir: I have the honor to inclose a copy of a letter just received from Mr. Joseph Schierberg, dated at Damme, in the Grand Duchy of Oldenburg, 2d instant. It seems to call for some stronger action than a vice-consular officer is able to exercise, however energetically disposed he may be. It is the old story—of which cases are springing up every day—of claims on American citizens with American passports, to perform German military service. His excellency Minister Wright, no doubt, fell into the error of supposing that my district extended over Oldenburg, from the circumstance plain enough to everybody in this country, that such an arrangement would be far more judicious and proper than the present one. I have replied to Mr. Schierberg that he should apply to Mr. Vice-consul Doering; but, in case of his absence or of his inability to render him the required assistance, to write to me again, and I would endeavor, in some way or other, to get a protest before the Oldenburg government. * *

I have the honor to be, with great respect, sir, your obedient, servant,

SAMUEL RICKER.

Hon. Lewis Cass,
Secretary of State, Washington.

Damme, Grand Dukedom of Oldenburg,
January 2d, 1860.

Dear Sir: I was arrested in this place on the 28th of December, 1859, for owing military service to the Grand Duke of Oldenburg, at eight o'clock in the morning, by an officer of the above-named government and taken to the "*Amt-House*," or before the magistrate of this town, who had a warrant for me, which he read to me; and he gave me the choice of being taken on foot to the capital of this country, the city of Oldenburg, or give bonds to the amount of eighteen hundred ($1,800) dollars in Prussian currency. I preferred the latter, and gave bonds for that amount. I emigrated from Damme in the year 1835, in the month of March or April, with all our family, my mother being a widow at that time, my father having died three years previous. I was at the time of our emigration to the United States nine years old. We arrived in Baltimore in June or July the same year, (1835,) and went to Cincinnati, Ohio, at which place I have resided ever since. I was naturalized in Cincinnati by a judge of the court of common pleas, when E. C. Roll was clerk of that court. I left Cincinnati at the age of thirty-one, on the 7th of September, 1859, for New York, and sailed on the Bremen steamer "New York," for Southampton, and went over to Havre, France; from thence to Paris, *via* Strasburg, to Frakfort-on-the-Main, where I staid several days at hotel "Landsberg;" from Frankfort to Hanover, and then to Osnabrück, and to this place, to visit some of my relations.

The above is a copy of a letter that I wrote to the Hon. Joseph A. Wright, United States minister at Berlin, Prussia, on the day of my arrest. I wrote to him also that I have a United States passport, signed by the Hon. Lewis Cass, (dated Washington, August 15, 1859,) Secretary of State; in which passport, my wife, three children, and servant are mentioned. I came to Europe on the advice of my doctor, on account of bad health, and I intend to return next summer to the United States.

The Hon. Joseph A. Wright, United States minister at Berlin, answers me as annexed.

Dear sir, you will confer a great favor to me by answering this letter. Myself and wife feel somewhat uneasy in this case. You will please answer at your earliest convenience.

Yours, respectfully, &c.,

JOSEPH SCHIERBERG.

Hon. SAMUEL RICKER,
U. S. Consul General, Frankfort-on-the-Main.

BERLIN, *December* 31, 1859.

DEAR SIR: Yours of the 28th instant is before me. The Oldenburg government has no right to your military service. Your arrest is a great outrage. You are an American citizen, and entitled to full protection. I am not, however, accredited to the government which has arrested you. You should write immediately to Mr. Ricker, our consul general at Frankfort-on-the-Main, who will promptly attend to your case and give all necessary instruction and aid. I believe he has a vice-consul at Oldenburg.

In haste, &c.,

JOSEPH A. WRIGHT.

Mr. JOSEPH SCHIERBERG,
Damme, &c.

Mr. Doering to Mr. Appleton.

[Extract.]

No. 1.] CONSULATE OF THE UNITED STATES,
Oldenburg, January 12, 1860.

SIR: * * * * * * * *

I have to inform the department of the arrest of an American citizen, Mr. Joseph Schierberg, from Cincinnati, by the Oldenburg government, as being held liable to military service; he having emigrated to the United States in his ninth year, with his mother. Mr. Schierberg, at his arrest in Damme, addressed himself to our minister in Berlin, his excellency Joseph A. Wright, but the same not being accredited to this government, referred Mr. Schierberg to Mr. Ricker, consul general of the United States in Frankfort. This consulate not being within the consular general district of Mr. Ricker, Mr. Schierberg was directed by the same to apply to me, as vice-consul of the Grand Duchy of Oldenburg, for redress.

Mr. Schierberg having given bonds for 1,800 thalers, was permitted to come to Oldenburg, and called on me for his protection as an American citizen. I called immediately on Mr. Von Råssing, minister of the foreign department, stated the circumstances of Mr. Schierberg, and asked for his release. The minister asserted the full justice of their claim upon Mr. Schierberg, and that the acquired citizenship of the

United States did not release him of his duty owing unto them. I told the minister that our government would protect Mr. Schierberg, and claim his release; showed him also the answer which Mr. Schierberg had received from Mr. Joseph A. Wright, our minister, and that of our consul general, Mr. Ricker, for the same purpose. I referred also to the same circumstances, which but lately had happened in the kingdom of Hanover, and also this government had given up their claim and released the man. The minister finally declared that they could not go to war with the United States, but this matter could only be settled in the regular diplomatic way. They would consider the matter till to-morrow. If they would come to another conclusion, he would send me word; but if not, it would have to be settled as he stated.

These are the particulars of my interview with the minister of the foreign department. As no word was sent to me the next day, I presumed they had concluded not to release Mr. Schierberg, but hold on to their claim. I wrote therefore to his excellency Joseph A. Wright, all these particulars, submitted the whole to him, and asked for further instructions, as the minister of the foreign department on a similar occasion had refused to acknowledge Mr. Epping, the former consul here, as the proper diplomatic person to interfere.

However, to preserve the friendly intercourse which heretofore has existed between this and our government, I made some other personal efforts for the release of Mr. Schierberg. This morning I called on the attorney general, to ascertain what other proceedings they would enter upon. Here I received the assurance that all further prosecution against Mr. Schierberg would be dropped, he having proved that he had emigrated in his ninth year, as Schierberg asserts, to the United States. This will likely have been done at this time, and Mr. Schierberg was at liberty. Also of these facts I have informed our minister in Berlin, in a postscript.

The attorney general told me he intended to apply for a law that all those who emigrated or had emigrated before the seventeenth year of their age should not be held liable to military duty at their return here; and by such a law he hoped all future conflicts with the United States would be avoided.

Should any other circumstances in this case occur, or any other of this kind, I shall keep the department advised.

I am, sir, very respectfully, your obedient servant,

C. H. DOERING,
United States Vice-Consul.

JOHN APPLETON, Esq.,
Assistant Secretary of State, Washington, D. C.

Mr. Ricker to Mr. Cass.

[Extract.]

No. 26.] CONSULATE GENERAL OF THE UNITED STATES OF AMERICA.
Frankfort-on-the-Main, January 19, 1860.

SIR : I have the honor to hand you herewith the copy of a second letter received from Joseph Schierberg, dated at Damme, the 16th instant.

* * * * * * * * *

In my dispatch No. 21, of the 14th instant, it is stated that by the present system of reclamation, Germany did not recover from the many thousands who yearly emigrate, more than some half a dozen or less, for each State. That statement is not exactly correct. *All* Germany regains to her use not more than half a dozen yearly ; but in the aggregate the number is equal to some half a dozen for each German State, of those returned German travelers who require consular protection ; of those who are police-hunted, arbitrarily oppressed, or in some other manner unjustly molested ; of those who are prevented from accomplishing the purpose for which they have returned—being kept out of their native State, and consequently obliged to leave business transactions unsettled, in many cases forfeiting to the advantage of their former governments estates inherited, &c., merely from fear of arrest and molestation, annoyances from which their American nationality should of right afford them ample security.

I have the honor to be, with great respect, sir, your obedient servant,
SAMUEL RICKER.

Hon. LEWIS CASS,
Secretary of State, Washington.

DAMME, GRAND DUCHY OF OLDENBURG,
January 16, 1860.

Your letter of the 4th instant came duly to hand on the evening of the 6th. The next morning I left for Oldenburg. I called on Mr. C. H. Doering, United States vice-consul, stated to him my case ; also gave him your letter and that of the Hon. Joseph A. Wright, United States minister at Berlin. He said he would do for me all he could. He called on the proper officers of this government. He informed them that the United States government would protect me ; but it appears that the Oldenburg government do not acknowledge Mr. Doering as the authorized person to interfere in such cases. I informed Mr. Doering that I was anxious to have my case settled as soon as possible, on account of releasing my security. Mr. Doering accompanied me to the military court-house. I was examined by the doctor, then sent to the State's attorney, who asked me more questions than I could answer. I told him at what age I emigrated with our family to the United States, &c., &c., the same I wrote you in my former letter.

The State's attorney then told me to go to Damme, and prove before the magistrate that I emigrated at the age I stated; which I have done. I supposed that would end the case, but I was mistaken. The *amtmann* or magistrate told me I had to appear at the capital on the 18th instant, or forfeit my bonds. I leave in the morning for Oldenburg. I will inform you what disposal they make of my case. I shall not pay a dollar if they should impose a fine on me, and I hope the United States government will protect me. Mr. Doering has done all for me that was in his power.

I am, &c.,

JOSEPH SCHIERBERG.

Hon. Mr. Ricker,
United States Consul General, Frankfort-on-the-Main.

Mr. Cass to Mr. Schleiden.

Department of State,
Washington, January 26, 1860.

Sir: Your note of the 28th of November last, relative to the claim of Bremen to surrender naturalized citizens of the United States to the governments of other German States, on the ground of their being deserters from the military service of those States, was duly received, and has been taken into consideration.

In reply, I have to state that, while you correctly represent that, by the laws of the United States, desertion from the army is made a crime, a person charged therewith must be clearly shown to have incurred the obligation to serve.

The views of the President upon the subject are contained in the accompanying extract from an instruction of the 8th of June last, from this department, to the minister of the United States at Berlin. As this instruction denies the right of the German governments to claim military service from returning naturalized citizens of the United States under the circumstances there set forth, the right of Bremen to surrender them in order that that service may be required of them elsewhere, cannot, of course, be acquiesced in. On this latter point, the opinions of this government were so fully communicated to you on the 9th of April last, that I do not think it necessary to repeat them now. It is proper to add, however, that I had no intention in that communication to intimate a doubt of the entire good faith of the government of Bremen in its intercourse with other governments, because no such doubt is entertained by the United States. It was quite necessary, however, to inform you that the arrest of our citizens in Bremen, under the circumstances mentioned in your note of the 28th of November last, for the purpose of their extradition, would not be regarded by this government as consistent with such faith.

I avail myself of this occasion to offer to you, sir, renewed assurances of my high consideration.

LEWIS CASS.

Rudolph Schleiden, Esq.,
&c., &c., &c.

Mr. Cass to Mr. Buchanan.

No. 15.] DEPARTMENT OF STATE,
Washington, February 4, 1860.

SIR: Your dispatches, to No. 34 inclusive, have been received.

I have already conveyed to you the approbation of the President of the views you have presented to the government of Denmark respecting the case of Mr. Smidt. With regard to the reimbursement you have demanded of the amount paid by Mr. Smidt for a substitute, your course is also approved; and, if necessary, you will make known to the minister of foreign affairs the expectation of this government that the justice of the claim will be recognized and the amount refunded.

But it is proper to observe that we have no right to ask the return of the sum paid by Mr. Smidt for a substitute, and the discharge of such substitute also. The pecuniary remuneration to Mr. Smidt will satisfy our just demand upon the government of Denmark.

I am, sir, your obedient servant,

LEWIS CASS.

JAMES M. BUCHANAN, Esq., *&c. &c.,*
Copenhagen.

Mr. Ricker to Mr. Cass.

[Extract.]

No. 51.] CONSULATE GENERAL OF THE UNITED STATES OF AMERICA,
Frankfort-on-the-Main, February 14, 1860.

SIR: I have the honor to hand annexed the copy of a letter just received from Mr. Joseph Schierburg, dated at Damme, the 13th instant.

The particulars of Mr. Schierburg's case were brought to your notice in my dispatches Nos. 4 and 26. You will now perceive that he has been liberated by the attorney, on the ground that the doctor had found him unfit, and that he had emigrated at an early age with his parents.

* * * * * * * *

I have the honor to be, with great regard, sir, your obedient servant,

SAMUEL RICKER.

Hon. LEWIS CASS,
Secretary of State, Washington.

DAMME, *February* 13, 1860.

DEAR SIR: I was discharged at Oldenburg, by the State's attorney, on the ground that the doctor found me unfit for service, and that I emigrated to the United States at an early age with my parents. I would have written to you before this, but I have been unwell since my return from Oldenburg. I took a bad cold in the stage coach.

Please accept my thanks for the interest you have taken in my behalf.

Yours, respectfully, &c.,

JOSEPH SHIERBURG.

Hon. Mr. RICKER,

U. S. Consul General, Frankfort-on-the-Main.

Mr. Helm to Mr. Cass.

No. 5.] CONSULATE GENERAL OF THE UNITED STATES OF AMERICA,
Havana, February 22, 1860.

SIR: I have the honor to inform you that, in the early part of the past month, the governor of Sagua la Grande issued an order summoning Gabino de Liaño, a native of Spain, but a naturalized American citizen, temporarily at that place, to surrender himself at the barracks for military duty. Mr. Liaño presented himself at the government house and exhibited to the governor his certificate of naturalization, together with his passport and *carta de domicilia*, in both of which he is described as an American citizen; notwithstanding which, the governor ordered him to surrender himself at the barracks, go to prison, or give bond in the penalty of $318, which is the indemnity for the conscription. To save himself from prison, he executed the bond, under protest.

The inclosed copy of my correspondence with his excellency the captain general, superior governor of Cuba, will put you in possession of all the facts necessary to a full understanding of this case.

You will perceive that the captain general takes the broad ground that natives of Spain, who have become naturalized citizens of another power without the authorization of Spain, are, under *any* and *all* circumstances, upon returning to the dominions of Spain, subject to military duty, and says that Mr. Liaño, though but nine years of age when he emigrated to the United States, has no alternative but to pay the penalty of the bond or surrender himself for military duty; and that, in the absence of instruction, I have, in the most earnest manner, protested against any act by which Mr. Liaño will be forced into the service of Spain, or compelled to pay the penalty of the bond coerced from him, and executed under protest.

I did not think the note of his excellency the captain general left room for argument, and therefore deemed it proper merely to state that the government of the United States would not consent that her adopted citizens, when temporarily abroad, even when visiting or temporarily residing in the country of their nativity, should be forced by a foreign power to perform military duty, from which position I shall not depart. And I must state that I am of opinion the captain general has given, or will give, the order to the governor of Sagua la

Grande to enforce the penalty of the bond, or compel Liaño to enter the service of Spain. Under these circumstances, I must ask full instruction in the premises at your earliest convenience.

I am, with profound respect, your obedient servant,

CH. J. HELM.

Hon. LEWIS CASS,
Secretary of State, Washington.

CONSULATE GENERAL OF THE UNITED STATES OF AMERICA,
Havana, January 18, 1860.

SIR: I have the honor to inform you that orders were recently issued by the lieutenant governor at Sagua la Grande for the arrest of Gavino de Liaño, a citizen of the United States, with the view of forcing him to perform military duty as a Spanish subject. The facts, as I am informed and believe, are as follows: Gavino de Liaño, when nine years of age, emigrated with his parents from Spain to America, and that when he arrived at the proper age he was admitted under our naturalization laws a citizen of the United States; that in May, 1858, he came to Cuba with a passport issued by the Spanish consul resident at San Francisco, in which he is described as an American citizen; that shortly after his arrival here he was compelled to take out, as an American citizen, a *carta de domicilia,* and has remained in this island, recognized in all his intercourse with officials and private individuals as a citizen of the United States; that when advised of the order for his arrest he presented himself in person to the governor and exhibited to him his certificate of naturalization, claiming his exemption from military duty and his rights as an American citizen; notwithstanding which, the governor ordered him to give security in the sum of $318 as the substitute for the conscription, go to prison, or surrender himself at the barracks; that to save himself from imprisonment he gave the security, under protest.

Mr. Liaño avers that in coming to Cuba he never intended to resume his original nationality, but that from the time he first landed at Havana to the present moment he has on all proper occasions proclaimed himself a citizen of his adopted country; that the *carta de domicilia* granted to him by this government is a full recognition of his American citizenship; in fact, it was because of his foreign citizenship that he was compelled to take out this *grant of temporary residence.* I presume that, under the foregoing statement of facts, it will not be contended that Mr. Liaño owes military service to the Spanish government, and must therefore request that your excellency cause the bond executed by Mr. Liaño to be canceled, and all further proceedings against him by reason of the foregoing to be dismissed.

I have the honor to be, with profound respect, your obedient servant,

CH. J. HELM.

His Excellency the Capt. Gen. DON FRANCISCO SERRANO,
Superior Governor of Cuba, &c., &c , &c.

[Translation.]

GOVERNMENT CAPTAIN GENERALCY AND SUPERINTENDENCY BY DELEGATION OF THE EVER FAITHFUL ISLAND OF CUBA. OFFICE OF THE GOVERNMENT SECRETARY, SECTION OF GOVERNMENT No. 3973.

HAVANA, *February* 14, 1860.

Being informed of the contents of your communication dated the 17th of January, in order to consider as exempted from the military service of Spain the young man Don Gavino de Liaño, as he appears inscribed as a citizen of the United States, I have to state that, even not taking into account the age he had when, with an uncle of his, he came from the peninsula to North America, for similar cases the royal decree of the 17th November, 1852, declares "that the foreigner obtaining naturalization in Spain, as well as the Spaniard obtaining it within the territory of another power, without the knowledge and authorization of his respective government, shall not exempt himself from the obligations which were consequent to his primitive nationality, although the subject of Spain may in other respects lose the quality of a Spaniard, conformably to what is prescribed in article 1st of the constitution of the monarchy." For which reason he has no recourse left to him but to enter the military service or redeem himself with the quota of indemnity.

God preserve you many years.

FRCO. SERRANO.

The CONSUL GENERAL OF THE UNITED STATES.

GOBIERNO CAPA. GENERAL Y SUPERINTENDENCIA DELEGADA DE HACIENDA DE LA SIEMPRE FIEL ISLA DE CUBA. SECRETARIA DE GOBIERNO, SECCION DE GOBIERNO No. 3973.

HABANA, 14 *de Febrero de* 1860.

Enterado de la comunicacion de V. S. fecha 17 de Enero en órden á considerar exento del servicio militar de España al jóven Don Gabino de Liaño por aparecer inscripto como ciudadano de los Estados Unidos, debo manifestar que, aun prescindiendo de la edad en que pasó con untio suyo de la peninsula al Norte América, en casos semejantes el real decreto de 17 de Noviembre de 1852, declara "que el estrangero que obtuviere naturalizacion en España, así como el Español que la obtuviere en el territorio de otra potencia, sin el conocimiento y autorízacion de su gobierno respectivo, no se libertará de las obligaciones que eran consiguíentes á su nacionalidid primitiva, aunque el súbdīto de España pièrda en otro concepto la calidad de Español, con arreglo á lo dispuesto en el artículo 1° de la constitucion de la monarquia." Por lo cual no le queda mas que entrar en el servicio milítar ó redimirse con la cuota de indemnizaciòn.

Dion guarde á V. S. muchos anos.

FRCO. SERRANO.

Sōr CÓNSUL GENL DE LOS ESTADOS UNIDOS.

CONSULATE GENERAL OF THE UNITED STATES OF AMERICA,
Havana, February 20, 1860.

SIR: I have the honor to acknowledge the receipt of your excellency's note of the 14th instant, in reply to my communication of the 17th ultimo, asking that the proceedings against Gavino de Liaño, a naturalized American citizen, temporarily residing at Sagua la Grande, who had been summoned by the governor of that place to surrender himself at the barracks for military service, be dismissed, and the bond coerced from him, and executed under protest, be discharged.

I had hoped, and from the conversation I had with your excellency on the subject did believe, that Mr. Liaño would not be pursued further, and hence the decision of your excellency, as communicated to me in your note, was read with great regret and some surprise.

The government of the United States will not consent that her adopted citizens when temporarily abroad, even when visiting or temporarily residing in the country of their nativity, shall be forced by a foreign power to perform military duty; and I must, in the most earnest and solemn manner, in the absence of instructions from my government, object to any act by which Mr. Liaño will be forced into the military service of Spain, or be compelled to pay the bond coerced from him as the indemnity for the conscription.

I have the honor to be, with personal regards and profound respect, your most obedient servant,

CHARLES J. HELM.

His Excellency the Capt. Gen. DON FRANCISCO SERRANO,
Superior Governor and Captain General of Cuba, &c., &c.

CONSULATE GENERAL OF THE UNITED STATES,
Havana, February 20, 1860.

SIR: I herewith inclose you a copy of my correspondence with his excellency the captain general, on the subject of the attempt by the governor of Sagua la Grande to force Gavino de Liaño, a naturalized American citizen, to perform military duty in the service of Spain.

I will thank you to instruct or advise Mr. Liaño not to pay the bond, as I am satisfied the government of the United States will protect him in his rights as an American citizen.

I am, sir, very respectfully, your obedient servant,

CHARLES J. HELM.

HUGH MARTIN, Esq.,
United States Consul at Matanzas.

Mr. Cass to Mr. Helm.

DEPARTMENT OF STATE,
Washington, March 3, 1860.

SIR: Your dispatch, No. 5, has been received, inclosing your correspondence with the captain general on the subject of a recent order issued by the governor of Sagua la Grande, summoning a naturalized citizen of the United States, temporarily residing at that place, to surrender himself at the barracks for military duty.

A copy of the correspondence which you have transmitted respecting this affair has been sent to the United States minister at Madrid, who has been requested to call the attention of the government of her Catholic Majesty, without delay, to this case, as one in which much interest is felt by the President, involving as it does the claim of a foreign government to interfere with the personal security and liberty of citizens of the United States whose interests may require them to return temporarily to the respective countries of which they were once inhabitants. This claim which, as you are aware, is denied by the government of the United States, has, in all recent cases, been yielded without hesitation, upon a representation of this government respecting it. These views are given in a dispatch of the 8th of July last, addressed to Mr. Wright, at Berlin, a printed copy of which you will receive with this communication.

Fortunately, such cases as the one in question are not likely to be of frequent occurrence, and the President indulges the confident hope that the government of her Catholic Majesty will at once direct its authorities in Cuba to put a stop to all further proceedings against Mr. Liaño, and, at the same time, take such measures as may prevent the recurrence of similar proceedings so likely to interrupt the friendly relations of the two countries.

I am, sir, your obedient servant,

LEWIS CASS.

C. J. Helm, Esq.,
United States Consul General, Havana.

Mr. Helm to Mr. Cass.

No. 7.] Consulate General of the United States of America,
Havana, February 28, 1860.

Sir: I have the honor to inform you that I received on yesterday a note from his excellency the captain general, superior governor of Cuba, informing me that he had resolved to cancel the bond executed by Gavino de Liaño, at Sagua la Grande, as the indemnity for the conscription, suspend all further proceedings against him, and submit the case to his government, with the recommendation that Gavino de Liaño be exempted from military duty; a copy of which, together with my reply, is herewith inclosed.

I am, sir, with great respect, your obedient servant,

CHARLES J. HELM.

Hon. Lewis Cass,
Secretary of State, Washington.

GOVERNMENT CAPTAIN GENERALCY AND SUPERINTENDENCY BY DELEGATION OF THE EXCHEQUER OF THE EVER FAITHFUL ISLAND OF CUBA.

OFFICE OF THE GOVERNMENT SECRETARY,
Havana, February 23, 1860.

I have received your communication of the 20th instant, in which you are pleased to present me some observations in respect to the declaration made by this superior civil government, in the case as to whether there is or not the obligation to enter the military service on the part of the young man Gavino de Liaño, a Spaniard by birth, now a citizen of the United States, residing at present in the town of Sagua la Grande, and demanded by the royal order of the 27th of May, 1858, as a conscript for the proportion of Santa Maria del Cazon in the peninsula.

Before entering into the merits of the case, taking notice of one of your remarks, I have to state that if, on your speaking to me confidentially upon this matter, I may have given you some expectations of a favorable result, it was in the understanding that it referred to a citizen of the United States, born in it, preserving his original nationality, and not subject to any of the obligations which the laws of Spain impose upon the natives of this country.

But the case is very different from that which I had understood. There appears in the *expediente* of the affair, in a manner which leaves no doubt that Gavino de Liaño was born in Spain; that at an early age he went to the United States, where he became naturalized, without the permission of the Spanish government; and that on his coming, at a later day, to the Island of Cuba, he fixed his residence at the said town of Sagua la Grande.

In this understanding, and considering the article 45th of the royal decree of 17th of November, 1852, in which it is definitely established that Spaniards obtaining letters of naturalization in a foreign country, without the authorization of her Majesty's government, shall, when they return to Spain, be subject to the same obligations as if they had never been naturalized in another country, I could not, in strict law, fail to apply to the young man, Gavino de Liaño, the sovereign command which has foreseen the case in which he finds himself.

According to the good principles of international policy, this question, in its present state, should be treated of at the court of Spain, directly between the minister plenipotentiary of the United States and her Majesty's government. Being desirous, however, of showing to you all deference, which you and the nation whose representative you are here deserve, recognizing that in the case of Gavino de Liaño there are some circumstances which may render it equitable that he be exempted from the military service; but in the impossibility of exceeding my powers, by leaving without effect the two sovereign commands before cited, I have resolved that the case be referred to her Majesty's government, with a report favorable to the pretension supported by you, and that until a definitive resolution be issued the proceedings against Liaño be suspended; that the bond be canceled; and that he be not compelled to perform military service. All of which I say to you for your information and in answer to your communication above mentioned. God preserve you many years.

FRCO. SERRANO.

The CONSUL GENERAL OF THE UNITED STATES, *in this city.*

CONSULATE GENERAL OF THE UNITED STATES OF AMERICA,
Havana, February 28, 1860.

SIR: I have the honor to acknowledge the receipt, on yesterday, of your note of the 23d instant, informing me that you had resolved to suspend all proceedings against Gavino de Liaño, and cancel the bond which he executed, under protest, as the indemnity for the conscription.

I shall, with great pleasure, forward a copy of your communication to Washington by the first mail, that the important international question involved in our correspondence may be acted on by the governments of her Catholic Majesty and the United States, either there or at Madrid.

I am, sir, with profound respect, your obedient servant,

CHARLES J. HELM.

His Excellency the Capt. Gen. DON FRANCISCO SERRANO,
Superior Governor of Cuba, &c., &c., &c.

Mr. Appleton to Mr. Helm.

DEPARTMENT OF STATE,
Washington, March 8, 1860.

SIR: Your dispatch No. 7 has been received, in which you state that the captain general has resolved to cancel the bond executed by Mr. Liaño as the indemnity for conscription, to suspend all further proceedings against him, and submit the case to his government, with the recommendation that Mr. Liaño be exempted from military duty.

The department has been much gratified to learn that the captain general has been induced to yield to your representations in this case, and relieve Mr. Liaño from the embarrassing condition in which he was placed. You will take an early opportunity of making known to the captain general how highly the courtesy which he has shown in this matter is appreciated by the government of the United States.

Your correspondence with the captain general has been read with interest and pleasure, and your proceedings receive the approval of the department.

I am, sir, your obedient servant,

JOHN APPLETON,
Assistant Secretary.

C. J. HELM, Esq.,
United States Consul General, Havana.

Mr. Ricker to Mr. Cass.

No. 61.] CONSULATE GENERAL OF THE UNITED STATES OF AMERICA,
Frankfort-on-the-Main, February 23, 1860.

SIR: Application has just been made to me for my official assistance in behalf of a Mr. Anton Weidmann, said to be a citizen of the United States, who is now in difficulty in Rhenish Bavaria, in consequence of a claim for personal military services.

I do not think it is within my power to assist Mr. Weidmann *effectually*, and an inadequate interference might even aggravate his position.

But it is proper that I should bring his case to your notice, and, by the present, I have the honor to do so, and to solicit, in his behalf, the needful protection against the outrage offered to him, and through him to every American citizen.

I have the honor to be, with great respect, &c.,

SAMUEL RICKER.

Hon. LEWIS CASS,
Secretary of State, Washington.

Mr. Buchanan to Mr. Cass.

[Extract.]

No. 45.] LEGATION OF THE UNITED STATES,
Copenhagen, February 26, 1860.

SIR: After I had closed my dispatch to you (No. 44) this morning, your dispatch (No. 15) came to hand.

I am truly glad to see that my course in regard to the case of the naturalized citizen, Mr. Boie Smidt, has been approved of by the President. You may rely on it, it is absolutely necessary to take strong ground in regard to the *just rights* of our naturalized citizens. They are constantly subjected to annoyances in Europe. I have several cases before me at present, but I do not apprehend much difficulty with any of them, if I can only myself be satisfied with the regularity and correctness of the *naturalization papers*. You will see, by my dispatch of to-day, that we have a new Danish ministry here; and I am gratified to believe that the new minister of foreign affairs is extremely well-inclined towards our government.

* * * * * * * *

I will have an immediate interview with his excellency, Mr. Hall, the new minister, in regard to the matter of Mr. Boié Smidt, and I doubt not it will, after a while, be satisfactorily arranged.

I have the honor to be, with great respect, your obedient servant,

JAMES M. BUCHANAN.

Hon. LEWIS CASS, *&c., &c., &c.*

Mr. Buchanan to Mr. Cass.

[Extract.]

No. 46.] LEGATION OF THE UNITED STATES,
Copenhagen, February 29, 1860.

SIR: I have the honor to inform you that on Monday last, the day after the reception of your dispatch No. 15, I addressed a note to his excellency Mr. Hall, the new minister of foreign affairs, asking an early interview with him, my object being to bring to his immediate notice the still unsettled case of Mr. Boie Smidt. Looking to the kind relations which have existed between Mr. Hall and myself, when he was at the head of the ministry of foreign affairs, and looking also to the fact that he and myself had had some correspondence, and much conversation, in respect to this case of Mr. Boie Smidt, whilst he (Mr. Hall) occupied that position, I thought it best to converse with him in person, rather than to address to him a formal communication.

* * * * * * * * *

At the time appointed I called on the minister of the foreign office. He received me with great kindness and cordiality. I explained to him the object of my visit, and I read to him that part of your dispatch terminating with the words "and the amount refunded;" the remainder of the dispatch I thought it better to reserve for further consideration,. inasmuch as I had been informed, but not by the Danish government, that the "substitute" had been already discharged. The minister heard patiently what I had to say, and I took occasion, among other things, mildly to remind him of what I had previously assured him, that the government of the United States would feel itself bound to vindicate the just rights of our naturalized citizens at all times and in all places.

The minister assured me that he had hoped the case of Mr. Smidt had been already settled, that he would take it into immediate consideration, and would determine it one way or another with as little delay as possible.

It is proper to say that although my interview with the minister was full, and, as far as it went, satisfactory to me, he by no means committed himself to any line of action. He desired time for examination and reflection, and I cheerfully acquiesced in the propriety of his taking it. The minister expressed his gratification that I have proposed to converse with him rather than to have addressed to him a formal note on the subject in question, and I assured him that it was always agreeable to me to converse freely with one who seemed so well disposed to do what might be just and proper.

I am inclined to think I may have some difficulty in obtaining the indemnity required, but still in the end I think I shall succeed.

I have the honor to be, with high respect, your obedient servant,

JAMES M. BUCHANAN.

Hon. LEWIS CASS,
Secretary of State.

Mr. Cass to Mr. Preston.

No. 25.] DEPARTMENT OF STATE,
Washington, March 1, 1860.

SIR: I have the honor herewith to transmit a copy of a dispatch of the 22d ultimo from the consul general of the United States at Havana to this department, on the subject of a recent order issued by the governor of Sagua la Grande, summoning a naturalized citizen of the United States, temporarily residing at that place, to surrender himself at the barracks for military duty.

It appears that Mr. Liaño, the individual alluded to, who is a native of Spain, answered the summons of the governor, and exhibited to him his certificate of naturalization, with other proofs of his American citizenship; notwithstanding which, however, he was ordered either to go to the barracks for the performance of the military service exacted of him, or give bond in the penalty of $318, as indemnity for the non-performance of such service. To escape being sent to prison, he executed the bond, under protest.

A copy of the correspondence respecting this affair which has taken place between the consul general of the United States and the captain general of Cuba accompanies the transcript of the former's dispatch, herewith sent.

You are requested to call the attention of the government of her Catholic Majesty, without delay, to this case, as one in which much interest is felt by the President, involving, as it does, the claim of a foreign government to interfere with the personal security and liberty of citizens of the United States whose interests may require them to return, temporarily, to the respective countries of which they were once inhabitants. This claim, which, as you are aware, is denied by the government of the United States, has, in all recent cases, been yielded without hesitation, upon representation of the views of this government respecting it. These views are given at length in a dispatch of the 8th of July last, addressed to Mr. Wright, at Berlin, a printed copy of which you will receive by the next mail.

Fortunately, such cases as the one in question are not likely to be of frequent occurrence; and the President indulges the confident hope that the government of her Catholic Majesty will at once direct its authorities in Cuba to put a stop to all further proceedings against Mr. Liaño, and at the same time take such measures as may prevent the recurrence of similar proceedings, so likely to interrupt the friendly relations of the two countries.

I am, sir, your obedient servant,

LEWIS CASS.

W. PRESTON, Esq., *&c.*, *&c.*, *Madrid.*

Mr. Cass to Mr. Ten Brook.

DEPARTMENT OF STATE,
Washington, March 7, 1860.

SIR: Your dispatch No. 8 has been received, with the draft of a communication which you propose to address to the Bavarian government, touching the case of Mr. Wittelshofer, and for which you desire the approval of the department. I am directed to acquaint you that subsequent to the receipt by the department of the first communication respecting the application of Mr. Wittelshofer, the whole subject of the rights of naturalized citizens of the United States, in connection with the claims of the several governments of which they were formerly subjects to their services for the performance of military duty, has received the careful consideration of the President.

The views entertained by the President upon this important subject are stated at length in a communication dated July 8, 1859, addressed to the United States minister at Berlin, a printed copy of which is transmitted herewith, for your information and guidance.

In place of the letter which you proposed to address to the Bavarian government, you are requested to lose no time in making known the views of the President to his excellency Baron Von Schrenck, the minister of the royal house and of foreign affairs, with whom you have had correspondence on the subject. You will be especially careful to assure his excellency that the American government has no desire to interfere in the slightest degree with the domestic affairs of Bavaria, or excuse the citizens of the United States who visit that kingdom for any crime which they may commit against its peace and order. It only demands, as it surely may rightfully do, that when its citizens who go there submit themselves in good faith to its laws, and conduct themselves in a peaceable and orderly manner, they shall be protected in their persons and property, and shall be permitted to enter and leave the kingdom without molestation.

The claim of any foreign government to interfere with the personal security and liberty of citizens of the United States whose interests may require them to return temporarily to their respective countries of which they were once inhabitants, and who have committed no crime or been guilty of no offense, is utterly denied by the government of the United States. In various recent cases of the arrest of naturalized citizens of the United States by foreign governments, for the performance of military service, such individuals have been released on a representation of the facts and a statement by the proper functionaries of the views of the American government in respect to this question.

Fortunately, such cases as that of A. Wittelshofer, or of Bernhard Schleck, who, as the department is to-day informed by the United States consul general at Frankfort, a copy of whose dispatch is herewith inclosed, has been called to the Bavarian army, and required to enter upon active service at Spire, on the 22d instant, are not likely to be of frequent occurrence, and the President indulges the confident hope that the Bavarian government will at once direct the proper authorities to put a stop to all further proceedings in the case of Schleck, and at the same time take such measures as may prevent the recurrence of similar proceeding so likely to interrupt the friendly relations of the two countries.

You are quite aware that it is only due to the courtesy of the Bavarian government to enter into a correspondence with a consular officer respecting the rights of naturalized citizens of the United States in Bavaria, a subject which more properly appertains to the duties of a diplomatic functionary, and that it may, without impropriety, decline any longer to continue with you the correspondence.

To meet this contingency, it has been thought proper to transmit a copy of this letter, and of the inclosures accompanying it, to the minister of the United States at Berlin, to whom you are requested to report your proceedings.

I am, sir, your obedient servant,

LEWIS CASS.

Andrew Ten Brook, Esq.,
United States Consul, Munich, Bavaria.

[Extract.]

No. 67.] Consulate General of the United States of America,
Frankfort-on-the-Main, February 28, 1860.

Sir: I have the honor to inform you that application has just been made to me for my official protection by Mr. Bernhard Schleck, citizen of the United States, bearer of passport No. 16,675, dated Washington, January 3, 1860.

The parents of Mr. Schleck died when he was about three years of age. He emigrated to America seven years ago, when at the age of about fourteen years, and has now come back to Rhenish Bavaria, his native country, to receive his paternal inheritance, amounting to something more than three thousand dollars, on which sum he has calculated to complete certain engagements in New York, and the loss of it will involve him in utter ruin.

Instead of friendly facilities to enable him to touch the capital, for which he expressly came, and then return to New York to attend to his business in that city, he has been called to the Bavarian army, and must enter upon active service, at Spire, on the 22d of next month. I suppose he might easily escape personal service; but it would be at the expense of the three thousand dollars fortune, on which Bavaria maintains a lien, and would no doubt be right glad to have an excuse to take into actual possession.

* * * * * * * *

I have the honor to be, with great respect, sir, your obedient servant,

SAMUEL RICKER.

Hon. Lewis Cass,
Secretary of State, Washington.

Mr. Cass to Mr. Preston.

No. 26.] Department of State,
Washington, March 8, 1860.

Sir: Since the date of my last instruction to you, a dispatch has been received at the department from Mr. C. J. Helm, the consul general of the United States at Havana, stating that he had received from the captain general of Cuba a note informing him that he had resolved to cancel the bond executed by Gavino de Liaño, at Sagua la Grande, as the indemnity for the conscription, suspend all further proceedings against him, and submit the case to his government with the recommendation that Gavino de Liaño be exempted from military duty. A copy of the dispatch of Mr. Helm, and its accompaniments, is herewith transmitted for your information.

Although it is not doubted that the intervention of this government in behalf of Mr. Liaño will result in his exemption from the military service exacted of him, the opportunity which his case presents is deemed a favorable one for pressing upon the government of her Catholic Majesty the necessity of its taking such precautionary measures as will prevent a recurrence of similar causes of complaint. You will, therefore, carry out the instructions contained in my last dispatch, and urge the speedy adoption of these measures on the part of her Majesty's government.

The views of the United States upon this subject, which are in accordance with the spirit of the age, will, it is confidently believed, finally prevail among all enlightened nations.

I am, sir, your obedient servant,

LEWIS CASS.

W. PRESTON, Esq., *&c.*, *&c.*, *Madrid.*

Mr. Ricker to Mr. Cass.

No. 72.] CONSULATE GENERAL OF THE UNITED STATES OF AMERICA,
Frankfort-on-the-Main, March 9, 1860.

SIR: In my No. 21 of the 14th January last, I brought to your notice the case of Mr. John Mägly, and at his urgent request, I now have the honor again to solicit your interference in his behalf. He has been required by the Bavarian government to perform military services, and has to enter upon active duties, at Spire, on the 22d of the present month.

* * * * * * * * * * *

I have the honor to be, &c.,

SAMUEL RICKER.

HON. LEWIS CASS,
Secretary of State, Washington.

Mr. Appleton to Mr. Ten Brook.

DEPARTMENT OF STATE,
Washington, March 18, 1860.

SIR: I transmit herewith a copy of a communication addressed to this department by S. Ricker, Esq., United States consul general at Frankfort, in relation to the case of Austin Weidmann, said to be a citizen of the United States, and who is now in difficulty in Bavaria. You will please report the facts of this case to the department for its consideration.

I am, sir, your obedient servant,

JOHN APPLETON,
Assistant Secretary.

A. Ten Brook, Esq.,
United States Consul, Munich.

Mr. Cass to Mr. Wright.

No. 30.]

Department of State,
Washington, March 30, 1860.

Sir: Herewith I have the honor to transmit a copy of a dispatch, dated the 7th instant, from the department to Mr. Ten Brook, consul of the United States at Munich, in reference to the case of Mr. Wittelshofer, which may possibly form the subject of a correspondence between yourself and the minister of foreign affairs at Bavaria.

Your dispatches to No. 119 of the 7th instant have been received.

I am, sir, your obedient servant,

LEWIS CASS.

Joseph A. Wright, Esq, *&c., Berlin.*

Mr. Appleton to Mr. Ricker.

Department of State,
Washington, April 5, 1860.

Sir: Your dispatches numbered 21 and 72, relating to the protection of naturalized citizens of the United States, have been received.

You will find the views entertained by the President upon this subject in a dispatch, a copy of which is herewith inclosed, addressed on the 7th ultimo to Mr. Ten Brook, the United States consul at Munich, and in a dispatch, dated July 8th, to the United States minister at Berlin, a printed copy of which is also transmitted for your information on this subject.

I am, sir, your obedient servant,

JOHN APPLETON.
Assistant Secretary.

S. Ricker, Esq.,
United States Consul General, Frankfort-on-the-Main.

MESSAGE

OF THE

PRESIDENT OF THE UNITED STATES,

COMMUNICATING,

In compliance with a resolution of the Senate, further information in relation to the compulsory enlistment of American citizens in the army of Prussia.

MAY 2, 1860.—Read, and ordered to be printed; and that 5,000 additional copies be printed for the use of the Senate.

To the Senate of the United States:

In compliance with the resolution of the Senate of the 2d of February, 1859, requesting information in regard to the compulsory service of citizens of the United States in the army of Prussia, I transmit an additional report from the Secretary of State, and the documents by which it was accompanied.

JAMES BUCHANAN.

WASHINGTON, *April* 30, 1860.

DEPARTMENT OF STATE,
Washington, April 30, 1860.

The Secretary of State has the honor to represent that, since the report of this department of the 10th of last month, relative to the compulsory service of citizens of the United States in the army of Prussia, has been printed, it has been discovered that the instruction to Mr. Wright, at Berlin, of the 12th of May last, was accidentally omitted. A copy of that instruction is consequently hereunto annexed.

Respectfully submitted.

LEWIS CASS.

The PRESIDENT.

Mr. Cass to Mr. Wright.

No. 18.] DEPARTMENT OF STATE,
Washington, May 12, 1859.

SIR: In the dispatch from this department of December 10, 1858, you were requested to procure and transmit reliable information respecting the law of Prussia relating to natives of that country naturalized in the United States and returning to the place of their birth, and were informed that, upon its receipt, the views of this government would be communicated to you upon various questions affecting that class of our citizens. Your letter transmitting this information has been received, has been submitted to the President, and I am now to convey to you his instructions for your guidance under the circumstances.

I need not repeat the considerations, heretofore adverted to, which induce European emigrants, naturalized in the United States, to desire to revisit the countries of their birth. It is certain that in some of these countries, Prussia particularly, serious impediments exist to the gratification of this desire, to the grave injury of the persons thus harassed, and with no obvious corresponding advantage to the countries themselves.

The grievances in Prussia, of which we have a right to complain, are of two descriptions, one being harsh regulations, which it is competent for the government of the country to impose, but which are so oppressive, and it is believed unnecessary, as to be scarcely consistent with that comity and courtesy which friendly States owe to one another; and the other being, in the opinion of the United States, in violation of the treaty between them and Prussia. I shall call your attention to these subjects of complaint.

The most friendly feeling has always existed between these two States, and the President confidently relies upon the disposition of the Prussian government to receive our representations in an amicable spirit, and to furnish such redress as the circumstances may justly call for. The change you anticipated in the government of Prussia, by the inauguration of a regency, and to which you look forward as an event that would probably prove favorable for the consideration of these subjects having taken place, the present time may afford you a proper opportunity to urge these questions upon that government, and you will not fail to commence your task by impressing upon the minister of foreign affairs the importance which is attached in this country to the accomplishment of the objects indicated.

The rights of the citizens of the United States and of Prussia to enter and reside in the territories of those powers respectively are prescribed and regulated by the treaty between them of May 1, 1828. It is therein provided, that "the inhabitants" (meaning thereby, by the practical exposition of the parties, their respective citizens) "shall mutually have liberty to enter the ports, places, and rivers of the territories of each party wherein foreign commerce is permitted." Baron Manteuffel, in the declaration contained in his note to you of November 9, 1857, "that, from the existing laws of Prussia, no former subject of the King, whatever his condition may be, has the right of claiming his readmission into Prussia," has advanced a pretension which this government considers palpably inconsistent with this clause of the treaty.

The right of entrance is unconditional and unlimited, and no distinction is recognized in the enjoyment of its benefits between native-born and naturalized citizens; nor is it competent for either of the parties to make such a distinction, and to restrict, at its pleasure, the operation of that instrument. Had there been any reason whatever to suppose that Prussia would assume this power, the treaty would not have been concluded, for this government has no constitutional authority to recognize classes among its citizens, and to embrace some of them in its treaty stipulations while others are excluded. It does not appear that the claim of a right to judge what American citizens shall be excluded from its benefits has ever been actually enforced, and its application in Mr. Dullye's case is clearly disclaimed. We may expect that it will be disavowed by the Prussian government, and the obligations of the treaty admitted, according to the plain import of the terms.

The reciprocal right of entrance into the territories of the parties having been thus provided for, provision was then made for residence therein in the following words: "They shall be at liberty to sojourn and reside in all parts whatsoever of said territories, in order to attend to their affairs, and they shall enjoy to that effect the same security and protection as natives of the country wherein they reside, on condition of their submitting to the laws and ordinances there prevailing."

This clause is sufficiently clear, in the judgment of this government, to preclude any controversy respecting its meaning, and yet Baron Manteuffel claims for the Prussian government a power of administration expressly at variance with the rights herein secured, and which, if exercised, would leave the treaty inoperative, so far as regards the question of residence. In his letter to you, he maintains that the Prussian "government has the incontestible right to decide, *per se*, whether or not it be expedient for it to allow a stranger to sojourn in Prussia," &c. The government of the United States, on the contrary, maintains that every American citizen has the incontestible right to enter the Prussian territories, and there to remain undisturbed, so long as he submits "to the laws and ordinances there prevailing." It is not denied that the right claimed by Baron Manteuffel is one of the attributes of national sovereignty, which any government may exercise when not restrained by conventional stipulations. But the United States and Prussia have contracted with each other that the power of expulsion shall not be assumed, unless under the circumstances prescribed by the treaty. The question, therefore, in any given case, is not what the parties might do, by the public law of the world, but what they may do, consistently with the obligations they have respectively incurred.

The condition of residence being submission to the laws and ordinances, it is competent for the government of the country having reason to believe that this condition has been violated, to direct an inquiry to be instituted, with a view to ascertain if there is any just ground of complaint against the suspected party. The ordinary criminal jurisdiction of the country is wholly independent of the treaty stipulations. These apply only to the power of expulsion. The manner of conducting this inquiry is not prescribed by the treaty, but it should, no doubt, be in conformity with the institutions of the country, and managed with fairness and impartiality. In the dispatch addressed to you from this department, and dated December 10, 1858, this subject was briefly considered, and the right of the Prussian authorities to inquire into the conduct of American citizens, in the same manner the conduct of Prussian citizens is inquired into, fully admitted; and this principle of administration leads necessarily to the admission made in the same dispatch, that our citizens resident in Prussia are subject to all the police regulations of the kingdom, and responsible to the tribunals intrusted with their maintenance. The difference, however, in the constitution and practice of the judicial courts, and of these police tribunals, leads to one of the practical grievances you have pointed out. The ordinary courts of justice are open, and their proceedings free to public observation and scrutiny, while parties accused are always heard in their defense. On the contrary, it appears that the police investigations are conducted in secret, and our citizens, in such cases, are kept in ignorance of the accusation and the accuser, and are thus deprived of the natural right of self-defense.

Independent of general principles of justice, which are violated by such a mode of investigation, there are obvious considerations why in the determination of a question of right, like that in M. Dullye's case, arising out of conventional obligations with another country, the proceedings should be open, with proper opportunity of defense, so as to carry with them a satisfactory conviction of their justice and impartiality. Every Prussian subject residing in the United States would be entitled, in the event of an accusation against him, to this process of examination, and it is difficult to conceive what reasonable objections there can be to the introduction of the same system into Prussia, and its extension to all cases where the rights of American citizens are concerned. Sudden ejection from Prussia might be seriously injurious to an American citizen, and if he is kept in ignorance of the charges against him, he may be the victim of personal hostility, and learn their existence by the judgment of expulsion only.

I fully concur with you in the opinion, that copies of the papers upon which an American citizen has been condemned, should be furnished upon application. Indeed, it is so obviously just that I have been unable to conjecture what reason can be given for the refusal. Baron Manteuffel misapprehends the relation of the government of the United States to their citizens, when he supposes that it cannot interest the government to know upon what evidence an American citizen has been excluded from the enjoyment of rights guaranteed by treaty stipulations. It interests this government at all times to know how the conventional engagements into which it enters are observed, and especially when they involve cherished personal rights. Without at all calling in question the good faith or impartiality of another government, it is certainly not unreasonable that this government should be furnished with the grounds of proceeding in any case which it may think demands its interposition. Without such a resource, it would have no means of judging how far its rights may have been respected or its citizens justly dealt with. The claim made by Baron Manteuffel of the exclusive right of judgment in these cases is not contested, but its possession furnishes an additional consideration in favor of the adoption of a mode of proceeding which would carry with it confidence in its administration.

You are authorized to bring this subject to the attention of the Prussian government, and to ask its favorable action in relation to it.

But the principal subject of complaint on the part of the United States, growing out of the treaty, results from the power assumed by the Prussian government to compel the performance of military service in cases which, in the opinion of this government, are not justified by that instrument. Prussia does not hold to the doctrine of perpetual allegiance, but recognizes the right of her native-born citizens to expatriate themselves, and to form new political ties in a new country.

And whatever may have been the conflicting views entertained on this subject in former times, it is believed that this right is now generally acquiesced in by all the leading nations of the earth. Practically, at least, it is not likely that the doctrine of perpetual allegiance will ever hereafter be insisted on. In this age of the world, the idea of controlling the citizen in the choice of a home, and binding him by the tie of a mere political theory to inhabit, for his lifetime, a country which he constantly desires to leave, can hardly be entertained by any government whatever. All, probably, that can be expected or obtained, in respect to citizens or subjects who wish to emigrate, is, that, before emigrating, they shall discharge faithfully the duties, whether past or present, which they owe to the country of their birth. This being done, they are free, doubtless, to find a new home in whatever portion of the world they may choose to live. In recognizing this doctrine, as she is understood to do, Prussia places herself fully in accord with the spirit of the age, and with what will, doubtless, hereafter be regarded as the settled law of the world. Preliminary, however, to the exercise of the right of expatriation in Prussia, it appears, by the information furnished you by Baron Manteuffel, that the permission of the government is required, and that the violation of this law is punishable by fine and imprisonment. It is not known whether this law is stringently enforced, or how far it is restrained in its application by considerations of age or condition, but it is not easy to reconcile its existence with a full admission of the right of expatriation. When a native Prussian leaves his country, even without permission, and becomes a naturalized citizen of the United States, can it be reasonably contended that he is liable to punishment, should he return to Prussia, merely because he so left? This would be to hold that he could be justly punished for having exercised an acknowledged right. It is indispensable that he should leave Prussia before he can find a new home elsewhere; and to punish him for his departure, is to punish him for changing his home. If this doctrine is maintained, it is easy to see how often and painfully two great nations may be brought in conflict with regard to their respective rights and duties in the case of a subject of the one who has become a naturalized citizen of the other. Such a person returns to the land of his birth, for example, claiming no protection in his original character as a native of the country, but relying on the government of his new home to see that he is not injured himself, while he does wrong to no one else. What is the duty towards him of this new government? Shall it permit him to be placed in prison, or otherwise punished, without any attempt whatever for his protection? Especially shall it do this when there is a treaty in full force between the two countries, which provides that the citizens or subjects of either shall be allowed to visit and reside in the territories of the other? These questions indicate very clearly in what way a collision of duty and authority might frequently arise among nations, if the act of expatriation is to be regarded as a grave offense, and punishable by fine and imprisonment. I am persuaded that the enlightened government of Prussia will not fail to appreciate this difficulty, and that your representations on the subject will not, therefore, be without effect.

In respect to the claim of military service, which is regarded by the States of Germany as of great importance, a manifest distinction is to be made between actual deserters from the army, and the withdrawal from the country of persons who have not yet been drafted into service. The former are undoubtedly under obligations to perform their military duty, whenever they return to their native State. But the mere contingency that he may be called into service cannot place the citizen or subject under the same obligation. The principle of compulsory military service exists in the United States, and all their citizens able to bear arms may be called out, if required, to defend the republic. But this liability which exists, till destroyed by physical disability, and becomes an active duty when called for by the state of the country, interferes with no man's right to travel at home or abroad, or to become a member of some other political community. And the same considerations apply to all the duties which men are required to perform under all governments, such as serving upon juries, where juries make part of the judicial system, the holding of civil offices, where the law imposes this duty, and various other kinds of obligatory service which the necessities of society require, and which from time to time during life must be performed. If the future liability to do military duty creates a perpetual obligation, wherever the party may be, and whatever other responsibilities he may have incurred, the same principle will enable a government to prevent its subjects or citizens from ever leaving its dominions, or changing their home. It would be a practical denial of all right of expatriation, and a full assertion of the doctrine of perpetual allegiance.

In stating these views I must not be understood as desiring to limit in any manner the jurisdiction of Prussia within its own territories, or to contest in the slightest degree its full control over its own municipal legislation. I appeal only to the express language of our treaty, and to those principles and that policy which are approved by Prussia herself.

So far as two of the points mentioned in your dispatch of the 18th of January are concerned, it is not supposed that there would be any serious difference of opinions between Prussia and the United States. I cannot believe that the claim of military duty will be insisted upon as against an American citizen who left Germany before the age when he became liable to military duty. Since the class of those who leave without permission after the age of liability, but before they have actually been called into service, cannot be a large one, it is hoped that a liberal disposition on the part of the two governments in respect to the few persons of the class who may desire to return to Prussia, will prevent the occurrence of any practical disagreement between Prussia and the United States.

Under our treaty with Prussia there can be no doubt that American citizens who owe no service to Prussia, and have broken no Prussian law, have a right to visit and reside in Prussian territories without being in any way molested by the government. And if they are charged with any offense, it seems only reasonable that their trial should be surrounded with all the usual safeguards of a court of justice. Or if, under any circumstances, their cases should require, in the opinion of the Prussian government, a summary examination, this government surely ought to be supplied with copies of the papers on which the proceeding was founded, and the reasons which led to its result. While Prussia has a perfect right to proceed against persons found within its jurisdiction, the government of those persons has an equal right to inquire whether the proceeding was reasonable, and the result which was reached just.

In discussing this subject with the Prussian government, you will will bear in mind its difficulties, and will aim to procure a modification of the existing system by an appeal to the justice and intelligence of the Prussian authorities, rather than by a peremptory demand, which might be calculated to defeat its own object.

I am, sir, your obedient servant,

LEWIS CASS.

JOSEPH A. WRIGHT, Esq.,
&c., &c., &c.

www.ingramcontent.com/pod-product-compliance
Lightning Source LLC
LaVergne TN
LVHW050513100826
845148LV00002B/323

* 9 7 8 1 4 2 5 5 2 1 8 0 6 *